Springer Series in Emerging Cultural Perspectives in Work, Organizational, and Personnel Studies

Series Editors

The Springer Series in Emerging Cultural Perspectives in Work, Organizational, and Personnel Studies publishes fully developed conceptual pieces that focus on current state-of-the-art topics and research that uses a cultural lens to examine topics related to work, organizations, and employees. Both theoretical and empirical works may be included.

Wendi L. Adair • Nancy R. Buchan
Xiao-Ping Chen • Leigh Anne Liu

What Isn't Being Said

Culture and Communication at Work

Springer

Wendi L. Adair
Department of Psychology
University of Waterloo
Waterloo, ON, Canada

Nancy R. Buchan
Sonoco International Business Department, Darla Moore School of Business
University of South Carolina
Columbia, SC, USA

Xiao-Ping Chen
Department of Management and Organization, Michael G. Foster School of Business
University of Washington
Seattle, WA, USA

Leigh Anne Liu
Robinson College of Business
Georgia State University
Atlanta, GA, USA

ISSN 2662-4672 ISSN 2662-4680 (electronic)
Springer Series in Emerging Cultural Perspectives in Work, Organizational, and Personnel Studies
ISBN 978-3-031-53644-1 ISBN 978-3-031-53645-8 (eBook)
https://doi.org/10.1007/978-3-031-53645-8

This Springer imprint is published by the registered company Springer Nature Switzerland AG
The registered company address is: Gewerbestrasse 11, 6330 Cham, Switzerland

This book is dedicated to Jeff Russell and Arie Lewin who created the opportunity for us to meet and sowed the seeds for this collaboration at Duke University's Fuqua School of Business over 20 years ago. Jeff Russell continues to work with us managing knowledge translation, practical applications, and cross-cultural communication training for education and corporate audiences through icEdge.com.

Acknowledgments

We gratefully acknowledge the support of several CIBER programs that allowed us to dig deep and develop these ideas for over 10 years. These CIBER schools include Duke University, the University of Colorado at Denver, University of Florida, Georgia Institute of Technology, University of Kansas, University of Memphis, Michigan State University, Ohio State University, University of Pennsylvania, Purdue University, University of South Carolina, University of California, Los Angeles, University of North Carolina at Chapel Hill, University of Washington, and University of Wisconsin.

Each author has received funding and/or support from their respective institutions for this work on contextualized communication in diverse and multicultural workplaces (Cornell University, University of Waterloo, University of South Carolina, University of Washington, Seattle, and Georgia State University). External research funding from the Social Science and Humanities Research Council of Canada (grant# 435-2014-1649) contributed to theory development and accompanying empirical work. Our graduate students who have significantly contributed to this work include Zhaleh Semnani-Azad (University of Waterloo, now at California State University, Northridge) and Suraj Sharma and Elena Poliakova (Georgia State University, now at California State University, Northridge, and IESEG France, respectively).

Contents

Author Biographies

Wendi L. Adair (Ph.D., Northwestern University) is Professor of Industrial-Organizational Psychology and Director of the Culture at Work Lab at University of Waterloo, Ontario. Wendi's current research examines the impact of culture on communication, for example what is said and what is not said, and interdependent work outcomes, such as communication effectiveness, conflict resolution, trust, and team performance. Her work appears in outlets including *Journal of Applied Psychology*, *Negotiation and Conflict Management Research*, *Journal of Cross-cultural Psychology*, and *Academy of Management Discoveries*. She is co-Principal Investigator of Indigenous Workways, a collaborative project among faculty and Indigenous Student Centres in Ontario to develop a sustainable solution to underemployment among Ontario's Indigenous workforce by empowering Indigenous youth with career mentors and opportunities, and Ontario employers with relational, respectful, reciprocal, and relevant workplace communication and climate practices. Wendi has served as Associate Editor of *Negotiation and Conflict Management Research* and President of the International Association for Conflict Management.

Nancy R. Buchan (PhD, University of Pennsylvania) is Associate Professor of International Business in the Moore School of Business at the University of South Carolina. Nancy's research combines the methodology of experimental economics with theory from psychology, sociology, and political science to understand the factors that influence the development of trust and cooperation in cross-cultural relationships and interactions. She has conducted primary research in more than 13 countries. She was the PI and co-leader of an NSF-funded (Human and Social Development), multidisciplinary team of researchers that conducted experiments among the general populations in multiple countries to study the effect of globalization on individual attitudes such as social identification and behaviors toward others locally, nationally, and globally. Her work has been published in the *Proceedings of the National Academy of Science*, the *American Economic Review*, the *American Journal of Sociology*, *Psychological Science*, the *Journal of Consumer Research*, the *Journal of International Business Studies*, and others. Nancy has been on the Editorial Boards of the *Journal of International Business Studies* and *Organizational Behavior and Human Decision*

Processes. She served for 4 years as the Associate Dean of Undergraduate Programs of the Moore School, overlapping with 5 years as Director of the Undergraduate International Business Program (ranked #1 for 23 consecutive years USNWR).

Xiao-Ping Chen (PhD, University of Illinois) is Philip M. Condit Endowed Chair Professor in the Michael G. Foster School of Business, University of Washington. She is an elected Fellow in the Academy of Management (AOM) and the American Psychological Association (APA). Her current research interests are on teamwork and leadership, Chinese guanxi, and cross-cultural communication and management. Her work appears in journals such as *Academy of Management Review*, *Academy of Management Journal*, *Journal of Applied Psychology*, *Organizational Behavior and Human Decision Processes*, *Management Science*, and *Journal of International Business Studies*. She has also published more than ten books in English and Chinese, including *Leadership of Chinese Private Enterprises: Insights and Interviews* (Palgrave McMillan), *A Journey Toward Influential Scholarship: Insights from Leading Management Scholars* (Oxford University Press), *Leading Across Cultures* (Tsinghua University Press), and *Empirical Methods in Organization and Management Research* (Peking University Press). Professor Chen is Editor-in-Chief of *Management and Organization Review* and Executive Editor of *Management Insights*. She also served as Editor-in-Chief of *Organizational Behavior and Human Decision Processes* (2010–2016). She served as President of International Association for Chinese Management Research (IACMR) and is the recipient of numerous teaching and research awards, including Scholarly Impact Award by *Journal of Management* (2019), Best Paper of Chinese Management Research by Peking University Press (2018), Dean's Leadership Award (2017), Distinguished Scholarly Contribution Award by IACMR (2016), Outstanding Ph.D. Mentor Award, Dean's International Research Award, and Charles E. Summer Teaching Award.

Leigh Anne Liu (PhD, Vanderbilt University) is Professor and Director of the Institute of International Business at Georgia State University's Robinson College of Business. Leigh Anne studies how culture and cognition influence intercultural interactions, including negotiation, conflict management, and collaboration at interpersonal, organization, and national levels. Her research appears in *Administrative Science Quarterly*, *Journal of Applied Psychology*, *Journal of International Business Studies*, among other outlets. She has co-authored a book *Doing Business in Emerging Markets* (Sage). Her research teams have received grants from the World Health Organization, the U.S. Department of Education, Research Grants Council of Hong Kong, and the European Commission. She was awarded the Fulbright-Hanken Distinguished Chair in 2020 by the U.S. Department of State, Fulbright Foreign Scholarship Board, and Fulbright Finland Foundation. She has been a Visiting Professor at University of South Australia, University of Toulouse in France, Hanken School of Economics in Finland, Peking University, and Nanjing University in China. Leigh Anne has served as an Associate Editor of *Journal of Business Research* and *Cross Cultural and Strategic Management*, a guest editor of *Human Resource Management*, and a member of the editorial boards of journals such as *Journal of International Business Studies*, *Academy of Management Review*, *International Business Review*, and *Management and Organization Review*.

Chapter 1
How Does Culture Communicate at Work? An Introduction

He who does not understand your silence will probably not understand your words. – Elbert Hubbard

In a curiously circular yet powerful statement, cultural anthropologist Edward T. Hall wrote, "Culture is communication and communication is culture" (Hall, 1959, p. 169). Certainly, many parts of culture, like language, dress, and religion, *communicate* a group's shared values, which are motivational in nature, and norms, which are behavioral. At the same time, communication itself is a cultural artifact that can be both visible and invisible. In the culture-as-an-iceberg metaphor (Schein & Schein, 2016), visible culture, such as traditional clothing and hairstyles, floats above the water like the tip of the iceberg. In contrast, invisible culture, such as values and norms, lays below the surface, providing a sturdy foundation that is not readily detectable. Communication norms, we argue, lay right at the surface of the water. Some features of communication that vary by culture, for example, verbal expression of emotion or frequency of conversational interruptions, are indeed visible to the human eye or audible to the human ear. However, other features of communication are difficult to detect. The complexity of interpreting communication, for example, a head nod or "yes" uttered in response to a request, lies in understanding the communication context and what isn't said. This book is about communication context – the unspoken, invisible meaning expressed not with words but around words, within relationships, through space, and across time. We will explore how cultural variation in communication norms, or the communication context surrounding a verbal message, can create ripples, or even waves, of miscommunication. We then unpack how diverse communication norms in a global workplace can work synergistically to support cross-cultural collaboration that positively impacts downstream organizational outcomes.

Like cultural values (Kwantes & Glazer, 2017), communication patterns become normative because they serve basic human needs and facilitate the fulfillment of a

W. L. Adair et al., *What Isn't Being Said*, Springer Series in Emerging Cultural Perspectives in Work, Organizational, and Personnel Studies,
https://doi.org/10.1007/978-3-031-53645-8_1

culture's values and survival, including human connection and collaborative work (Adair et al., 2009; Triandis, 1977). These patterns become shared among members of a cultural group, reinforced through socialization at home, school, and work, and thus are perpetuated over time into something rather sticky and hard to change (Brett et al., 1997). While situational factors can influence the activation and accessibility of cultural values and thinking patterns, indicating a certain level of fluidity (Hong et al., 2000), adapting culturally normative communication patterns is effortful and not always possible in a fast-paced and dynamic workplace (Molinsky, 2007). Hence, the challenges of communicating effectively across cultures can frustrate understanding, relationship-building, and ultimately collective performance in organizations (Merkin et al., 2014; Szkudlarek et al., 2020).

When we teach cross-cultural communication in teams, we often begin with a series of questions (e.g., When a meeting is scheduled for 9:00 am, what time do you arrive? What time do you expect to get down to work?) for teams to uncover and discuss the diversity of communication norms they hold. We then use a vignette to show how diverse communication norms can create communication challenges. One scenario involves a cross-functional team (Mattieu, he/him, from Paris, France), Charlie (they/them, from Hamilton, Canada), Winnie (she/her, from Chengdu, China), Ash (he/him, from Hyderabad, India), and Jasmin (she/her, from South Carolina, U.S.) scheduled to meet in-person at 9:00 am. Ash arrives at 8:55 am and notices that Jasmin is already there with her laptop open. A few minutes after 9:00, Charlie, Winny, and Mathieu arrive. Based on this simple description, we discuss what different team members might be thinking, if anything, about their teammates, given their arrival times.

We then introduce a snapshot of the team's first three speaking turns. Once sitting down, they start with self-introductions:

Jasmin: *My name is Jasmin and I grew up in South Carolina and have lived in New York for the past 3 years. I got my MBA at...*

Mathieu: *Thank you Jasmin. I am Mathieu from France. Let's keep it short so we can get down to business.*

Ash: *Hello, I am Ash.*

Here again, we stop to discuss the verbal messaging. What does it mean that Jasmin speaks first? That Mathieu interrupts her? What might the impact of Mathieu's "get down to business" message be for the task and relationship components of the team's upcoming work?

After discussing the team's verbal interaction, we then show the same team interaction with additional detail on accompanying nonverbal communication.

Jasmin speaks first.

Jasmin: *My name is Jasmin and I grew up in South Carolina and have lived in New York for the past 3 years. I got my MBA at...*

Mathieu interrupts her.

Mathieu: *Thank you Jasmin. I am Mathieu from France. Let's keep it short so we can get down to business,* he says hastily, emphasizing a desire to focus on the task at hand.

Jasmin is visibly surprised and quite taken aback, literally moving her upper body away from the table. She abruptly stops speaking and looks away, barely concealing an angry expression.

Seeing this, Charlie and Winny don't say a word but just look down at the table; Ash looks towards Mathieu and moves his chair closer.

Ash: *Hello, I am Ash, glad to be here.*

As our students readily agree, in this multicultural team, nonverbal communication speaks volumes. We clearly see the negative affect Jasmin experiences after feeling cut off. Mathieu's request now seems more controlling and dominating. We notice the awkwardness Charlie and Winny are feeling and wonder how it will impact their participation. We wonder if Ash's subtle glance and chair shuffle signify a message of support for Mathieu's interjection and perhaps the beginnings of a subgroup formation. This description highlights what we call the communication context – the nonverbal cues that surround a verbal message, residing in culturally normative paralanguage and body language, dictated by unspoken power and relationship status, conveyed through physical and sensory space and attached to the way we move through time (Adair et al., 2016; Hall, 1976).

Now, imagine the same scenario yet again, taking place in Atlanta. Mathieu's interruption is particularly egregious in the Southern United States, where things move more slowly and personal information is welcomed. What if the meeting were held in Paris, where personal information is typically not shared in a first meeting? Suddenly Mathieu is merely guiding culturally appropriate meeting norms. What if we told you the meeting takes place in a floundering organization facing cutbacks? Suddenly everyone's awkwardness and verbal expressions take on a note of desperation. These descriptions highlight situational factors that can influence what is said, what isn't said, and how a message is interpreted. Organizational behavior scholars' recent calls for studying cross-cultural communication "in context" often refer to these valid and important forms of situational context, including political, organizational, and economic factors that ascribe meaning (Gelfand et al., 2013; Liu et al., 2018; Szkudlarek et al., 2020). We agree that cross-cultural communication in organizations needs to be considered within situational context, and we argue that it also needs to be examined *through* communication context. As we will unpack throughout this volume, culture-based communication norms governing what to say and how to say it influence how employees interact through the message, relationship, space, and time domains of communication context. A broader, more holistic treatment of communication accounts for the role of relationships and nonverbal cues within space and time (Szkudlarek et al., 2020; Sharma & Liu, 2023) as well as for cues as to what is contained in a message not limited to the words used (Adair et al., 2016). As we will discuss, effective cross-cultural communication in the workplace requires an understanding of the socio-cultural roots of verbal and nonverbal communication styles in the self and others, a recognition of the complex psychological and situational factors that underlie faulty attribution and motivate adaptation, and engaged listening for nonverbal cues in all four domains that are often unnoticed or misinterpreted.

The "Culture" in Cross-Cultural Communication

In the twenty-first century's diverse, global, and increasingly virtual workplace, cross-cultural communication is a daily challenge. Culture is defined as a group's shared values and norms that are learned and reinforced through the group's symbols and institutions (Kroeber & Kluckhohn, 1952; Triandis, 1972). When organizational personnel come from different cultural backgrounds and/or work across international boundaries, communication challenges may arise from cultural variations in communication goals, norms, and behaviors (Adair et al., 2001; Liu & Adair, 2017) rooted in a variety of distinct values such as power distance (Ting-Toomey, 2005) or relational ideologies about the appropriateness of non-task related communication at work (Sanchez-Burks et al., 2000). Culture-based communication norms govern the *what* and *how* of messaging, guiding reliance on and attention to nonverbal cues that may emphasize, supplement, and sometimes even contradict the accompanying verbal message (Adair et al., 2016; Hall, 1959, 1976). Culture and communication are closely intertwined and reciprocally influence each other (Sharma & Liu, 2023). This means that while culture influences communication through language, nonverbal and verbal communication also shape culture by reinforcing and challenging cultural values and norms.

Cultural values define what is important and motivating for a social group (Hofstede, 1980). On the other hand, norms are rules for appropriate or expected behavior (Morris et al., 2015). Thus people who belong to groups with strong values for individualism, defined as an understanding of the self as an individual actor, tend to have more direct communication norms. Members of groups with strong values for collectivism, defined as an understanding of the self based on group membership and obligations to those groups, tend to have more indirect communication patterns (Gudykunst et al., 1996; Gudykunst, 2003; Markus & Kitayama, 1991). A meta-analysis of 60 studies examining the relationship between Hofstede's (1980) cultural values and communication patterns confirmed that values for individualism, power distance, masculinity, and uncertainty avoidance were all related to specific communication patterns for directness and indirectness, but also communication norms that go beyond directness/indirectness, such as sensitivity and propensity to interrupt (Merkin et al., 2014).

Gelfand et al. (2011) found that the cultural norm of tightness, wherein social groups have more rigidly defined and enforced social norms, can also be communicated both explicitly and implicitly. Specifically, the degree of tightness can influence communication styles in formality, conflict management, and perception of silence. In tight cultures such as Singapore or Japan, people prefer to use formal titles to reflect social hierarchies, avoid being expressive or confronting conflicts to maintain harmony, and use silence as a sign of respect and attentiveness. In Finland, "silence is not equated with failure to communicate but as an integral part of social interaction" (Lewis, 2006, p. 333). On the other hand, members of loose cultures, such as Brazil, favor informality, are open to direct confrontation and debate, and view silence as rudeness or lacking engagement (Gelfand, 2018).

Hall (1976) described these cultural differences in whether meaning is contained primarily in the explicit verbal code versus more implicit nonverbal cues as low and high communication context, respectively (Hall, 1976). Communication context is shared knowledge and common ground that permits interlocutors to say less to be understood (Trompenaars & Hampden-Turner, 2011). It is also described as the implicit norms that define how people interact, relate, and exchange information (Hall, 1976). Low/high communication context as a cultural construct defines communication norms and patterns shared by a group of people within a geographical region or national boundaries (Hall, 1976; Trompenaars & Hampden-Turner, 2011). Beyond directness and indirectness, low/high communication context encompasses the nonverbal communication fields of proxemics (use of space), gaze (eye contact), kinesics (the use of body motions, such as gestures) and haptics (use of touch) (Gudykunst, 2003; Hall, 1959, 1976). In high-context cultures, communication serves relational, social, and informational functions (Cohen, 1997). At the individual level, employees may vary in their context dependence, defined as the degree to which one relies on and attends to nonverbal, contextual cues embedded in the message surrounding the words, the relationship with one's counterpart, the physical and sensory environment where communication takes place, and temporal components of the interaction (Adair et al., 2016). In cross-cultural workplace communication, employees send and receive messages to fulfill organizational functions using different forms of low and high-context communication.

Communication Functions in Organizations

Communication is woven into every organizational process, from internal visioning and external marketing to personnel selection, teamwork, and conflict management. Communication translates organizational goals into goal-related behavior and occurs through oral-verbal, written-verbal, and nonverbal channels (Greenbaum, 1974). Greenbaum further describes four functional networks in which communication occurs: regulatory (e.g., direction and feedback), innovative (e.g., problem-solving and adaptation to change), integrative (e.g., employee well-being, community building), and informative (e.g., training and information exchange). In other words, the functions of communication at work, whether verbal or nonverbal, face-to-face or virtual, spoken or conveyed implicitly, are to exchange information, manage relationships, influence others, and coordinate action (Postmes, 2003). Within an organization, communication can occur downwardly from management to employees to convey the vision and define goals; upwardly from subordinates to superiors to identify problems and offer suggestions for improvement; and laterally among peers to coordinate, collaborate, and build consensus.

Haslam (2004) explains that from a motivational perspective, organizational communication fulfills multiple needs. At the intrapersonal level, employees can fulfill security needs by asking questions and gathering information to reduce uncertainty or affiliation needs by chatting with colleagues over lunch. At the interpersonal level, employees use communication to influence and obtain desired resources or seek self-improvement-oriented feedback. Communication is also a means through which organizational needs for performance and sustainability are met, for example, through coordinated teamwork and leader visioning (Haslam, 2004). Communication is at the heart of the interdependent and collaborative work that is organizational behavior.

From a social identity perspective, employees self-categorize to define membership in different groups at work (Tajfel, 1981; Turner et al., 1987). Shared in-group identity facilitates communication through shared motivations, cognitions, norms, and social networks (Postmes, 2003). This shared social identity gives group members access to communication repertoires and meanings that are more difficult for out-group members to decipher (Katz & Kahn, 1972; Haslam, 2004). For example, in a tech company, employees in programming may have different communication norms from employees in operations, just as Chinese employees may have different communication norms from U.S. employees. However, it should be noted that employees have multiple intersecting identities with different social groups. For example, one employee's social identity may include Chinese, female, and programming, while another's includes nonbinary, Californian, and operations. Communication helps form and reinforce individual and organizational identities, as well as a shared understanding that enables collective sensemaking in organizations (Postmes, 2003; Weick, 1969).

In multicultural workplaces and international businesses, employees from similar cultural backgrounds have shared communication norms that facilitate in-group communication effectiveness (Szkudlarek et al., 2020). Further, communication across group boundaries is subject to barriers from intergroup comparisons, biases, and processes that can impede effective communication (Turner et al., 1987). Overcoming the challenges of cross-cultural communication in the workplace means developing skills and strategies to communicate effectively across intergroup boundaries, distinct communication norms, and unfamiliar patterns of verbal and nonverbal meaning (Molinsky, 2007, 2013).

Notably, researchers have tackled cross-cultural communication across various organizational spheres, as reflected in the organizational topics of each chapter in this volume. As our review of the literature will show, this prior work emphasizes verbal expression, language, emotion display, speaking up, and communication climate. A thorough treatment of nonverbal communication is lacking in the existing body of knowledge. As Greenbaum (1974) noted, "organizational communication should be construed as including all behavior-modifying stimuli, both verbal and nonverbal. It includes gestures and facial expressions as well as the spoken word in conversation and meetings" (Greenbaum, 1974, p. 740). We propose a holistic consideration of nonverbal communication, including four domains of communication context, that promises to fill the gap in research and offer practical strategies for cross-cultural communicators.

Managing the Cross-Cultural Communication Challenge

Interpersonal, cross-cultural communication is a dynamic process of sensemaking, contextualization, and recontextualization informed by cultural, situational, and individual factors (Osland & Bird, 2000). The uncertainty inherent in cross-cultural encounters can increase anxiety, reinforce in-group/out-group boundaries, and prompt automatic cultural responses (Gudykunst & Nishida, 2001), in this case reliance on culturally-normative communication styles. To reduce uncertainty and create shared social bonds, cross-cultural communicators may adjust their language, for example, what they say and how they say it (e.g., pitch, rate of speech), to be more similar to their counterparts (Giles et al., 1991). Through such accommodation processes (converging to or diverging from one's interlocutor), people navigate self-categorization and shared social membership. Communication adaptation as a social identity process is also evident among bilingual and multilingual employees (e.g., Bourhis, 1994) and people of color in a White dominant workplace who often codeswitch to be seen and heard as equals (McCluney et al., 2021). However, communication adaptation is costly in terms of cognitive resources and psychological stamina and difficult to finesse, leaving many cross-cultural and inter-ethnic workplace communications subject to miscommunication and misunderstanding (Molinsky, 2007).

To improve our understanding of communication in intercultural work, researchers have called for more context-rich approaches (Henderson, 1987; Liu et al., 2018; Szkudlarek et al., 2020). The nuances of effective cross-cultural communication can only be unpacked against the backdrop of organizational environments and workplace interactions in which they take place (Bjerregaard et al., 2009; Hinds et al., 2011). Cultural norms and individual styles influence communication codes. Still, far from being static, those patterns are constantly unfolding and adapting against a social and political backdrop amidst a "complex and dynamic environmental mosaic" (Bjerregaard et al., 2009, p. 208).

Effective workplace communication positively impacts task performance, job satisfaction, trust, and firm performance (Miller et al., 1990). Yet, cross-cultural communication is prone to misunderstandings that impede effectiveness and often lead to conflict (Adair et al., 2016; Erez & Earley, 1993; Liu et al., 2010), limiting the ability of organizational actors to optimize their work. The intersection of culture and communication at work creates a challenge and an opportunity for managers and employees to foster connection and collaboration through communication practices. First, employees need knowledge and awareness of the diverse identities and associated low/high context communication norms that people bring to the workplace. Second, self- and other awareness of culturally normative patterns of nonverbal expression and interpretation will give employees from diverse backgrounds the ability to pause, identify, and interpret information in nonverbal cues that can be easily overlooked and misinterpreted. Third, employees need to recognize areas of organizational life that are common miscommunication hotspots and become skilled in adopting a flexible communication style that includes attention to one's own nonverbal messaging, engaged listening for counterparts' nonverbal cues, and a willingness to collaboratively construct shared understanding.

How exactly do these three steps pave the way for effective intercultural communication at work? To answer this question, we first take a deep dive into the ecological and cultural underpinnings of communication style across groups and individuals. We introduce a communication model that focuses on four sources of nonverbal messaging where managers and employees from different cultural backgrounds are most likely to miss nuanced but essential information (Chap. 2). Then, we review theories from communication, industrial-organizational psychology, and cross-cultural psychology that explain the challenges of intercultural communication and various paths to adaptation for communication effectiveness, relationship building, and collaboration (Chap. 3).

With this introductory landscape established, we then discuss cross-cultural communication in six workplace settings (Chap. 4: Multicultural Teams; Chap. 5: Cross-cultural Negotiation and Conflict Management; Chap. 6: Voice, Silence, Gossip, and feedback in a Diverse Workplace; Chap. 7: Multicultural Leadership; Chap. 8: Workplace Incivility; and Chap. 9: Virtual Cross-Cultural Communication). In our concluding chapter, we offer propositions for how and when seemingly hidden messages can influence effective intercultural workplace communication, focusing on interpersonal connection and finding common ground.

An Ecological Model of Culture and Communication

Drawing on theories from anthropology and social psychology, we suggest that culture is an adaptive system linking people to the contexts in which they live (Keesing, 1974; Gudykunst & Ting-Toomey, 1988). Furthermore, culture relates to individual and collective actions or interactions through a number of interrelated systems, including the ecological, subsistence, socio-cultural, individual, and inter-individual (social) systems (Erez & Earley, 1993; Triandis, 1977). The model proposed in Chap. 2 predicts that individuals who share a common language, who interact frequently because of shared physical locale, and who have shared perceptions of rules, methods, group norms, roles, customs, and values are likely to share the same subjective culture (Triandis, 1972; Erez & Earley, 1993). Accordingly, "behavioral patterns," "customs" (Harris, 1968, p. 16), "unstated assumptions," and "standard operating procedures" (Triandis, 1994, p. 6) are adapted and internalized among individuals within cultures making such patterns distinct, and similarly, distinct communication and interaction styles develop and become implicit. These implicit behavioral patterns, unstated assumptions, and standard operating procedures are manifested in contextual cues – particularly in nonverbal communication – within the domains of the message, relationship, time, and space.

Our model supports the idea that culture and communication are intricately intertwined; culture may be a group-level phenomenon, but culture itself is enacted and sustained at the individual level through communication and interaction between actors in specific organizational contexts (Van Maanen & Barley, 1984). The model applies to any social group in and with which we need to communicate effectively – national cultures, ethnicities, genders, generations, professions (lawyers and social workers, for instance), and even across corporate functional areas in a single workplace (such as engineering, marketing, and accounting). In addition to shared values and beliefs, each of these cultural groups may develop standard operating procedures, normative behavioral patterns, and unwritten scripts, allowing the group members to communicate with one another and be understood.

The Psychology of Cross-Cultural Communication

Effective communication can be challenging for employees from different cultural backgrounds due to psychological, cognitive, and communication factors. Intercultural encounters arouse anxiety and stress due to parties' unfamiliar cultural norms and behavioral scripts (Avery et al., 2009; Gudykunst & Nishida, 2001). Employees may worry that they aren't expressing themselves clearly, aren't being understood, and are not getting the complete message from their counterparts. Distinct communication norms challenge encoding, transmission, and decoding processes (Hall, 1976; Harzing et al., 2011; Molinsky, 2007). Such uncertainty naturally causes anxiety and inefficiency in communicating. To reduce uncertainty and facilitate understanding, most employees will try to adapt to their counterparts' communication styles (Gudykunst & Nishida, 2001).

In addition to uncertainty reduction motives, adaptation in cross-cultural communication may occur to improve information exchange and build relationships (Gallois et al., 2005). Employees from minority culture groups may adapt their communication style to be heard and fit in with the cultural majority (Avery et al., 2009). The language spoken, a team's demographic composition, and a superior's presence are examples of situational factors that influence the activation and accessibility of distinct communication styles in bilingual and multilingual employees (Hong et al., 2000; Morris et al., 2015). Chapter 3 reviews the many theoretical models informing adaptation in cross-cultural communication.

Organizational Spheres

Global Teams

Effective communication is essential for global teams to manage diverse cultural perspectives and approaches (Wang et al., 2019). Chapter 4 reviews research on multicultural team communication challenges as well as communication climates and practices that reduce misunderstanding and frustration (e.g., Lisak et al., 2016; Stahl & Maznevski, 2021). Existing recommendations are based on Western models of teamwork that emphasize speaking up and being explicit and direct in team meetings (Behfar et al., 2006; Gibson & Gibbs, 2006). Future research focusing on high-context team members' indirect communication will build theory and practical applications for global team collaboration and performance.

Negotiation and Conflict Management

Workplace conflicts are disagreements or incompatibility in interests or values between and among employees. Negotiation is a joint decision-making process where parties communicate to resolve conflicting needs and interests. Extant literature on cross-cultural conflict management and negotiation has largely focused on the message domain of communication, namely norms for direct vs indirect expression and conflict management. Chapter 5 presents a holistic analysis of four domains of communication context in negotiation and conflict management and proposes that in addition to managing the message context through engaged listening, negotiators and conflict managers can explore relationships, time orientation, and space sensitivity as potential opportunities for building consensus.

Voice, Silence, Gossip, and Feedback

Voice, silence, gossip, and feedback are examples of dyadic and small group communication in organizations that may look very different in low and high context cultures. Employees are guided by communication norms when they speak up (or remain silent) with recommendations for process improvements, reinforce organizational norms through informal gossip, or seek and receive performance feedback (Brady et al., 2017; Morrison, 2011; Ashford & Cummings, 1983). Communication norms are manifested through the message domain, where directness and clarity are emphasized more by low-context communicators (e.g., Lam et al., 2019; Sully De Luque & Sommer, 2000) and the relationship domain, where high-context employees let status and power determine the appropriateness of speaking up and seeking feedback (e.g., Ren et al., 2022; Ward et al., 2016). Chapter 6 discusses how nonverbal cues in the message, relationship, time, and space domains create challenges for misinterpretation across cultures and offers opportunities for research on mechanisms to reduce misunderstandings.

Leadership

Leadership is a process through which one individual influences a group of individuals to achieve a common goal. Communication plays a central role in social influence: what is communicated and how it is communicated can determine the breadth and depth of leadership effectiveness. Chapter 7 reviews the literature on how cultural norms of communication in the domains of message, relationship, time, and space context affect leadership effectiveness across cultures. More importantly, propositions are developed regarding how leaders might deal with challenges in nonverbal communication norms to achieve effective cross-cultural communication at work.

Incivility

Workplace incivility or deviance refers to voluntary behaviors that violate organizational norms and threaten the well-being of others. Incivility can be communicated both verbally and nonverbally. Chapter 8 reviews the subtle and nonverbal communication of ostracism, silent treatment, and social exclusion, as well as the explicit verbal and nonverbal forms of incivility such as abusive supervision, bullying, and microaggressions in the workplace. We propose how navigating the message, relationship, time, and space domains of communication context can potentially mitigate the negative impact of workplace uncivil communication.

Virtual Communication

The use of virtual interactions for professional communication has exploded in recent years. Communication mediums vary in the amount of information they can transmit, the depth of detail articulated, and the richness of messages conveyed to facilitate clear understanding. In mediums that are more information rich (e.g., consider Zoom meetings vs email), context will be more easily recognized and understood, and nonverbal messages will be more fluently encoded and decoded. Chapter 9 discusses nonverbal communication in virtual interactions related to the message, relationship, time, and space domains of communication context. The challenges of encoding and decoding nonverbal communication in each domain through a virtual medium are presented, as well as possible ways to overcome the challenges.

Pathways to Collaboration

In the final chapter we review the recommendations within this book for creating culturally inclusive communication climates. Focusing on the Interactive Model of Contextualized Communication, our propositions ultimately speak to the center of the model, maximizing the zone of overlap wherein communicators' culturally normative communication styles are acknowledged, respected, and adapted for the sake of communication effectiveness and shared understanding. There is an inherent divide when individuals communicate because no person can truly know the other's field of experience, the cultural communication context. This divide is exacerbated by nonverbal language presenting multiple or hidden meanings. Yet, to the extent that there is overlap in the speakers' fields of experience, effective communication can ensue. The sender's intention and the receiver's interpretation are more likely to be in sync, the more deeply they each understand the cultural context of the other and the message, relationship, time, and space contexts in which the signal was encoded or decoded. Such effective communication can then be the seedbed for finding common ground and collaboration.

Conclusion

Explaining the complexity of cross-cultural workplace communication, Szkudlarek and colleagues note: "Each intercultural encounter generates a novel combination and unknown results that are negotiated through the interplay among individuals' background, characteristics, situational circumstances, and contextual cues (Casrnir, 1999; Nardon, 2017)" (Szkudlarek et al., 2020, p. 2). The call is for management and organizational scholarship to integrate nonverbal communication concepts in future international business and organizational behavior research (Bonaccio et al., 2016; Szkudlarek et al., 2020). Employees are social beings who need to be understood and to belong. Estimates that over half of communication is contained in nonverbal messaging demonstrate our awareness of and attention to the importance of subtle and implicit meaning (Burgoon et al., 1996). This volume emphasizes the importance of understanding patterns of cultural variation in what nonverbal cues are used, what the cues mean, and what is done with the information decoded from nonverbal messaging. The next challenge for cross-cultural organizational scholars is to include implicit, high-context nonverbal communication in research and theory development.

References

Adair, W. L., Okumura, T., & Brett, J. M. (2001). Negotiation behavior when cultures collide: The United States and Japan. *Journal of Applied Psychology, 86*(3), 371–385.

Adair, W. L., Buchan, N., & Chen, X. P. (2009). Conceptualizing culture as communication in management and marketing research. In C. Nakata (Ed.), *Beyond Hofstede: Culture frameworks for global marketing and management* (pp. 146–180). Macmillan Palgrave.

Adair, W. L., Buchan, N. R., Chen, X. P., & Liu, D. (2016). A model of communication context and measure of context dependence. *Academy of Management Discoveries, 2*(2), 198–217.

Ashford, S. J., & Cummings, L. L. (1983). Feedback as an individual resource: Personal strategies of creating information. *Organizational Behavior and Human Performance, 32*(3), 370–398.

Avery, D. R., Richeson, J. A., Hebl, M. R., & Ambady, N. (2009). It does not have to be uncomfortable: The role of behavioral scripts in Black–White interracial interactions. *Journal of Applied Psychology, 94*(6), 1382–1393. https://doi.org/10.1037/a0016208

Behfar, K., Kern, M., & Brett, J. (2006). Managing challenges in multicultural teams. In Y. R. Chen (Ed.), *National culture and groups* (pp. 233–262). Emerald Group Publishing Limited.

Bjerregaard, T., Lauring, J., & Klitmøller, A. (2009). A critical analysis of intercultural communication research in cross-cultural management: Introducing newer developments in anthropology. *Critical Perspectives on International Business, 5*(3), 207–228. https://doi.org/10.1108/17422040910974695

Bonaccio, S., O'Reilly, J., O'Sullivan, S. L., & Chiocchio, F. (2016). Nonverbal behavior and communication in the workplace: A review and an agenda for research. *Journal of Management, 42*(5), 1044–1074. https://doi.org/10.1177/0149206315621146

Bourhis, R. (1994). Bilingualism and the language of work: The linguistic work environment survey. *International Journal of the Sociology of Language, 105–106*, 217–266.

Brady, D. L., Brown, D. J., & Liang, L. H. (2017). Moving beyond assumptions of deviance: The reconceptualization and measurement of workplace gossip. *Journal of Applied Psychology, 102*(1), 1–25.

Brett, J. M., Tinsley, C. H., Janssens, M., Barsness, Z. I., & Lytle, A. L. (1997). New approaches to the study of culture in I/O psychology. In C. P. Earley & M. Erez (Eds.), *New perspectives on international industrial/organizational psychology* (pp. 75–129). Wiley.

Burgoon, J. K., Buller, D. B., & Woodall, W. G. (1996). *Nonverbal communication: The unspoken dialog*. McGraw-Hill.

Casrnir, F. L. (1999). Foundations for the study of intercultural communication based on a third-culture building model. *International Journal of Intercultural Relations, 23*(1), 91–116.

Cohen, R. A. (1997). *Negotiating across cultures: International communication in an interdependent world.* US Institute of Peace Press.

Erez, M., & Earley, P. C. (1993). *Culture, self-identity, and work.* Oxford University Press.

Gallois, C., Ogay, T., & Giles, H. (2005). Communication accommodation theory: A look back and a look ahead. In W. B. Gudykunst (Ed.), *Theorizing about intercultural communication* (pp. 121–148). Sage.

Gelfand, M. J. (2018). *Rule makers, rule breakers: How tight and loose cultures wire our world.* Scribner.

Gelfand, M. J., Raver, J. L., Nishii, L., Leslie, L. M., Lun, J., Lim, B. C., et al. (2011). Differences between tight and loose cultures: A 33-nation study. *Science, 332*(6033), 1100–1104.

Gelfand, M. J., Brett, J., Gunia, B. C., Imai, L., Huang, T. J., & Hsu, B. F. (2013). Toward a culture-by-context perspective on negotiation: Negotiating teams in the United States and Taiwan. *Journal of Applied Psychology, 98*(3), 504–513.

Gibson, C. B., & Gibbs, J. L. (2006). Unpacking the concept of virtuality: The effects of geographic dispersion, electronic dependence, dynamic structure, and national diversity on team innovation. *Administrative Science Quarterly, 51*(3), 451–495.

Giles, H., Coupland, J., Coupland, N., & Oatley, K. (Eds.). (1991). *Contexts of accommodation: Developments in applied sociolinguistics* (Vol. 10). Cambridge University Press.

Greenbaum, H. H. (1974). The audit of organizational communication. *Academy of Management Journal, 17*(4), 739–754.

Gudykunst, W. B. (2003). *Cross-cultural and intercultural communication*. Sage.

Gudykunst, W. B., & Nishida, T. (2001). Anxiety, uncertainty, and perceived effectiveness of communication across relationships and cultures. *International Journal of Intercultural Relations, 25*(1), 55–71.

Gudykunst, W. B., & Ting-Toomey, S. (1988). *Culture and interpersonal communication*. Sage.

Gudykunst, W. G., Matsumoto, Y., Ting-Toomey, S., & Nishida, T. (1996). The influence of cultural individualism–collectivism, self-construals, and individual values on communication styles across cultures. *Human Communication Research, 22*(4), 510–543.

Hall, E. T. (1959). *The silent language*. Random House.

Hall, E. T. (1976). *Beyond culture*. Anchor Press.

Harris, M. (1968). *The rise of anthropological theory*. Crowell.

Harzing, A. W., Köster, K., & Magner, U. (2011). Babel in business: The language barrier and its solutions in the HQ-subsidiary relationship. *Journal of World Business, 46*(3), 279–287.

Haslam, S. A. (2004). *Psychology in organizations: The social identity approach*. Sage.

Henderson, L. S. (1987). The contextual nature of interpersonal communication in management theory and research. *Management Communication Quarterly, 1*(1), 7–31.

Hinds, P., Liu, L., & Lyon, J. (2011). Putting the global in global work: An intercultural lens on the practice of cross-national collaboration. *Academy of Management Annals, 5*(1), 135–188.

Hofstede, G. (1980). *Culture's consequences: International differences in work-related values*. SAGE.

Hong, Y., Morris, M. W., Chiu, C., & Benet-Martinez, V. (2000). Multicultural minds: A dynamic constructivist approach to culture and cognition. *American Psychologist, 55*, 709–720.

Katz, D., & Kahn, R. L. (1972). *The social psychology of organizations* (2nd ed.). Wiley.

Keesing, R. (1974). Theories of culture. *Annual Review of Anthropology, 3*, 73–97.

Kroeber, A. L., & Kluckhohn, C. (1952). *Culture: A critical review of concepts and definitions*. Papers. Peabody Museum of Archaeology & Ethnology, Harvard University.

Kwantes, C. T., & Glazer, S. (2017). *Culture, organizations, and work: Clarifying concepts*. Springer International Publishing.

Lam, C. F., Lee, C., & Sui, Y. (2019). Say it as it is: Consequences of voice directness, voice politeness, and voicer credibility on voice endorsement. *Journal of Applied Psychology, 104*(5), 642–658.

Lewis, R. D. (2006). *When cultures collide: Leading across cultures* (3rd ed.). Nicholas Brealey International.

Lisak, A., Erez, M., Sui, Y., & Lee, C. (2016). The positive role of global leaders in enhancing multicultural team innovation. *Journal of International Business Studies, 47*(6), 655–673.

Liu, L. A., & Adair, W. L. (2017). Intercultural communication in international negotiation. In Y. Y. Kim & K. McKay-Semmler (Eds.), *The international encyclopedia of intercultural communication*. Wiley-Blackwell. https://doi.org/10.1002/9781118783665.ieicc0048

Liu, L. A., Chua, C. H., & Stahl, G. K. (2010). Quality of communication experience: Definition, measurement, and implications for intercultural negotiations. *Journal of Applied Psychology, 95*(3), 469–487.

Liu, L. A., Adair, W. L., Tjosvold, D., & Poliakova, E. (2018). Understanding intercultural dynamics: Insights from competition and cooperation in complex contexts. *Cross Cultural & Strategic Management, 25*(1), 2–31.

Markus, H. R., & Kitayama, S. (1991). Culture and the self: Implications for cognition, emotion, and motivation. *Psychological Review, 98*(2), 224.

McCluney, C. L., Durkee, M. I., Smith, R. E., II, Robotham, K. J., & Lee, S. S. L. (2021). To be, or not to be… Black: The effects of racial codeswitching on perceived professionalism in the workplace. *Journal of Experimental Social Psychology, 97*, 104199.

Merkin, R., Taras, V., & Steel, P. (2014). State of the art themes in cross-cultural communication research: A systematic and meta-analytic review. *International Journal of Intercultural Relations, 38*, 1–23. https://doi.org/10.1016/j.ijintrel.2013.10.004

Miller, K. I., Ellis, B. H., Zook, E. G., & Lyles, J. S. (1990). An integrated model of communication, stress, and burnout in the workplace. *Communication Research, 17*(3), 300–326.
Molinsky, A. (2007). Cross-cultural code-switching: The psychological challenges of adapting behavior in foreign cultural interactions. *Academy of Management Review, 32*(2), 622–640.
Molinsky, A. L. (2013). The psychological processes of cultural retooling. *Academy of Management Journal, 56*(3), 683–710.
Morris, M. W., Hong, Y. Y., Chiu, C. Y., & Liu, Z. (2015). Normology: Integrating insights about social norms to understand cultural dynamics. *Organizational Behavior and Human Decision Processes, 129*, 1–13.
Morrison, E. W. (2011). Employee voice behavior: Integration and directions for future research. *Academy of Management Annals, 5*, 373–412. https://doi.org/10.1080/19416520.2011.574506
Nardon, L. (2017). *Working in a multicultural world: A guide to developing intercultural competence*. University of Toronto Press.
Osland, J. S., & Bird, A. (2000). Beyond sophisticated stereotyping: Cultural sensemaking in context. *Academy of Management Perspectives, 14*(1), 65–77.
Postmes, T. (2003). A social identity approach to communication in organizations. In S. A. Haslam, D. van Knippenberg, M. J. Platow, & N. Ellemers (Eds.), *Social identity at work: Developing theory for organizational practice* (pp. 81–89). Psychology Press.
Ren, R., Ma, L., Wang, H., & Ju, D. (2022). Implicit voice delivery: Its antecedents, consequences, and boundary conditions. *Management and Organization Review, 18*(1), 43–72.
Sanchez-Burks, J., Nisbett, R. E., & Ybarra, O. (2000). Cultural styles, relationship schemas, and prejudice against out-groups. *Journal of Personality and Social Psychology, 79*(2), 174–189. https://doi.org/10.1037/0022-3514.79.2.174
Schein, E. H., & Schein, P. A. (2016). *Organizational culture and leadership* (5th ed.). Springer.
Sharma, S., & Liu, L. A. (2023). Culture and communication. In M. J. Gelfand & M. Erez (Eds.), *Oxford handbook of cross-cultural organizational behavior*. Oxford University Press.
Stahl, G. K., & Maznevski, M. L. (2021). Unraveling the effects of cultural diversity in teams: A retrospective of research on multicultural work groups and an agenda for future research. *Journal of International Business Studies, 52*(1), 4–22.
Sully De Luque, M. F., & Sommer, S. M. (2000). The impact of culture on feedback-seeking behavior: An integrated model and propositions. *Academy of Management Review, 25*(4), 829–849.
Szkudlarek, B., Osland, J. S., Nardon, L., & Zander, L. (2020). Communication and culture in international business–Moving the field forward. *Journal of World Business, 55*(6), 101126.
Tajfel, H. (1981). *Human groups and social categories*. Cambridge University Press.
Ting-Toomey, S. (2005). The matrix of face: An updated face-negotiation theory. In *Theorizing about intercultural communication* (Vol. 4, pp. 71–92). Sage.
Triandis, H. C. (1972). *The analysis of subjective culture*. Wiley.
Triandis, H. C. (1977). *Interpersonal behavior*. Brooks/Cole.
Triandis, H. C. (1994). *Culture and social behavior*. McGraw Hill.
Trompenaars, F., & Hampden-Turner, C. (2011). *Riding the waves of culture: Understanding diversity in global business*. Nicholas Brealey International.
Turner, J. C., Hogg, M. A., Oakes, P. J., Reicher, S. D., & Wetherell, M. S. (1987). *Rediscovering the social group: A self-categorization theory*. Basil Blackwell.
Van Maanen, J., & Barley, S. R. (1984). Occupational communities: Culture and control in organizations. *Research in Organizational Behavior, 6*(1), 287–365.
Wang, J., Cheng, G. H. L., Chen, T., & Leung, K. (2019). Team creativity/innovation in culturally diverse teams: A meta-analysis. *Journal of Organizational Behavior, 40*(6), 693–708.
Ward, A. K., Ravlin, E. C., Klaas, B. S., Ployhart, R. E., & Buchan, N. R. (2016). When do high-context communicators speak up? Exploring contextual communication orientation and employee voice. *Journal of Applied Psychology, 101*(10), 1498–1541.
Weick, K. E. (1969). *The social psychology of organizing*. Addison Wesley.

Chapter 2
The Secret Code of Nonverbal Communication

Nonverbal communication is an elaborate secret code that is written nowhere, known by all. – Edward Sapir

Edward Hall's statement that "culture is communication and communication is culture" (Hall, 1959, p. 169) reflects the view of many anthropologists who consider culture an adaptive system. That is, culture is a system that links individuals to the ecological setting or context in which they live (Keesing, 1974; Gudykunst & Ting-Toomey, 1988). Within this anthropological perspective, culture can be boiled down to "behavioral patterns associated with particular groups of people, to 'customs' or to a people's 'way of life'" (Harris, 1968, p. 16). It is within these particular groups that the secret code of nonverbal communication is known by all.

Triandis (1980) further elaborated on culture from a social psychological perspective, suggesting that culture can be viewed as a function of interrelated systems, including the ecological, subsistence, socio-cultural, individual, and inter individual systems, and that it is through this framework of interrelated systems that we can understand culture and its relation to individual and collective actions and interactions (Erez & Early, 1993). Specifically, Triandis (1977) proposed that the ecological system refers to the physical environment, including the resources, geography, flora, and fauna surrounding a people. The subsistence system refers to the methods by which individuals in a society will use ecological resources to survive, e.g., hunting and fishing, gathering food, and creating industry. The socio-cultural system refers to institutional behavior, family structure, norms, roles, and values as they exist outside the individual (i.e., within society or the ecological context) (Triandis, 1977). The individual system refers to individual aspects of behavior, values, perceptions and attitudes, learning, and motivational patterns; finally, the interindividual system refers to the socialization system, that is, to social behaviors such as social networks and child rearing (Bhagat & McQuaid, 1982; Triandis, 1977).

In this chapter we develop a framework of culture and contextualized communication. We propose that individuals who share a common language, who interact

W. L. Adair et al., *What Isn't Being Said*, Springer Series in Emerging Cultural Perspectives in Work, Organizational, and Personnel Studies,
https://doi.org/10.1007/978-3-031-53645-8_2

frequently because of shared physical locale, and who have shared perceptions of rules, norms, roles, customs, and values – that is, a shared subjective culture – rely on and attend to similar nonverbal cues in the communication context surrounding message, relationship, time, and space (Adair et al., 2016). Within a shared subjective culture, "behavioral patterns," "customs" (Harris, 1968, p. 16), "unstated assumptions," and "standard operating procedures" (Triandis, 1994, p. 6) are adapted and internalized among individuals such that distinct communication patterns develop and become implicit and adaptive.

Our model (see Fig. 2.1 and to be explained in the rest of this chapter) supports the idea that culture and communication are intricately intertwined. Culture may be a group-level phenomenon, but culture itself is enacted and sustained at the individual level through communication and interaction between actors in specific organizational contexts (Brannen & Salk, 2000; Van Maanen & Barley, 1984). Context is related to the unspoken, unformulated, implicit rules governing how information is handled and how people interact and relate (Hall, 1976). These rules are often deeply embedded in culture at an aggregate level, in the collective's commonly shared values and norms (Hall, 1976; Triandis, 1972).

Given the different levels of interaction then, an obvious question one might ask is, how does the individual become in sync with the cultural strategies of others enacted at the group level? As Shteyneberg (2010) proposes, it may be that groups maintain social attunement through vigilant monitoring for stimuli experienced by others in the group. Results from Shteyneberg's experiments with nonverbal stimuli and implicit cues suggest that individuals align to the group by way of fast and frugal heuristics (Gigerenzer, 2004): i.e., "if those in my social group experience the stimuli, it is mentally prioritized," (Shteynberg, 2010, p. 688). Thus, individuals are constantly scanning the environmental context for cues as to the communication

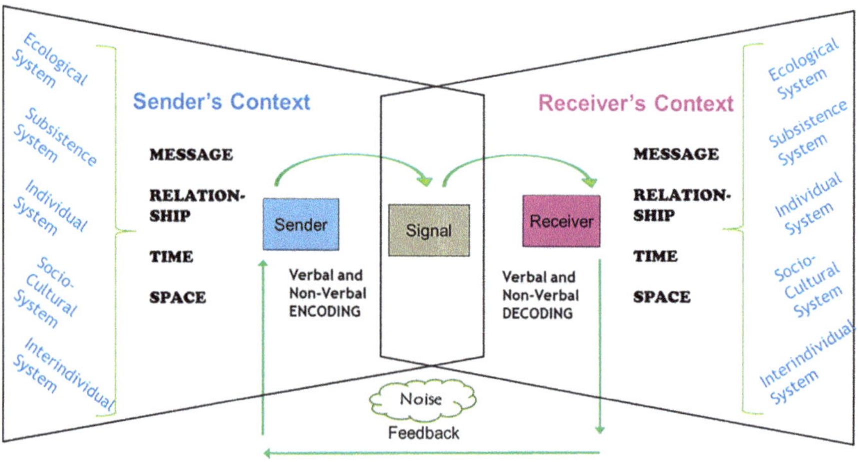

Fig. 2.1 Interactive model of contextualized communication. (Developed based on Schramm (1954, p. 3))

strategies and norms of their group. In adhering to perceived descriptive norms, individuals are, in a sense, on autopilot that "automatically guides immediate responses in a socially safe direction" (Morris et al., 2015, p. 7). Furthermore, people have social radar that is, "acting in line with the injunctive norms of identity groups is a looping process of sending a signal and having it reflected back in order to validate one's position" (Morris et al., 2015, p. 7). These theories thus support the idea that understanding the interaction context is central to understanding how culture is enacted in communication.

Regarding culture, one important thing to note is that as the cohesion or social identity of a collective develops, group-level values, norms, and beliefs also develop. These specific and often implicit values, norms, and beliefs can emerge in any number of groups throughout society. As such, the model suggested here applies to every societal group in and with which we need to communicate effectively – national cultures, ethnicities, genders, generations, professions (lawyers versus social workers, for instance), and even across corporate functional areas in a single workplace (such as engineering versus marketing versus accounting). In addition to values, norms, and beliefs, each of these cultural groups may develop standard operating procedures, behavioral patterns, and unwritten scripts, allowing the members of the group to communicate with one another and be understood both verbally and nonverbally.

Culture, Communication, and Context Dependence

Contextual cues are integral to the meaning-making of verbal and, more particularly, nonverbal messages. Hall argued that "without context, the (linguistic) code is incomplete since it encompasses only part of the message" (1976, p. 86). Context-dependent communication is not only about how people convey information but also about the degree to which they attend to and use contextual cues in their environment to reason and relate to others in social interaction (Adair et al., 2016). People who are high-context communicators attend to and rely heavily on cues in their interaction environment to relay or interpret meaning. Low-context communicators tend not to use such cues; for them, meanings tend to be captured literally and explicitly in the words used. Communication as a system linking individuals to the subjective cultural or ecological context in which they live (Hall, 1959) can be distilled into four key (non-orthogonal) components (Adair et al., 2009, 2016): the message, relationship, time, and space domains of communication context. These four domains comprise an individual's context dependence, defined as the individual's internalized standard operating procedures for communication and social interaction characterized by a subjective cultural dependence on direct or indirect messages, and attention to contextual cues in the relationship, temporal and spatial domains of the interaction to convey or interpret meaning (Adair et al., 2016).

The Message Domain of Communication Context

The message domain of communication context is defined by the nonverbal cues that convey implied and inferred meaning accompanying a verbal message (Adair et al., 2016). People lower in context dependence communicate directly and explicitly; they do not rely heavily on their environment to convey meaning. In contrast, people higher in context dependence tend to use implicit language or communicate indirectly, relying on information (cues) contained in the context surrounding the speaker – for example, in the socio-cultural system (e.g., institutional and family norms) and the interindividual or social system (e.g., social behaviors and networks) – to convey meaning. Within the individual system in high-context communication, people rely on internal context – information contained in the individual, for example, in nonverbal cues or the life experience one brings to a social interaction. Because high-context communication is indirect and implicit, listeners take a more active role than in low-context cultures; listeners engage in search and inference behind and beneath the words spoken to interpret meaning. Indeed, because in high-context cultures, "it's not what is said, but how one says it" that imparts meaning, the listener needs to be highly attuned to gestures, posture, eye gaze, and tone of voice to fully understand all that was conveyed. In contrast, in low context cultures where individuals "say what they mean and mean what they say," the meaning is clear from the words used and such search and inference is not needed.

For example, for people in low-context cultures, silence is an uncomfortable form of auditory space interpreted as a void to be filled (Hasegawa & Gudykunst, 1998). Thus, in a study of interactional involvement among low-context US Americans, fewer silences and more conversational interruption and turn-taking signaled better interaction management (Coker & Burgoon, 1987). In contrast, for East Asian communicators, who are higher in context dependence, silence is not an empty space but a communicative act that can carry multiple meanings (Lebra, 1987; Gudykunst et al., 1996). In Japan, for example, silence may indicate disapproval or disagreement, but it can also signal truthfulness, seriousness, or support for one's interlocutor (Lebra, 1987).

The Relationship Domain of Communication Context

The relationship domain of communication context is defined by the unspoken relational cues that influence how people communicate with others (Adair et al., 2016), which is highly related to the social and socio-cultural norms regarding role responsibilities and attention to status that are initially taught in the household and reinforced in school and the workplace. The relationship indicators include the interlocutor's age, gender, ethnicity, job title, and status. They also include how long they have known each other, what interactional history they had before, how much they trust each other, and how similar or different they are in terms of age, gender, status, etc. For example, Gudykunst (1983) found that in initial meetings, people in high-context cultures ask more questions about strangers' backgrounds than members of low-context cultures; they search for relationship context. Once a friendship bond is established, no more questions will be asked or doubts will be raised. But if no clear relationship can be established, the communication style will be rather different. Instead of warmth, coldness, or even hostility will ensue. This is because the relationship context influences what is said and also how it is said, allowing for the use of implicit scripts and reliance on internalized norms (Lewis, 2010).

Similarly, the relationship context is influenced by the extent to which the parties compartmentalize their personal relationships from their work relationships, or the specific vs. diffuse involvement in relationships (Trompenaars & Hampden-Turner, 1997). Ashforth and colleagues propose that cultures vary in the degree to which roles are segmented versus integrated and how individuals transition from one role to another (Ashforth et al., 2000). This degree of compartmentalization will often determine the extent of verbalized information required in a given transaction. Hall and Hall (2002) offer some examples:

> Japanese, Arabs, and Mediterranean peoples, who have extensive information networks among family, friends, colleagues, and clients and who are involved in close personal relationships, are high-context. As a result, for most normal transactions in daily life they do not require, nor do they expect, much in depth background information… Low-context people…compartmentalize their personal relationships, their work, and many aspects of day-to-day life. Consequently, each time they interact with others they need detailed background information. (pp. 200–201)

The relationship context also influences the degree to which face-saving measures will be employed in communication. Cohen writes that in high-context cultures, "language is a social instrument – a device for preserving and promoting social interests as much as a means for transmitting information" (1997, p. 32). Adjusting or adapting one's own communication style to a counterpart is a social and relational component explained by Communication Accommodation Theory (CAT) – the tendency for people to reduce interpersonal and group boundaries through communication responses that are similar or complementary to a counterpart's communication style (Gallois et al., 2005; see Chap. 3). Such social and relational tendencies are emphasized in high-context cultures. In contrast, in low-context cultures, language "performs on the whole an informational rather than socially lubricative function" (Cohen, 1997, p. 33). And, importantly, face-work can often be done without a single word spoken – through facial expressions, brow movements, body orientation, and touch (Trees & Manusov, 1998) – and apologies can be conveyed or conflicts avoided. Such mutual understanding via communication without words is called *moqi* in Chinese (Chen & Cole, 2023) and is commonly observed in high-context cultures such as Japan and Mexico.

Previous research has shown significant cultural differences in how much people value relationship harmony and relational order/hierarchy (Hofstede, 1980; Bond, 1993; Triandis, 1977, 1988). In particular, people in cultures that inherited Confucian values (e.g., China, Japan, Korea) tend to focus more on maintaining relational harmony and relational order than do people in more individualistic cultures (e.g., the United States, Canada) (Brewer & Chen, 2007). The relationship focus even becomes a distinct characteristic of Chinese society, in which "guanxi" permeates every aspect of human interaction, including interpersonal communication in the workplace. Guanxi is an informal, personal, and particularistic connection between two individuals (Chen et al., 2004). Unlike the professionalism emphasized in compartmentalized cultures that discourage the mix of work and life, in Chinese organizations, people tend to develop informal, personal, and particularistic relationships with their colleagues and superiors (Chen et al., 2009; Chen & Peng, 2008), through which both cognitive and affective trust are built. Due to the particularistic nature of guanxi, people in China adopt differential treatments to those with a close vs distant guanxi (Chen et al., 2004, 2013; Law et al., 2000); one such treatment is communication style. The guanxi between the two interlocutors will largely determine their communication frequency, communication setting (e.g., private or public, in office or over dinner), and communication style (demeanor).

For instance, when there is only a role-based relationship between a supervisor and a subordinate, communication only happens when it is mandatory, in a formal setting, regarding job-related issues. In such a relational context, the supervisor is likely to show authority by keeping a distance and exhibiting an assertive tone in communication. In contrast, the subordinate tends to listen more and talk less, often taking notes and showing respect by not directly looking into the eye of the supervisor while maintaining eye contact. However, when there is close guanxi between the subordinate and the supervisor, they are likely to communicate more frequently in both formal and informal settings (e.g., restaurants, coffee shops, social events, weddings, and birthday parties). In this relational context, their status difference will appear smaller, and they tend to communicate in a more relaxed and natural manner.

The Time Domain of Communication Context

Time is part of a socio-cultural system – it is socially constructed and reflects cultural variation in pace of life, time horizons, temporal focus, and simultaneous versus sequential task involvement (Bluedorn, 2002; Brislin & Kim, 2003; Brislin & Lo, 2006; MacDuff, 2006). Some cultures view time as fluid and have a more holistic and cyclical notion of time and events, influenced by nature, seasons, customs and traditions. In contrast, other cultures view time as a tangible commodity controlled by the clock and have a more linear and sequential perception of time, influenced by technology and industrialization (Aldulaimi & Abdeldayem, 2018; Fulmer et al., 2014; Levine, 2008; Lewis, 2010). Temporal communication focuses on the manner in which people organize and react to time. "Time talks. It speaks more plainly than words. The message it conveys comes through loud and clear." (Hall, 1959, p. 1). Thus, we define the time context of communication as the cues within a communication environment that convey meaning associated with interlocutors' understanding of time (Adair et al., 2016).

In polychronic cultures," people tend to engage in simultaneous information processing, have fluid attitudes toward time, and view punctuality and deadlines as artificial constraints relative to the reality of human relationships (Hall, 1959). For the polychronic individual, catching up with a friend you've run into on the way to your office is much more important than arriving "on time" for a meeting with a new associate. People from monochronic cultures, on the other hand, process information in a serial fashion, which is reflected in a segmented and sequential approach to clock time, schedules, and deadlines. For them, time can be measured, saved, spent, invested, or lost. For the monochronic person, it seems inconceivable and rude that in a business meeting their polychronic partner would arrive "late" for the meeting and then allow constant interruptions – phone calls, messages, and even other people (Gesteland, 1999; Hall, 1960; Hall & Hall, 2002). This distinction between the strict, objective, monochronic view of time and the more fluid, contextual, polychronic view of time is captured in the time domain of context dependence.

Temporal communication conveys a nonverbal message, but the meaning is likely to be understood only if the listener is similar to the speaker in terms of high or low contextualization. Being "on time" may convey respect for low-context communicators, and "being late" might convey rudeness. But, for high-context communicators who view time more fluidly, worries about "on time" arrival might convey someone is uptight; rather, the priority is on tending to the relationship in front of you at the moment, regardless of how long it takes.

For example, individuals in Arab cultures tend to view time as flexible and adaptable rather than rigid and fixed. They value relationships more than schedules and do not like to rush things or miss out on opportunities to connect with others. They also believe in fate and destiny and that things happen when they are supposed to happen. For example, when someone says, "I will meet you tomorrow at 10 a.m., inshallah," they are not only expressing their intention to meet, but also acknowledging that there may be unforeseen events or opportunities that could affect their schedule. The phrase may also indicate flexibility and adaptability to changing circumstances and can be a way of coping with uncertainty and complexity in a fluid time culture.[1] As such, it is not uncommon for Arabs to be late, even when a strict clock time is given, and such "lateness" for a meeting or an appointment is not considered rude or disrespectful but rather normal and acceptable (van Eerde & Azar, 2020).

[1] Note this refers to managing environmental uncertainty, not uncertainty stemming from an intercultural interaction, which is addressed by Anxiety Uncertainty Management theory (Gudykunst, 1983) in Chap. 3.

The Space Domain of Communication Context

The ecological and physical environment where we are located influences proxemics, our perception of space, and how we use space to communicate. The most obvious is the level of the physical boundary; one can stake territory or communicate power by maintaining (or infringing on another's) invisible bubble of space or by choosing a corner office on a top floor. Less obvious is when space communication works at the level of the other senses. "Few people realize that space is perceived by all the senses, not by vision alone. Auditory space is perceived by the ears, thermal space by the skin, kinesthetic space by the muscles, and olfactory space by the nose" (Hall & Hall, 2002, p. 11). Thus, factors such as the use of silence, interruption, emotion, and body language also come into play. How people define and interpret these different forms of space in communication and social interaction provides another piece of contextual information that differentiates low- and high-context cultures.

One example of how space communicates in different cultures is the meaning associated with personal space. In high-context Latin cultures, people share space in communication. Touching someone's shoulder, speaking loudly, and using expressive hand gestures are all ways of saying, "I am listening and engaged in this conversation with you." Such a communication style would be considered overbearing and aggressive in more high-context East Asian cultures where personal space between communicators is reserved for listening, reflection, and respect (Hall & Hall, 2002; Mandal, 2014). In Indigenous cultures, the physical space between two people is communication itself. Each party is responsible for what they put into that space, making sure it is the right time and place to release their words and that the people receiving those words will, in turn, act responsibly with them (Verbos & Humphries, 2014). Speakers and listeners are equal participants and equally responsible for the knowledge shared and cocreated in the communication space (Wilson, 2008). We see these principles enacted in Indigenous sharing circles used for problem-solving, conflict management, and strategizing (Redpath & Nielsen, 1997). Emotion and body language are also important elements of space context. The tone of conversation or the volume of speech is one cue, as are facial expressions, hand gestures, and body movement, the meanings of which vary greatly across cultures (Cohen, 1997; Hall, 1966). As would be expected, individuals in high-context cultures are more likely to be attuned to auditory and physical cues. Thus, as with time, both attention to space and space itself communicate information.

Communication Context as Culture

The culture-as-an-iceberg metaphor is useful here in that it illustrates that the visible part of a culture (e.g., surface characteristics such as dress, language, food, music) is small relative to the massive invisible foundation (e.g., values, norms, beliefs, human nature), that floats beneath the water (Schein & Schein, 2016). One should also note that similar to the danger inherent in icebergs for sea-going ships, what is hidden below the surface can be most perilous to cross-cultural communication precisely because of how much is unknown. Groups develop cultural systems that relate to survival, sense of control, and predictability within their physical and social environment. We replicate and reinforce culture through socialization, education, and institutional support and persist with adaptive behaviors that work for us.

The communication context is located at the intersection of hidden values and visible behaviors. Here, the opportunity exists to establish a deep connection with others during interaction via understanding the cues in this context. We suggest that nonverbal information derives from the communication context, including that which resides within the communicator (e.g., through emotions, eye contact, body movement, use of silence and tone of voice); and that which resides outside the communicator (e.g., the temporal setting and location of the interaction, the physical and social surroundings – including the relationship between the interlocutors, and the channel through which the communication is happening). This nonverbal information, both within and outside the communicator, is yielded from the basic elements of the communication context (Adair et al., 2009, 2016; Hall, 1976).

When communicating with others, it is from the context of our interactions that we draw cues about the meaning of messages sent or received. Some of these messages are manifested in verbal communication in low context culture (for example, a German businessperson using all of their counterpart's titles in an introduction to acknowledge their higher status in the relationship). Some of the messages are manifested in nonverbal behaviors that can also be observed (for example, a Japanese businessperson using the appropriately deep bow in deference to a superior). Many nonverbal behaviors are not visible and are more difficult to detect (for example, the implicit meaning of the extent of time you are made to wait for your meeting with a high-ranking government official in Saudi Arabia whom you have never met). To fully understand the meaning of verbal and nonverbal language, one must understand the message, relationship, time, and space contexts in which the meaning is transmitted and received (Fig. 2.2).

The Roots of Individual Contextualization and Nonverbal Communication

Communication is at the heart of international business (Brannen, 2004a). In addition to the relational function of communication explained by CAT (Gallois et al., 2005; Chap. 3 in this volume), the purpose of communication is also to convey meaning and establish understanding through information exchange (Beamer & Varner, 2008; Brannen, 2004b). While the information can be transmitted both verbally (i.e., through coded, explicitly worded messages) and nonverbally (i.e., through visual cues and paralanguage displayed by one's interlocutor and by cues in

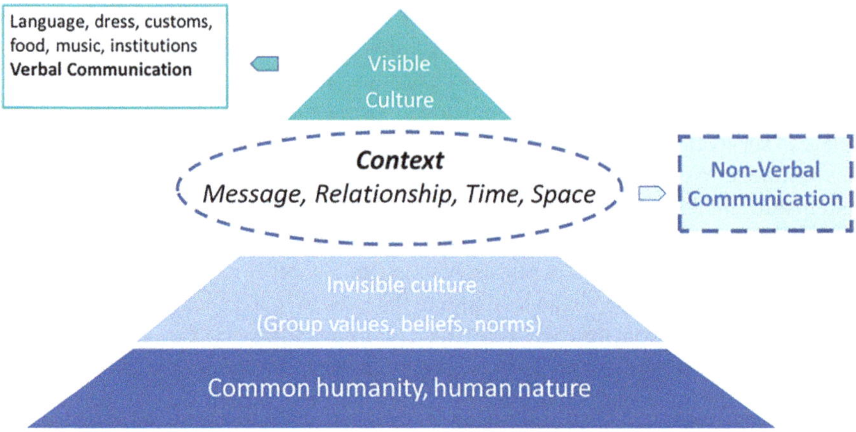

Fig. 2.2 A contextualized version of Schein & Schein's iceberg model of communication (2016, p. 28)

the communication environment), researchers estimate that nonverbal communication transmits approximately 65% of the meaning in an interaction (Birdwhistell, 1955; Burgoon et al., 1996).

The relationship between context and communication was highlighted by Trompenaars and Hampden-Turner (2011, p. 111): "Context has to do with how much you have to know before effective communication can occur, how much shared knowledge is taken for granted by those in conversation with each other, how much reference there is to tacit common ground." In other words, communication context can be defined as the shared knowledge and tacit common ground that are taken for granted by those in conversation. The more shared knowledge and tacit common ground between two interlocutors, the higher the context of communication. In such a case, meaning can be deciphered, and understanding can be established with little use of verbal explicit messages. On the other hand, the less shared knowledge and tacit common ground between two interlocutors, the lower the context of communication. In this case, much verbal explicit messaging needs to be used to convey meaning and establish understanding.

Because context is related to the unspoken, unformulated, implicit rules governing how information is handled and how people interact and relate, these rules are often deeply embedded in culture at an aggregate level, defined as a social group's commonly shared values and norms (Hall, 1976; Triandis, 1972). It follows then that the unspoken, unformulated, implicit rules governing how information is handled are highly related to individual cultural values regarding how people view themselves and their relationship with others, i.e., self-construal (Markus & Kitayama, 1991). We demonstrated in prior research that people with an interdependent self-construal are also more likely to rely on cues in the context to gather meaning; that is, they are likely to be a high-context communicator (Adair et al., 2016). Based on Markus and Kitayama's (1991) theory, people with a stronger independent self-construal are likely to think of themselves as autonomous and independent and organize their behavior in reference to their own internal repertoire of thoughts, feelings, and actions rather than by reference to those of the people around them (Markus & Kitayama, 1991). For these individuals, a more self-centered approach is adopted in communication such that they rely little on the communication context to convey meaning. In other words, they rely mostly on explicit verbalized thoughts and ideas and tend to use a context-free approach to manage information exchange.

By contrast, for people with a stronger interdependent self-construal, "one's thoughts, feelings, and actions are made meaningful in reference to the thoughts, feelings, and actions of others in the relationship, and consequently, others are crucially important in the very definition of the self" (Markus & Kitayama, 1991, p. 570). For these individuals an other-centered approach will be adopted; they are likely to be context-dependent or sensitive to nonverbal cues in communication by paying much attention to the four domains of context (i.e., message, relationship, time, and space) to convey and understand meaning (Adair et al., 2016; Singelis & Brown, 1995). Depending on the relationship between the interlocutors, the temporal nature of the conversation, and the location where the conversation happens, interdependently minded individuals will choose the words they use and the manner, facial expression, and physical distance they exhibit to convey a particular meaning.

The Process of Contextualized Communication

The interaction model of communication introduced by Schramm (1954), depicted in Fig. 2.3, suggests that communication is a two-way process by which participants – a sender and a receiver – impart meaning through encoding and decoding their thoughts into transmitted signals given their particular fields of experience. These fields of experience reflect each individual's lived experiences, including

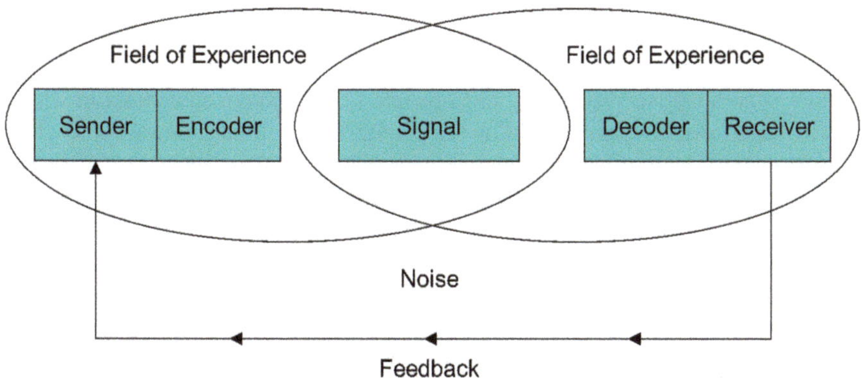

Fig. 2.3 Illustration of Schramm's interactive model of communication. (Schramm, 1954, p. 3)

culture. When sending and receiving such signals, it is important to understand the manner in which one's field of experience influences how meaning will be encoded and how the signal will be decoded or understood. The greater the overlap in fields of experience, the more likely the signal sent will be understood by the receiver. If there is no overlap, the intended meaning and the meaning interpreted may be quite different, and it will be very difficult for any real communication to occur.

We elaborate on Schramm's model to reflect a more comprehensive role of cultural context in the communication process. Specifically, we suggest that the fields of experience for the sender and receiver encompass all that Hall (1959) and Triandis (1977, 1980) proposed culture to be – the ecological, subsistence, individual, socio-cultural and interindividual contexts influencing the communicator. Furthermore, senders and receivers communicate thoughts or ideas based on their fields of experience, which influence a multitude of factors affecting how the message is encoded and decoded. For example, the language in which the thought or idea is coded, the posture of the speaker and responder, gestures, expression and tone of voice used to convey meaning, the communication setting or time it was delivered, the extent of touching (haptics) or eye contact (gaze) used during the delivery, are all manifestations of these culturally contextualized fields of experience, and all can influence meaning. As with Schramm's original model, if there is no or little overlap in the speakers' fields of experience, or cultural contexts as presented here, they will have much difficulty in encoding or decoding thoughts or ideas understood with the intended meaning by both communicators.

However, the greater the overlap between the environmental contexts of the Sender and the Receiver, transmitted thoughts and ideas are likely to be more clearly understood. The communication process then sends, receives, and returns messages, which are likely to occur more easily and efficiently, with less noise due to the deeper understanding of each other's context. This ease of communication and the efficiency of it leads to the greater likelihood of collaboration between the two interlocutors (Fig. 2.4).

Summary

Culture is an adaptive system that links people to the ecological context in which they live and interact. Communication is a manifestation of that cultural context and is itself an expression of culture, be it at the ecological, subsistence, socio-cultural, interindividual, or individual levels. As such, the communication patterns of each individual differ depending on whether, for example, they live in close-knit agricultural communities versus in more heterogenous and autonomous city dwellings, or whether they have an independent or interdependent self-construal.

Communicators encode and decode messages in ways consistent with their own cultural context, using both verbal and nonverbal means to get their message across. The extent to which the communicators' fields of experience overlap will determine whether the intended message matches the interpreted one. Culturally contextualized communication will typically carry meanings beneath the messages and

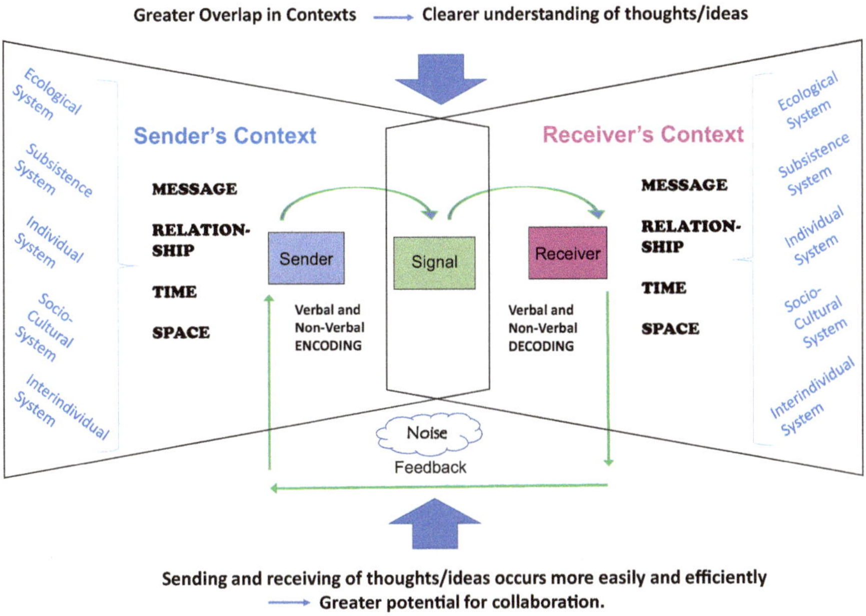

Fig. 2.4 Interactive model of contextualized communication. (Developed based on Schramm (1954, p. 3))

implicit cues based on the unwritten scripts and norms of the communicator. The model presented here provides an understanding of how such cues might come about and how the meanings might be transmitted and manifested.

References

Adair, W., Buchan, N. R., & Chen, X. P. (2009). Conceptualizing culture as communication in management and marketing research. In C. Nakata (Ed.), *Beyond Hofstede: Cultural frameworks for global marketing and management* (pp. 146–180). Macmillian Publishers Limited.

Adair, W. L., Buchan, N. R., Chen, X. P., & Liu, D. (2016). A model of communication context and measure of context dependence. *Academy of Management Discoveries, 2*(2), 198–217.

Aldulaimi, S. H., & Abdeldayem, M. M. (2018). The economic value of time in Arab culture: New evidence using Zimbardo Time Perspective Inventory (ZTPI). *American Journal of Social Sciences and Humanities, 3*(1), 63–72.

Ashforth, H. E., Kreiner, G. E., & Fugate, M. (2000). All in a day's work: Boundaries and micro role transitions. *Academy of Management Review, 25*(3), 472–491.

Beamer, L., & Varner, I. I. (2008). *Intercultural communication in the global workplace*. McGraw-Hill Irwin.

Bhagat, R. S., & McQuaid, S. J. (1982). Role of subjective culture in organizations: A review and directions for future research. *Journal of Applied Psychology, 67*(5), 653–685.

Birdwhistell, R. L. (1955). Background to kinesics. *ETC: A Review of General Semantics, 13*(1), 10–18.
Bluedorn, A. C. (2002). *The human organization of time: Temporal realities and experience*. Stanford University Press.
Bond, M. H. (1993). Emotions and their expression in Chinese culture. *Journal of Nonverbal Behavior, 17(4)*, 245–262.
Brannen, M. Y. (2004a). When Mickey loses face: Recontextualization, semantic fit, and the semiotics of foreignness. *Academy of Management Review, 29*(4), 593–616.
Brannen, M. Y. (2004b). *Global meeting grounds: Negotiating complex cultural contexts across organizations*. Oxford University Press.
Brannen, M. Y., & Salk, J. E. (2000). Partnering across borders: Negotiating organizational culture in a German-Japanese joint venture. *Human Relations, 53*(4), 451–487.
Brewer, M. B., & Chen, Y. R. (2007). Where (who) are collectives in collectivism? Toward conceptual clarification of individualism and collectivism. *Psychological Review, 114*(1), 133.
Brislin, R. W., & Kim, E. S. (2003). Cultural diversity in people's understanding and uses of time. *Applied Psychology: An International Review, 52*(3), 363–382.
Brislin, R. W., & Lo, K. D. (2006). Culture, personality, and people's uses of time: Key interrelationships. In J. C. Thomas, D. L. Degal, & M. Hersen (Eds.), *Comprehensive handbook of personality and psychopathology* (Vol. 1, pp. 44–61). Wiley.
Burgoon, J. K., Buller, D. B., & Woodall, W. G. (1996). *Nonverbal communication: The unspoken dialog*. McGraw-Hill.
Chen, X. P., & Cole, B. M. (2023). Achieving mutual understanding without saying a word: The conceptualization of Moqi and a nomological network. *Management and Organization Review, 19*(1), 3–31.
Chen, X. P., & Peng, S. (2008). Guanxi dynamics: Shifts in the closeness of ties between Chinese coworkers. *Management and Organization Review, 4*(1), 63–80.
Chen, C. C., Chen, Y. R., & Xin, K. (2004). Guanxi practices and trust in management: A procedural justice perspective. *Organization Science, 15*(2), 200–209.
Chen, Y., Friedman, R., Yu, E., Fang, W., & Lu, X. (2009). Supervisor–subordinate guanxi: Developing a three-dimensional model and scale. *Management and Organization Review, 5*(3), 375–399.
Chen, C. C., Chen, X. P., & Huang, S. S. (2013). *Guanxi* and social network research: Review and future directions. *Management and Organization Review, 9*(1), 167–207.
Cohen, R. (1997). *Negotiating across cultures: Communication obstacles in international diplomacy*. United States Institute of Peace Press.
Coker, D. A., & Burgoon, J. K. (1987). The nature of conversational involvement and nonverbal encoding patters. *Human Communications Research, 13*(4), 463–494.
Erez, M., & Early, P. C. (1993). *Culture, self-identity, and work*. Oxford University Press.
Fulmer, C. A., Crosby, B., & Gelfand, M. J. (2014). Cross-cultural perspectives on time. *Time and Work, 2*, 53–75.
Gallois, C., Ogay, T., & Giles, H. (2005). Communication accommodation theory: A look back and a look ahead. In W. B. Gudykunst (Ed.), *Theorizing about intercultural communication* (pp. 121–148). Sage.
Gesteland, R. R. (1999). *Cross-cultural business behavior: Marketing, negotiating and managing across cultures*. Copenhagen Business School Press.
Gigerenzer, G. (2004). Fast and frugal heuristics: The tools of bounded rationality. In D. Koehler & N. Harvey (Eds.), *Blackwell handbook of judgment and decision making* (pp. 62–88). Blackwell.
Gudykunst, W. B. (1983). Uncertainty reduction and predictability of behavior in low-and-high context cultures. *Communication Quarterly, 31*, 49–55.
Gudykunst, W. B., & Ting-Toomey, S. (1988). *Culture and interpersonal communication*. Sage.
Gudykunst, W. B., Matsumoto, Y., Ting-Toomey, S., Nishida, T., Kim, K., & Heyman, S. (1996). The influence of cultural individualism-collectivism, self construals, and individual values on communication styles across cultures. *Human Communication Research, 22*(4), 510–543.

Hall, E. T. (1959). *The silent language*. Random House.

Hall, E. T. (1960). The silent language in overseas business. *Harvard Business Review, 38*(3), 87–96.

Hall, E. T. (1966). *The hidden dimension*. Doubleday.

Hall, E. T. (1976). *Beyond culture*. Random House.

Hall, E. T., & Hall, M. R. (2002). Key concepts: Underlying structures of culture. In J. M. Martin, T. K. Nakayama, & L. A. Flores (Eds.), *Readings in cultural communication: Experiences and contexts*. McGraw Hill.

Harris, M. (1968). *The rise of anthropological theory*. Crowell.

Hasegawa, T., & Gudykunst, W. B. (1998). Silence in Japan and the United States. *Journal of Cross-Cultural Psychology, 29*(5), 668–684.

Hofstede, G. (1980). *Culture's consequences: International differences in work-related values*. Sage.

Keesing, R. (1974). Theories of culture. *Annual Review of Anthropology, 3*, 73–97.

Law, K. S., Wong, C. S., Wang, D., & Wang, L. (2000). Effect of supervisor–subordinate guanxi on supervisory decisions in China: An empirical investigation. *International Journal of Human Resource Management, 11*(4), 751–765.

Lebra, T. S. (1987). The cultural significance of silence in Japanese conversation. *Multilingua, 6*(4), 343–357.

Levine, R. V. (2008). *A geography of time: On tempo, culture, and the pace of life*. New York, NY: Basic Books.

Lewis, R. (2010). *When cultures collide* (pp. 171–211). Nicholas Brealey Publishing.

MacDuff, I. (2006). Your pace or mine? Culture, time and negotiation. *Negotiation Journal, 22*(1), 31–45.

Mandal, F. B. (2014). Nonverbal communication in humans. *Journal of Human Behavior in the Social Environment, 24*(4), 417–421.

Markus, H. R., & Kitayama, S. (1991). Culture and the self: Implications for cognition, emotion, and motivation. In R. F. Baumeister (Ed.), *The self in social psychology. Key readings in social psychology* (pp. 339–371). Psychology Press/Taylor & Francis.

Morris, M. W., Hong, Y. Y., Chiu, C. Y., & Liu, Z. (2015). Normology: Integrating insights about social norms to understand cultural dynamics. *Organizational Behavior and Human Decision Processes, 129*, 1–13.

Redpath, L., & Nielsen, M. O. (1997). A comparison of native culture, non-native culture and new management ideology. *Canadian Journal of Administrative Sciences/Revue Canadienne des Sciences de l'Administration, 14*(3), 327–339. https://doi.org/10.1111/j.1936-4490.1997.tb00139.x

Schein, E. H., & Schein, P. A. (2016). *Organizational culture and leadership* (5th ed.). Springer.

Schramm, W. (1954). How communication works. In W. Schramm (Ed.), *The process and effects of mass communication* (pp. 3–26). University of Illinois Press.

Shteynberg, G. (2010). A silent emergence of culture: The social tuning effect. *Journal of Personality and Social Psychology, 99*(4), 683–689.

Singelis, T. M., & Brown, W. J. (1995). Culture, self, and collectivist communication: Linking culture to individual behavior. *Human Communication Research, 21*(3), 354–389.

Trees, A. R., & Manusov, V. (1998). Managing face concerns in criticism: Integrating nonverbal behaviors as a dimension of politeness in female friendship dyads. *Human Communication Research, 24*(4), 564–583. https://doi.org/10.1111/j.1468-2958.1998.tb00431.x

Triandis, H. C. (1972). *The analysis of subjective culture*. Wiley.

Triandis, H. C. (1977). *Interpersonal behavior*. Brooks/Cole.

Triandis, H. C. (1980). Values, attitudes, and interpersonal behavior. In H. E. Howe & H. M. Page (Eds.), *Nebraska symposium on motivation*. University of Nebraska Press.

Triandis, H. C. (1988). Collectivism and individualism: A reconceptualization of a basic concept in cross-cultural psychology. In G. K. Verma & C. Bargley (Eds.), *Personality, attitudes, and cognition* (pp. 60–95). McMillan.

Triandis, H. C. (1994). *Culture and social behavior*. McGraw Hill.

Trompenaars, F., & Hampden-Turner, C. (1997). *Riding the waves of culture: Understanding diversity in global business* (2nd ed.). McGraw Hill.

Trompenaars, F., & Hampden-Turner, C. (2011). *Riding the waves of culture: Understanding diversity in global business*. Nicholas Brealey International.

van Eerde, W., & Azar, S. (2020). Too late? What do you mean? Cultural norms regarding lateness for meetings and appointments. *Cross-Cultural Research, 54*(2–3), 111–129.

Van Maanen, J., & Barley, S. R. (1984). Occupational communities: Culture and control in organizations. *Research in Organizational Behavior, 6*(1), 287–365.

Verbos, A. K., & Humphries, M. (2014). A Native American relational ethic: An Indigenous perspective on teaching human responsibility. *Journal of Business Ethics, 123*, 1–9. https://doi.org/10.1007/s10551-013-1790-3

Wilson, S. 2008. *Research is ceremony: Indigenous research methods*. Halifax, NS: Fernwood Publishing.

Chapter 3
The Quest for Understanding and Connection: Theoretical Perspectives on Communication

Great communication begins with connection. – Oprah Winfrey, television producer and host, author, philanthropist

The problem with communication… is the illusion that it has taken place. – George Bernard Shaw

The previous chapter identified macro systems that define social norms that influence an individual's tendencies to communicate more directly in words and more indirectly through nonverbal cues in the message, relationship, time, and space domains of communication context. In cross-cultural communication, the sender and receiver often see and define the world differently, with different norms governing the context of communication. Whether information is stated directly in words or implicitly through nonverbal cues defines the message context. The relationship context describes norms for communication conveyed in a transactional manner or modified to accommodate the needs of relationships and networks. Within the temporal domain, low-context communicators move according to punctual, clock-based scheduling norms, whereas high-context communicators have more flexible, event-based timeframes. In the space domain, some high-context communicators transmit meaning through communal conversation spaces full of hand gestures and dramatic expression, and others through a conversation space that allows for personal distance, silent pauses, and physical stillness. Opportunities for miscommunication and misunderstanding proliferate the encoding, transmission, and decoding processes when employees have different nonverbal communication styles, creating barriers to interpersonal connections and collaboration.

The encoding-transmission-decoding processes in cross-cultural communication have been examined through multiple fields of inquiry. The social psychology of identity and intergroup relations explains why individuals identify with groups (e.g., a nation, an organization) and why groups draw boundaries that tend to reinforce similar within-group and different between-group communication patterns (Brewer, 1991; Hogg & Reid, 2006). Thus, cross-cultural communication at work may be ineffective because a sender uses one cultural lens to encode information and a receiver uses a different cultural lens to decode the information. For example,

W. L. Adair et al., *What Isn't Being Said*, Springer Series in Emerging Cultural Perspectives in Work, Organizational, and Personnel Studies,
https://doi.org/10.1007/978-3-031-53645-8_3

at a work-related cocktail party, US Americans tend to use direct and explicit messages with constant eye contact and stand within one-meter radius of personal space with colleagues, while Latino Americans use fast-paced messages with animated gestures and closer than one-meter personal space, especially with culturally similar others; and East Asians prefer implicit messages and little direct eye contact, with about one-meter radius of personal space (e.g., Hall, 1963, 1966; Morrison & Conaway, 2006). Using different communication codes, the East Asian employee may interpret their Latin American counterpart as overbearing; the Latin American employee may interpret their US counterpart as uptight, and the US employee may think their East Asian employee is not having fun.

Employees with culturally distinct communication norms often try to improve understanding by adjusting their communication style (Adair & Brett, 2005). Communication scholars explain the motivation to adjust one's style to accommodate a counterpart's style through interpersonal needs for affiliation and individual needs to reduce uncertainty (Giles et al., 1991; Gudykunst, 2004). Beyond strategic adaptation to improve communication effectiveness, individuals may naturally adjust to one another through psychological processes of subconscious mimicry and emotional recognition and contagion (Sato et al., 2013). Finally, characteristics of the individual and setting can influence whether an employee adjusts their communication style, as will be explained with reference to literature on code-switching and dynamic constructivism (e.g., Hong et al., 2000).

Clearly it is no easy task to understand the many cultural, individual, and situational variables that can explain when employees in a multicultural workplace might adjust their communication styles. Furthermore, the complexity of the dyadic process model illustrates that even when one party adjusts its style, the other party might fail to notice or might simultaneously adjust their own style (Adair et al., 2009). In this latter case, each person might speak the other's language, simply shifting the inefficiencies from decoding to encoding. In highlighting these challenges and the theories most useful for understanding them, this chapter aims to provide theoretical foundations for research on cross-cultural communication at work.

Theoretical Perspectives on Cross-Cultural Communication Adaptation

Communicators face more uncertainty in intercultural than intracultural settings due to unfamiliar cultural norms and behavioral scripts that challenge the encoding, transmission, and decoding processes. Such uncertainty naturally causes anxiety and inefficiency in communicating. Given these challenges, many people adapt their behaviors to accommodate culturally different others both to improve understanding and to build relationships. Situational factors also influence the likelihood of communication adaptation, as explained by the selected cognitive and linguistic models of cross-cultural communication presented here.

Anxiety/Uncertainty Management

Based in Uncertainty Reduction Theory (Berger & Calabrese, 1974), Anxiety/Uncertainty Management Theory (AUM) delineates factors that influence successful communication in cross-cultural encounters with strangers or cultural outgroups. When we communicate with someone from a cultural outgroup, our lack of familiarity with our counterpart's norms and scripts for a given situation creates uncertainty about how the communication will unfold (Gudykunst, 1993). When each party brings its own culturally normative scripts and expectations, even an ordinary interaction can become stressful and anxiety filled (Stephan et al., 1999). Anxiety is "the affective (emotional) equivalent of uncertainty" evident in feelings of apprehension and unease when interacting with cultural outgroup members (Gudykunst & Nishida, 2001, p. 59; Stephan & Stephan, 1985). To eliminate anxiety, we try to reduce uncertainty and increase feelings of control in cross-cultural interactions (Heine et al., 2006; Kruglanski & Webster, 1996).

The need for AUM's uncertainty reduction mechanism is shown in higher levels of stress and anxiety in intercultural compared to intracultural encounters (Gudykunst & Shapiro, 1996). Mendes et al. (2002) found patterns of cardiovascular responses in intergroup interactions that support the argument for intergroup anxiety as a threat response to stress. Importantly, this intercultural anxiety negatively impacts communication effectiveness (Gudykunst & Nishida, 2001). Because significant psychological resources are being devoted to reducing anxiety, fewer resources may be available for encoding and decoding messages (Avery et al., 2009).

In summary, AUM proposes that individuals are motivated to reduce feelings of anxiety caused by uncertainty and that doing so will improve communication effectiveness, defined as a message being received and interpreted as the sender intended (Gudykunst, 1993). Uncertainty reduction might be accomplished through adjusting or adapting one's communication style to the cultural context, a skill that models of intercultural competence aim to measure and develop (see Leung et al. (2014) for a comprehensive review). However, uncertainty can also be reduced by resorting to one's well-known, prescriptive group norms (Hogg, 2000), a process that inhibits adaptation. Removing oneself from an uncomfortable situation is another coping strategy noted to be suboptimal in intercultural negotiations when integrative solutions take time and information exchange to discover (Adair et al., 2001). Among the various strategies of reducing uncertainty, compared to strategies of using force to impose one's own approaches or avoidance, findings from AUM laid the foundation that active communication can be the more sustainable way of reducing uncertainty on multiple fronts.

Communication Accommodation Theory and Identity Negotiation Theory

According to Communication Accommodation Theory (CAT), people reduce interpersonal and group boundaries through communication responses that converge, for example, are similar or complementary to a counterpart's communication style (Giles et al., 1991). Communication acts that diverge from a counterpart's style increase social distance (Giles et al., 1991). In other words, people tend to adjust their communication style, for example the words they use or their tone of voice, for different counterparts to increase or decrease relational bonds. CAT helps us understand why employees may adjust their communication style when speaking with some counterparts and not others. Although CAT is not a culture theory per se, as noted in Chap. 2, its emphasis on both the informational and relational functions of communication aids in understanding the social lubricative function of communication in high-context cultures (Cohen, 1997).

According to CAT, communication has both informational and relational functions (Gallois et al., 2005). The relational function refers to communicators' motivation to build a connection with their counterparts. People who wish to reduce interpersonal distance and build relationships are more likely to accommodate their counterpart's communication style by engaging in converging, similar, or complementary communication acts; people who wish to maintain individual distinctiveness will avoid accommodation by engaging in divergent communication acts (Brewer, 1991; Giles et al., 1991; Ting-Toomey, 1993). Here, CAT relies on psychological theories of similarity and attraction that explain our tendencies to prefer people similar to us (Byrne, 1971). Accommodating a counterpart's communication style means becoming more similar to them, thus creating the foundation for a stronger relationship.

In addition to the relational motivation component, CAT has a strong foundation in social categorization theory, whereby group identification reinforces boundaries defining ingroups and outgroups (Tajfel & Turner, 1979). CAT lends itself well to cross-cultural contexts where there is a heightened awareness of distinct group membership and effective communication requires bridging these boundaries (Gallois et al., 1995). Thus, managers and employees working collaboratively in a diverse workplace are motivated to adjust or adapt their communication style to accommodate their counterparts and reinforce a shared ingroup identity (Gallois et al., 1995). However, as the theory notes, power, context, values, communication goals, and other factors can influence this motivation (Gallois et al., 2005), as will be discussed more below.

A third facet of CAT that is important for consideration in cross-cultural workplace communication is the role of perception and attribution. CAT is a dyadic process model, meaning that it predicts bi-directional communication patterns. The relational and informational benefits of communication accommodation depend on both parties perceiving, whether consciously or subconsciously, that their communication styles are becoming more similar (e.g., Rohr et al., 2022). CAT posits that a counterpart must (1) perceive the accommodation and (2) attribute positive intentions to the accommodation. Just as social norms and expectations influence one's motivation to adjust communication, they also influence how a communication adjustment is perceived (Gallois et al., 2005). For example, a counterpart might perceive an adjustment as a power move, attribute manipulative motivations to their counterpart, and respond with a divergent, rather than convergent, communication act. The success of the communication dance thus depends on the unfolding processes of person A's communication act; followed by person B's perception, attribution, and communication response; followed by person A's perception, attribution, and communication response, and so on (See Chap. 2, Fig. 2.1). Research on close relationships shows that over time, committed partners who use more social mimicry that signals liking and affiliation are more satisfied with their quality of relationships (Silver & Gottman, 1994; Rohr et al., 2022), while unreciprocated positive gestures and discourse can lead to defensiveness and dissolution of relationships (e.g., Fowler & Dillow, 2011). These findings are potentially applicable to professional relationships at the workplace and among business partners at the organizational level.

National culture is just one intergroup context where communication accommodation may occur and facilitate communication. Communication across generations, ethnicity, gender, physical abilities, and social class are some other examples of intergroup contexts that employees encounter on a daily basis at work. Also based on Social Identity Theory (Tajfel, 1981; Brewer & Miller, 1996), Ting-Toomey's (1999) Identity Negotiation Theory explains that encountering someone from another culture makes our own cultural identity salient, prompting patterns of communication that serve to balance our needs for ingroup inclusion and outgroup differentiation and to feel secure across our multiple identities. On the one hand, communication accommodation is essential to facilitate relationship building; on the other hand, intergroup accommodating communication acts that rely on group stereotypes, such as speaking more loudly to a senior citizen, can backfire, creating more, rather than less, interpersonal distance (Palomares et al., 2016).

In summary, CAT explains patterns of communication style convergence and divergence as a function of interpersonal relationship management. Although accommodation can occur quite naturally, it may not be smooth or effective given low- and high-context employees' distinct modes of communication. Preparation for cross-cultural interactions, cultural intelligence, and high-context communication norms are some factors associated with flexibility across low- and high-context communication styles (Adair et al., 2001; Earley & Ang, 2003; Lee et al., 2013).

Cross-Cultural Code-Switching

Cross-cultural codeswitching refers to the intentional adaptation of one's behavior in a foreign environment to conform to the cultural norms of that setting to ensure appropriate behavior (Molinsky, 2007). Cross-cultural code-switching behaviors include modifications in both verbal and nonverbal language and communication style. Notably, the theory goes beyond the relationship-building motive of CAT and includes employees' motivations to fit in, do good work, and take others' perspectives. Code-switching also explores downstream effects on employee well-being that are not addressed in the process-oriented CAT. For example, literature on expatriate employee effectiveness explores cross-cultural adaptation as a purposeful, strategic approach to impression management, acceptance, and work effectiveness (Bird et al., 1999; Black et al., 1991; Earley & Ang, 2003).

Cross-cultural code-switching occurs when employees from foreign or minority cultures adapt their culturally normative behavior to fit the norms of their organization's home culture (Molinsky, 2007). By adjusting their behavior, employees can avoid the negative consequences of norm violation and improve interpersonal relationships with colleagues (Pornpitakpan, 1999; Thomas & Ravlin, 1995). In fact, being able to adapt one's communication behaviors in a cross-cultural setting, like a cultural chameleon, is one facet of cultural intelligence (Earley & Ang, 2003; Earley & Peterson, 2004).

When employees adjust their communication behaviors to fit in or be heard in a multicultural or foreign workplace, they adopt communication norms that might be unnatural and uncomfortable. The new communication action may conflict with the employee's social role norms, for example, a Middle Eastern female employee speaking forcefully to a North American male superior. The behavior may conflict with the employee's previous understanding of task-related norms, such as when to ask for help. For these reasons, cross-cultural code-switching may have a negative psychological toll on the code-switcher (Molinsky, 2007). At the same time, when an employee successfully code-switches and performs well, they may experience positive emotions such as pride and confidence that can boost, rather than deplete, psychological resources (Molinsky, 2007). Molinsky (2013) describes the process of adapting to a new cultural environment as *cultural retooling*. This process initially instigates internal conflict and evolves from conflict to ambivalence and finally authenticity.

Cross-cultural code-switching applies to adjustments in language as well as communication style. Multicultural organizations may adopt English as the lingua franca, meaning employees who are non-native speakers of English are frequently code-switching language, idioms, and terminologies. Language may be the hardest code to master as it takes years to learn and speak fluently. Many researchers have noted that despite English as a lingua franca, multinational companies face frequent communication challenges (Feely & Harzing, 2003; Harzing & Feely, 2008; Steyaert et al., 2011). Beyond the cognitive load and psychological labor non-native English speakers bear in such workplaces, there are social costs. For example, native English speakers may receive preferential treatment and form cliques that exclude non-native English speakers (Neeley, 2013). In a study of German and Japanese corporate headquarters and subsidiary managers, Harzing et al. (2011) identified several factors positively impacting day-to-day communication effectiveness. They found that for multilingual individuals, linguistic code-switching (bilingual or multilingual speakers alternating between languages in a single interaction (Heller, 1988)) had a positive impact on communication effectiveness. However, this ability is not easily fostered. Other strategies included active listening, repetition, and adopting a richer mode of communication (e.g., phone instead of email). Similarly, when working in multicultural teams, employees with high language competence and cultural intelligence report lower avoidance behaviors, leading to higher levels of voice and performance (Peyrols Wu & Ng, 2021).

While effective in bridging social distance and improving understanding, the practice of code-switching is behaviorally and psychologically taxing, often leading to exhaustion and burnout for cultural minorities (Leong & Ward, 2000; Molinsky, 2007). Furthermore, through code-switching, employees may stifle unique ways of thinking and expression that are the essence of "value-in-diversity" perspectives (Cha & Roberts, 2019). To ensure minority group employee inclusion and equal participation, organizations must create voice pathways and value minority voices equally (Farndale et al., 2015).

Mimicry

In the workplace, employees and managers may find themselves unwittingly imitating each other's communication style due to subconscious mimicry. Humans have been found to mimic counterparts' movements, facial expressions, tone of voice, and verbal expressions without any particular motivation or benefit of such behavior (Bandura, 1977; Chartrand & Bargh, 1999). This chameleon effect has been explained by an automatic social perception-behavior link (Bargh et al., 1996) similar to the social perception-cognition link in stereotype activation (Devine, 1989). The perception-behavior link can be activated by language, as evidenced in priming research. For example, participants who completed tasks surreptitiously embedded with words related to the elderly stereotype, for example, "Florida" and "wrinkle," were then observed to embody stereotype consistent behavior on an unrelated task, in this case walking more slowly than participants who were primed with words unrelated to an elderly stereotype (Bargh et al., 1996). The tendency for humans to subconsciously mimic the actions of others is related to developing rapport and social connection, similar to the more effortful CAT and code-switching processes discussed above (Chartrand & Bargh, 1999).

Behavioral matching occurs when one person adjusts their posture or body movement to mimic their counterpart (LaFrance, 1979). In the workplace when power dynamics are at play, the perception-behavior activation may trigger complementary matching; for example, a manager exhibiting an expansive dominant posture triggers a more closed, submissive body posture in a subordinate, which occurs at a subconscious level and nevertheless predicts liking and affiliation (Tiedens & Fragale, 2003). Another form of subconscious mirroring is facial mimicry, which has been proposed to explain the finding that couples grow to resemble one another, because years of facial mimicry could cause the emergence of similar facial lines (Zajonc et al., 1987). A similar automatic social synchronization occurs with emotional contagion, a shared emotional state that develops from automatic postural, expression, and vocal mimicry (Hatfield et al., 1994).

Subconscious mimicry as a social glue has widespread implications for workplace interactions and communication. Barsade and colleagues argued that emotional contagion influences such workplace domains as teamwork, leadership, and decision-making (Barsade et al., 2018). The authors modeled both sender and receiver characteristics related to culture as predictors of emotional contagion and argued that more expressive communicators would facilitate emotional contagion. Also, receivers' cultural values and demographic characteristics (e.g., age, gender), can facilitate emotional contagion in the workplace, a prediction supported by work demonstrating greater attention to relational cues and indirect meaning at work in East Asian than North American cultures (Sanchez-Burks et al., 2003). Also of note, given the current trend toward virtual work, is the prevalence of emotional contagion across digital and virtual media (Goldenberg & Gross, 2020).

Together, the literature on anxiety/uncertainty management theory (AUM), communication accommodation theory (CAT), identity negotiation theory, codeswitching, and mimicry suggests that employees may consciously and subconsciously adjust their verbal and nonverbal communication patterns at work. When employees represent multiple cultures, certain communication styles may be more susceptible to mimicry than others. For example, nonverbal cues that convey emotion and expression are more likely to be "caught" and adopted in counterparts' communication styles (Van Kleef et al., 2012). Also, as noted above, high-context communicators are more likely to be attuned to their counterparts' style and adjust for understanding and/or relational attunement (Adair et al., 2001).

Dynamic Constructivist Perspectives

Dynamic constructivism is a theory that explicitly models the interaction between individual, interpersonal, and situational factors to explain behavior, such as communication adaptation, in multicultural individuals. Hong et al. (2000) studied bicultural individuals in Hong Kong and California, where Chinese descendants have been broadly exposed to North American culture. They found that when a situation is saturated with US American cultural images, these bicultural communicators would make decisions and express messages appropriate for the US culture; when a situation is primed with Chinese cultural images, they would communicate according to Chinese cultural norms. Hong et al. (2000) proposed that culture's influence on individual behaviors, such as communication, is dynamically constructed by the individual agency and the situation.

Benet-Martínez and Hong (2014) showed that for people with bicultural identities, such as Hong Kong Chinese or Chinese living in California, those who are high on bicultural identity integration (BII) would embrace both cultures with a higher level of language skills so that they can easily switch codes and adapt to either cultural setting. However, those with a lower level of BII would perceive the two cultural identities as contradictory to each other and experience difficulties in code-switching. They might feel higher levels of uncertainty, anxiety, and stress in either cultural setting that could inhibit code-switching (Benet-Martínez & Hong, 2014).

Advancing the dynamic constructivist view of culture's influence on individuals, Morris et al. (2015) proposed *polyculturalism*, suggesting cultures affect individuals not as independent categories but as partial and plural interacting systems. In other words, culture is not only determined by separate ancient origins that are historically stable but by continuous and evolving interactions with other cultures in a multicultural landscape. Accordingly, an individual's communication style may not be singularly prescribed by steady categories based on national values but rather by a dynamic configuration of situated and plural cues. In the polycultural framework, individuals learn about other cultures not through explicit "do" and "don't" lists but through implicit immersion and interactions in culturally specific settings through social learning.

To summarize, the dynamic constructivist view and the polycultural framework suggest that intercultural communicators are likely to use a holistic set of situational cues to exchange ideas and emotions with culturally different others. Therefore, employees in multicultural workplaces are likely to be sensitive to their communication environment, from which they learn to adjust their expressions, message encoding, transmission, and decoding processes.

Summary

In a diverse and multicultural workplace, adapting and adjusting communication behaviors to one's counterpart fulfills psychological, relational, and task needs. Communicating more like one's interlocutor can reduce intercultural anxiety and uncertainty, create interpersonal connections, and increase chances of being seen and heard. Communication style can also shift based on subtle interpersonal and situational cues that signal affiliation or cultural identity. These motivations and mechanisms apply to all forms of communication, although to date literature has focused primarily on language and verbal expression, as will be unpacked in subsequent chapters. Because the use and meaning of nonverbal cues vary across culture groups, we propose a closer look at adaptation in nonverbal cues that carry meaning across the four domains of communication context. Each of the following chapters discusses culture and nonverbal communication in a different organizational sphere, focusing on how senders and receivers from different cultural backgrounds can establish common ground and communicate effectively.

References

Adair, W. L., & Brett, J. M. (2005). The negotiation dance: Time, culture, and behavioral sequences in negotiation. *Organization Science, 16*(1), 33–51.

Adair, W. L., Okumura, T., & Brett, J. M. (2001). Negotiation behavior when cultures collide: The United States and Japan. *Journal of Applied Psychology, 86*(3), 371–385.

Adair, W. L., Taylor, M. S., & Tinsley, C. H. (2009). Starting out on the right foot: Negotiation schemas when cultures collide. *Negotiation and Conflict Management Research, 2*(2), 138–163.

Avery, D. R., Richeson, J. A., Hebl, M. R., & Ambady, N. (2009). It does not have to be uncomfortable: The role of behavioral scripts in Black–White interracial interactions. *Journal of Applied Psychology, 94*(6), 1382–1393. https://doi.org/10.1037/a0016208

Bandura, A. (1977). Self-efficacy: toward a unifying theory of behavioral change. *Psychological Review, 84*(2), 191.

Bargh, J. A., Chen, M., & Burrows, L. (1996). Automaticity of social behavior: Direct effects of trait construct and stereotype activation on action. *Journal of Personality and Social Psychology, 71*(2), 230–244.

Barsade, S. G., Coutifaris, C. G., & Pillemer, J. (2018). Emotional contagion in organizational life. *Research in Organizational Behavior, 38*, 137–151.

Benet-Martínez, V., & Hong, Y.-Y. (2014). *The Oxford handbook of multicultural identity*. Oxford University Press.

Berger, C. R., & Calabrese, R. J. (1974). Some explorations in initial interaction and beyond: Toward a developmental theory of interpersonal communication. *Human Communication Research, 1*(2), 99–112.

Bird, A., Osland, J. S., Mendenhall, M., & Schneider, S. C. (1999). Adapting and adjusting to other cultures: What we know but don't always tell. *Journal of Management Inquiry, 8*(2), 152–165.

Black, J. S., Mendenhall, M., & Oddou, G. (1991). Toward a comprehensive model of international adjustment: An integration of multiple theoretical perspectives. *Academy of Management Review, 16*(2), 291–317.

Brewer, M. B. (1991). The social self: On being the same and different at the same time. *Personality and Social Psychology Bulletin, 17*(5), 475–482.

Brewer, M. B., & Miller, N. (1996). *Intergroup relations*. Brooks/Cole.

Byrne, D. (1971). *The attraction paradigm*. Academic Press.

Cha, S. E., & Roberts, L. M. (2019). Leveraging minority identities at work: An individual-level framework of the identity mobilization process. *Organization Science, 30*(4), 735–760.

Chartrand, T. L., & Bargh, J. A. (1999). The chameleon effect: The perception–behavior link and social interaction. *Journal of Personality and Social Psychology, 76*(6), 893–910.

Cohen, R. (1997). *Negotiating across cultures: Communication obstacles in international diplomacy*. United States Institute of Peace Press.

Devine, P. G. (1989). Stereotypes and prejudice: Their automatic and controlled components. *Journal of Personality and Social Psychology, 56*(1), 5–18.

Earley, P. C., & Ang, S. (2003). *Cultural intelligence: Individual interactions across cultures*. Stanford University Press.

Earley, P. C., & Peterson, R. S. (2004). The elusive cultural chameleon: Cultural intelligence as a new approach to intercultural training for the global manager. *Academy of Management Learning and Education, 3*, 100–115.

Farndale, E., Biron, M., Briscoe, D. R., & Raghuram, S. (2015). A global perspective on diversity and inclusion in work organisations. *The International Journal of Human Resource Management, 26*(6), 677–687.

Feely, A. J., & Harzing, A. W. (2003). Language management in multinational companies. *Cross Cultural Management: An International Journal, 10*(2), 37–52.

Fowler, C., & Dillow, M. R. (2011). Attachment dimensions and the four horsemen of the apocalypse. *Communication Research Reports, 28*(1), 16–26.

Gallois, C., Giles, H., Jones, E., Cargile, A. C., & Ota, H. (1995). Accommodating intercultural encounters: Elaborations and extensions. In R. L. Wiseman (Ed.), *Intercultural communication theory* (pp. 115–147). Sage.

Gallois, C., Ogay, T., & Giles, H. (2005). Communication accommodation theory: A look back and a look ahead. In W. B. Gudykunst (Ed.), *Theorizing about intercultural communication* (pp. 121–148). Sage.

Giles, H., Coupland, J., & Coupland, N. (Eds.). (1991). *Contexts of accommodation: Developments in applied sociolinguistics (Studies in emotion and social interaction)*. Cambridge University Press.

Goldenberg, A., & Gross, J. J. (2020). Digital emotion contagion. *Trends in Cognitive Sciences, 24*(4), 316–328.

Gudykunst, W. B. (1993). Toward a theory of effective interpersonal and intergroup communication: An anxiety/uncertainty management (AUM) perspective. In R. L. Wiseman & J. Koester (Eds.), *Intercultural communication competence* (pp. 33–71). Sage.

Gudykunst, W. B. (2004). *Bridging differences: Effective intergroup communication*. Sage.

Gudykunst, W. B., & Nishida, T. (2001). Anxiety, uncertainty, and perceived effectiveness of communication across relationships and cultures. *International Journal of Intercultural Relations, 25*(1), 55–71.

Gudykunst, W. B., & Shapiro, R. B. (1996). Communication in everyday interpersonal and intergroup encounters. *International Journal of Intercultural Relations, 20*(1), 19–45. https://doi.org/10.1016/0147-1767(96)00037-5

Hall, E. T. (1963). A system for the notation of proxemic behavior. *American Anthropologist, 65*(5), 1003–1026. https://doi.org/10.1525/aa.1963.65.5.02a00020

Hall, E. T. (1966). *The hidden dimension*. Anchor Books.

Harzing, A. W., & Feely, A. J. (2008). The language barrier and its implications for HQ-subsidiary relationships. *Cross-Cultural Management: An International Journal, 15*(1), 49–61.

Harzing, A. W., Köster, K., & Magner, U. (2011). Babel in business: The language barrier and its solutions in the HQ-subsidiary relationship. *Journal of World Business, 46*(3), 279–287.

Hatfield, E., Cacioppo, J. T., & Rapson, R. L. (1994). *Emotional contagion*. Cambridge University Press.

Heine, S. J., Proulx, T., & Vohs, K. D. (2006). The meaning maintenance model: On the coherence of social motivations. *Personality and Social Psychology Review, 10*(2), 88–110.

Heller, M. (1988). Strategic ambiguity: Codeswitching in the management of conflict. In M. Heller (Ed.), *Codeswitching: Anthropological and sociolinguistic perspectives* (pp. 77–96). Mouton de Gruyter.

Hogg, M. A. (2000). Subjective uncertainty reduction through self-categorization: A motivational theory of social identity processes. *European Review of Social Psychology, 11*, 223–255.

Hogg, M. A., & Reid, S. A. (2006). Social identity, self-categorization, and the communication of group norms. *Communication Theory, 16*(1), 7–30.

Hong, Y., Morris, M. W., Chiu, C., & Benet-Martinez, V. (2000). Multicultural minds: A dynamic constructivist approach to culture and cognition. *American Psychologist, 55*, 709–720.

Kruglanski, A. W., & Webster, D. M. (1996). Motivated closing of the mind: "Seizing" and "freezing". *Psychological Review, 103*(2), 263–283.

LaFrance, M. (1979). Nonverbal synchrony and rapport: Analysis by the cross-lag panel technique. *Social Psychology Quarterly, 42*(1), 66–70.

Lee, S., Adair, W. L., & Seo, S. J. (2013). Cultural perspective taking in cross-cultural negotiation. *Group Decision and Negotiation, 22*, 389–405.

Leong, C. H., & Ward, C. (2000). Identity conflict in sojourners. *International Journal of Intercultural Relations, 24*(6), 763–776.

Leung, K., Ang, S., & Tan, M. L. (2014). Intercultural competence. *Annual Review of Organizational Psychology and Organizational Behavior, 1*(1), 489–519.

Mendes, W. B., Blascovich, J., Lickel, B., & Hunter, S. (2002). Challenge and threat during social interactions with White and Black men. *Personality and Social Psychology Bulletin, 28*(7), 939–952.

Molinsky, A. (2007). Cross-cultural code-switching: The psychological challenges of adapting behavior in foreign cultural interactions. *Academy of Management Review, 32*(2), 622–640.
Molinsky, A. L. (2013). The psychological processes of cultural retooling. *Academy of Management Journal, 56*(3), 683–710.
Morris, M. W., Chiu, C.-Y., & Liu, Z. (2015). Polycultural psychology. *Annual Review of Psychology, 66*, 631–659.
Morrison, T., & Conaway, W. A. (2006). *Kiss, bow, or shake hands*. Adams Media.
Neeley, T. B. (2013). Language matters: Status loss and achieved status distinctions in global organizations. *Organization Science, 24*(2), 476–497.
Palomares, N. A., Giles, H., Soliz, J., & Gallois, C. (2016). Intergroup accommodation, social categories, and identities. In H. Giles (Ed.), *Communication accommodation theory: Negotiating personal relationships and social identities across contexts* (pp. 123–151). Cambridge University Press.
Peyrols Wu, C., & Ng, K. Y. (2021). Cultural intelligence and language competence: Synergistic effects on avoidance, task performance, and voice behaviors in multicultural teams. *Applied Psychology, 70*(4), 1512–1542.
Pornpitakpan, C. (1999). The effects of cultural adaptation on business relationships: Americans selling to Japanese and Thais. *Journal of International Business Studies, 30*(2), 317–337.
Rohr, M. R., Kämpf, M. S., & Kunzmann, U. (2022). Love and imitation: Facial mimicry and relationship satisfaction in younger and older couples. *The Journals of Gerontology: Series B, 77*(7), 1210–1218. https://doi.org/10.1093/geronb/gbab193
Sanchez-Burks, J., Lee, F., Choi, I., Nisbett, R., Zhao, S., & Koo, J. (2003). Conversing across cultures: East-West communication styles in work and nonwork contexts. *Journal of Personality and Social Psychology, 85*(2), 363–372.
Sato, W., Fujimura, T., Kochiyama, T., & Suzuki, N. (2013). Relationships among facial mimicry, emotional experience, and emotion recognition. *PLoS One, 8*(3), e57889. https://doi.org/10.1371/journal.pone.0057889
Silver, N., & Gottman, J. (1994). *Why marriages succeed or fail: What you can learn from the breakthrough research to make your marriage last*. Simon & Schuster.
Stephan, W. G., & Stephan, C. W. (1985). Intergroup anxiety. *Journal of Social Issues, 41*(3), 157–175.
Stephan, W. G., Stephan, C. W., & Gudykunst, W. B. (1999). Anxiety in intergroup relations: A comparison of anxiety/uncertainty management theory and integrated threat theory. *International Journal of Intercultural Relations, 23*(4), 613–628.
Steyaert, C., Ostendorp, A., & Gaibrois, C. (2011). Multilingual organizations as 'linguascapes': Negotiating the position of English through discursive practices. *Journal of World Business, 46*(3), 270–278.
Tajfel, H. (1981). *Human groups and social categories*. Cambridge University Press.
Tajfel, H., & Turner, J. C. (1979). An integrative theory of intergroup conflict. In W. G. Austin & S. Worchel (Eds.), *The social psychology of intergroup relations* (pp. 33–53). Wadsworth.
Thomas, D. C., & Ravlin, E. C. (1995). Responses of employees to cultural adaptation by a foreign manager. *Journal of Applied Psychology, 80*(1), 133–146.
Tiedens, L. Z., & Fragale, A. R. (2003). Power moves: Complementarity in dominant and submissive nonverbal behavior. *Journal of Personality and Social Psychology, 84*(3), 558–568.
Ting-Toomey, S. (1993). Communication resourcefulness: An identity negotiation perspective. In R. L. Wiseman & J. Koester (Eds.), *Intercultural communication competence* (pp. 72–111). Sage.
Ting-Toomey, S. (1999). *Communicating across cultures*. Guilford Publications.
Van Kleef, G. A., Homan, A. C., & Cheshin, A. (2012). Emotional influence at work: Take it EASI. *Organizational Psychology Review, 2*(4), 311–339.
Zajonc, R. B., Adelmann, P. K., Murphy, S. T., & Niedenthal, P. M. (1987). Convergence in the physical appearance of spouses. *Motivation and Emotion, 11*(4), 335–346.

Chapter 4
Listening and Speaking Without Words: Effective Communication in Multicultural Teams

To effectively communicate, we must realize that we are all different in the way we perceive the world and use this understanding as a guide to our communication with others. – Tony Robbins

Multicultural teams are characterized by a diversity of worldviews and experiences such that team members have different ways of perceiving the world and communicating with others. Such diversity offers potential for process improvements, product innovation, and peak performance (see Wang et al., 2019, for a review). Yet despite the benefits of members' diverse knowledge and perspectives (Gibson et al., 2014), many multicultural teams fail to reach synergistic potential due to coordination, communication, and identity challenges (Earley & Mosakowski, 2000; Lau & Murnighan, 1998; Stahl et al., 2010). Still, others fail to capitalize on diversity because team members subconsciously assimilate to organizational and societal cultural norms, including communication norms, thus suppressing the diversity and uniqueness they bring to the table (Ely & Thomas, 2001). Due to the prevalence and costs of poor multicultural team communication, diverse and global teams must be proactive in understanding and managing communication processes to facilitate collaboration (Bui et al., 2019).

Teams are two or more individuals working interdependently towards a common goal (Devine, 2002; Hackman, 2002). Teams foster collaboration and accountability among groups of employees (Gibson & Zellmer-Bruhn, 2001). Team tasks, for example generating, executing, negotiating, and choosing (McGrath, 1984), require sharing and elaborating on information, which can be challenging in diverse teams that lack effective communication and process management (Van Knippenberg et al., 2004). A recent meta-analysis found that team diversity based on social categories, such as culture, was positively related to communication openness and subsequent team performance in small- and medium-sized teams (Bui et al., 2019). So, what communication barriers stymie the effectiveness of some culturally diverse teams? One such barrier is the presence of diverse native languages that can challenge team members' expression and interpretation, even when using English as a

W. L. Adair et al., *What Isn't Being Said*, Springer Series in Emerging Cultural Perspectives in Work, Organizational, and Personnel Studies,
https://doi.org/10.1007/978-3-031-53645-8_4

lingua franca (Neeley et al., 2012), and also their ability to form strong relationships (Kalra & Szymanski, 2023). Team members working in different time zones, if the team is globally dispersed, presents other challenges for time management and electronic communication (Hinds & Mortensen, 2005; Chap. 9, this volume). But even beyond language and time zones, effective team communication depends on correctly seeing, hearing, and interpreting information in nonverbal messaging that varies across cultures (Behfar et al., 2006).

Communication norms are rooted in our cultural upbringing, meaning that communication-related diversity extends well beyond native languages in multicultural teams (Adair et al., 2016). Within the message context, team members may attend more or less to subtle cues in body language and emotional expression. Based on their relationship context dependence, they may consider parties' status, or not, when deciding how to send and encode messages. Team members may also use and interpret meaning embodied in movement through the time and space contexts to varying degrees. With multiple people talking, listening, and responding at once, there is potential for nonverbal-communication-based misunderstanding in the contexts of message, relationship, time, and space. By managing effective nonverbal communication across low- and high-context communication norms, multicultural teams can reduce relationship and task conflict, build trust and cohesion, and improve efficiency and performance (Marlow et al., 2017; Sogancilar & Ors, 2018). In other words, effective communication is key to bridging cultural diversity so multicultural teams can build connections and common ground that will facilitate leveraging their differences in collaborative work (DiStefano & Maznevski, 2000).

This chapter begins with a non-exhaustive review of the literature on multicultural team processes and outcomes, focusing on communication as a key challenge and core competency. We organize this literature review according to the four domains of communication context: message, relationship, time, and space. The chapter concludes with recommendations for future research examining nonverbal communication in multicultural teams as a pathway to challenges (e.g., relationship conflict) and synergies (e.g., trust).

Communication in Multicultural Teams

Work teams are "a collection of individuals with different cultural backgrounds, who are interdependent in their tasks, who share responsibility for outcomes, who see themselves and are seen by others as an intact social entity embedded in one or more larger social systems, and who manage their relationships across organizational boundaries and beyond" (Cohen & Bailey, 1997, p. 241). The large number of multinational mergers and organizations operating internationally, labor market mobility, and virtual work all contribute to the prevalence of teams whose members come from diverse cultural backgrounds. In a meta-analysis of 108 multicultural team studies, researchers found that cultural diversity had positive effects on team processes and outcomes, for example, decreasing task conflict and increasing creativity (Stahl et al., 2010). Furthermore, teams realized these benefits in the presence of surface (i.e., visible characteristics) and deep levels (e.g., cultural values and beliefs about teamwork) of cultural diversity (Stahl et al., 2010). In a retrospective revisiting those findings, Stahl and Maznevski's (2021) review unpacked related individual (e.g., cultural intelligence, multiculturalism), team (e.g., creativity), and environmental (e.g., geographic configuration, organizational climate) factors. But within-team language and communication dynamics remain an understudied area.

Cross-cultural teamwork challenges begin with different conceptualizations and mental models for teamwork rooted in distinct cultural values and ways of seeing the world. Every aspect of teamwork, including communication practices, may be conceptualized differently across cultures. Gibson and Zellmer-Bruhn (2001) identified distinct teamwork metaphors reflecting sports, military, family, and community at one corporation's facilities in six different national cultures. When multicultural team members had different metaphors (e.g., sports team vs family) guiding their expectations for team process and outcome, communication challenges ensued (Gibson & Zellmer-Bruhn, 2001). It takes time working together for multicultural teams to develop a shared mental model for teamwork that includes a common understanding of task and relationship functions, including motivations, values, and communication norms (Adair & Liu, 2011; Adair & Ganai, 2013; Earley & Mosakowski, 2000). Effective communication such that messages are understood fully and as intended helps global teams create a shared teamwork mental model, which can likewise facilitate team communication (DiStefano & Maznevski, 2000).

Even when multicultural teams develop a shared mental model for their goals, processes, and procedures (Adair & Ganai, 2013), the execution must be managed across diverse languages and communication styles. Team members from low-context cultures are accustomed to direct and impersonal expression, moderate personal space and body language levels, and associating timeliness with respect and responsibility (Adair et al., 2016; Hall, 1976). Team members from high-context cultures rely more on *how* the message is conveyed and what is not said to express and interpret meaning. For them, relationships and events dictate how to communicate and move through time. Body language and personal space can be extremely close and expressive or extremely distant and reserved (Adair et al., 2016; Hall, 1976). Given these differences, it is not surprising that ineffective communication and misunderstanding are regularly cited as top multicultural team challenges (Sogancilar & Ors, 2018).

The enactment of high- and low-context communication norms is evident across all stages and processes of multicultural teamwork. For example, an analysis of publicly available email communication from a culturally heterogeneous United Nations team found that high-context team members began messages with a formal opening and setting the stage, avoiding explicit statements of problems, whereas low-context team members opened with proposals and a goal statement, and directly stated problems (Zakaria, 2017). At later stages of teamwork, high-context team members revealed decisions with humility and appreciation, whereas team members from low-context cultures asked questions and announced decisions (Zakaria, 2017). While early stages are essential for building connections, effective communication maintains common ground and facilitates collaboration throughout all team stages. Next, we review and organize research on global teams informing communication across the message, relationship, time, and space contexts, followed by recommendations for future research focused on contextualized communication.

Global Team Communication and Message Context

Effective communication across the message context occurs when team members from high-context cultures receive explicit messages without taking offense or reading into them, openly share information and engage in debate, and approach conflict without shutting down. At the same time, low-context team members must attend to and understand high-context teammates' implicit, nonverbal, and indirect messages, unpacking what is and isn't said and why. Global team communication climates that emphasize openness, equal participation, and inclusion offer one approach to effective communication within the message context.

Understanding Messages and Their Intent

When lower and higher context communicators work together in global teams, culturally distinct patterns of expression and interpretation can create challenges for comprehension. Managers of multinational corporations in Turkey reported that high-context team members could perceive communication directness as rude (Sogancilar & Ors, 2018). More high-context communicators who prefer consensus building can also perceive debate and confrontation by direct, low-context team members as too aggressive (Behfar et al., 2006; Brett et al., 2006). Low-context team members, in turn, may perceive high-context consensus builders as inefficient and passive (Behfar et al., 2006) or even incompetent and dishonest (Mariam & Chen, 2022). When team members attribute another's communication style to negative personality traits or incorrectly assume that communication style signals intent, relationship conflict is bound to ensue (Adair et al., 2016).

Executives working on multicultural teams report frequent misunderstandings due to differences in what is said or not said and the meaning of what is said (Behfar et al., 2006). For example, "yes" and "no" carry different meanings across cultures (Hall, 1976), so relying on direct, low-context interpretations of agreement or disagreement can lead to false consensus (Behfar et al., 2006). Cultural variation in whether silence indicates thinking, disinterest, agreement, or disagreement is common in multicultural teams, along with different opinions on the need for and appropriate expression of apology (Behfar et al., 2006). These examples demonstrate common cultural differences in message expression and interpretation that can lead to misunderstanding and faulty attributions about teammates.

Communication Climate for Low- and High-Context Participation and Inclusion

Multicultural team researchers have turned to communication climate as a situational factor that can help to overcome misunderstanding and avoid communication-based intragroup tension. A psychologically safe communication climate (PSCC) encourages open and inclusive exchange of opinions and ideas, trust, mutual respect, and constructive controversy (Gibson & Gibbs, 2006). The PSCC construct includes elements of psychological safety (e.g., "Members are able to say what they think"), open and non-judgemental conflict management (e.g., "When there's a problem, members talk about it," "Members are free to be assertive about what they think and feel"), and emotional intelligence (e.g., "People use words that are considerate of others' feelings"). PSCCs have been found to reduce the negative effects of both geographic dispersion and national diversity on team innovation (Gibson & Gibbs, 2006). Opening virtual communication with more relationally (vs task) oriented messages is one predictor of PSCCs in global teams (Glikson & Erez, 2020). However, it should be noted that this communication climate is decidedly low-context, requiring high-context team members to adjust their culturally normative styles.

In another study, researchers found that inclusive communication in co-located multicultural teams facilitated communication effectiveness and team innovation (Lisak et al., 2016). Inclusive communication is an active approach wherein all team members, both low- and high-context, adjust their style to promote cross-cultural understanding. Team members may carefully choose words, focus on clarity in expression, and check for understanding. Meaningful participation, a major component in Janssens and Brett's (2006) model of fusion teamwork (the other is coexistence), is a form of dialogue giving each team member responsibility and space to contribute unique information they have to offer. These authors recommend appreciating, acknowledging, and respecting cultural differences, including communication style, as a first step to improving multicultural team communication effectiveness. Helping low-context team members develop high-context communication skills and communication flexibility may be the next step in creating inclusive communication climates in global teams.

Global Team Communication and Relationship Context

Effective multicultural team communication across the relationship context occurs when low-context team members adjust their style to help high-context team members avoid direct conflict and save face. At the same time, high-context team members must ensure all messages imbued with indirectness or formality are clearly understood. All team members should be on the lookout and ready to disable communication barriers due to perceived power, language-in-use, and subgroup formation. Research on role- and status-based norms, language-in-use, team identity, and subgroup formation offers a foundation to explore the role of relationship context and effective communication in multicultural teams.

Role-Based Communication Norms

In high-context cultures, communication occurs within a web of relationships that defines lines of communication and status norms governing what is said to whom (Hall, 1976). High-context team members adhere to different communication norms depending on their relationship with other team members, whereas low-context team members tend not to adjust what they say and how they say it depending on relationship status (Adair et al., 2016). Role-based communication norms will be more noticeable and fixed in tight cultures with strong norms and low tolerance for deviance (Gelfand, 2019). When team members from low-context cultures ignore role or status-based lines and norms of communication in more hierarchical cultures, team processes and performance suffer (Behfar et al., 2006). Such challenges can be managed with an awareness of team members' contextualized communication norms and an ability to adapt one's own communication style, e.g., behavioral cultural intelligence (Wu & Ng, 2021).

Power and Status from Language Fluency and Language-in-Use

Different levels of language proficiency and language-in-use impact the relationship context in communication by creating power asymmetries (Hinds et al., 2014). Language diversity can also create faultlines (Kalra & Szymanski, 2023) and decrease trust in multicultural teams based on how team members perceive and react to language barriers (Tenzer et al., 2014). Impediments to understanding in multicultural teams with multiple native languages at the table can slow down decision-making and decrease efficiency. Language proficiency–based status barriers can limit communication frequency by non-native speakers and make it difficult for more low-context communicators to understand messages that are highly contextualized in the team's relationships.

Speaking and understanding a non-native language takes more cognitive effort and time than speaking one's native tongue (Volk et al., 2014). Non-native speakers report challenges decoding both verbal and nonverbal cues (Hinds et al., 2014), as found in German and Japanese companies and their subsidiaries (Harzing et al., 2011). Research shows that multicultural team members with low language fluency and cultural intelligence may engage in avoidance to reduce uncertainty (Wu & Ng, 2021). And non-native speakers may avoid communication entirely (Lauring & Klitmøller, 2015).

When non-native speakers process information more slowly and participate less, native English speakers in multicultural teams have a distinct advantage that leads to real and perceived power differences (Hinds et al., 2014). More fluent team members tend to talk more and get more credit, leading to perceptions of unfairness (Behfar et al., 2006). The greater a team member's language proficiency relative to other team members, the more position- and expert-based power benefits they derive (Tenzer & Pudelko, 2017). Particularly in teams without a psychologically safe communication climate, asymmetrical power can greatly impact communication effectiveness.

When an international company institutes English as a lingua franca, being a native English speaker can lead to increased status, as found in a Japanese company, and being a non-native speaker can lead to decreased status, as found in a French company (Neeley, 2013; Neeley & Dumas, 2016). Being ascribed status or claiming status may be particularly relevant in multicultural teams where members high on relationship context dependence are looking for status and power markers when sending and receiving messages (Adair et al., 2016). For example, in carefully crafting messages for more powerful team members, high-context team members may omit or disguise information to convey respect and/or save face (Ting-Toomey, 2005).

Communication with Subgroups and Intrateam Conflict

Team identity is a robust predictor of communication effectiveness in multicultural teams (Shan et al., 2021). However, team identity can be threatened when small groups of team members who speak the same language or share culture-based teamwork norms create subgroup fractures in the team. Subgroups occur in teams when boundaries between small groups of team members become stronger than the boundary defining the superordinate team (Lau & Murnighan, 1998, 2005). These boundaries are called faultlines, connoting a breaking up of the team into smaller units that share demographic characteristics, local dialects, task expertise, or other attributes such as shared cultural norms (Kalra & Szymanski, 2023; Lau & Murnighan, 1998, 2005). Importantly, these fractures boost within-subgroup cohesion and between-subgroup discrimination (Lau & Murnighan, 1998). The presence of faultline-based subgroups impacts the relationship context because coordination and collaboration function better within close-relationship subgroups than in the larger team as a whole.

In general, diversity research has shown that identity-based subgroup formation has the potential to create fractures in a cohesive team identity and reduce information exchange, although these processes are dependent on faultline strength and salience as well as the type of information and team member ties (Bezrukova et al., 2009; Carton & Cummings, 2013; Meyer et al., 2014). In a study of student project teams, nationality-based faultlines were found to restrict non-task-related communication without negatively impacting team performance (Jiang et al., 2012). However, education-based faultlines restricted task-information exchange, negatively impacting team outcomes (Jiang et al., 2012). Thus, when faultlines create subgroups and decrease information exchange, the impact on team performance may depend on the type of communication that is restricted.

The distinction between task and non-task-related communication is relevant for multicultural teams because communication norms in some high-context cultures emphasize attention to socio-emotional cues in the workplace, whereas in low-context cultures, workplace communication tends to be more task-focused (Sanchez-Burks, 2002; Sanchez-Burks et al., 2000). In general, relationship-oriented communication, as opposed to task-oriented communication, promotes social connections among team members (Keyton, 2000). Thus, restriction of relationship-oriented communication due to culture-based subgrouping could reinforce faultline-based fractures in multicultural teams.

However, not all research supports the negative effects of subgroups on communication in global teams. In the team learning literature, Gibson and Vermeulen (2003) found a positive effect of demographic-based subgroup strength on team learning (measured by communication, codification, and experimentation), which the authors explained through a positive cohort effect boosting open communication and idea exchange in global teams. In fusion teamwork, subgroup synergies are also emphasized, where multicultural teams tackle process challenges by first breaking into task-focused subgroups and then reintegrating into the superordinate group (Janssens & Brett, 2006). One study suggests that the negative effects of restricted cross-subgroup communication in multicultural teams can be buffered by introducing conflict because engaging in conflict management requires cross-subgroup communication and information elaboration (Adair et al., 2017). What hasn't yet been explored is how relationship context dependence influences what is said, how it is said, and to whom it is said both within and across subgroups.

Global Team Communication and the Time and Space Contexts

Existing literature on time and space context in multicultural teams focuses on temporal and geographical dispersion (O'Leary & Cummings, 2007). Temporal dispersion characterizes teams whose members work across multiple time zones (Jimenez et al., 2017). Research on geographically dispersed teams tends to compare co-located teams that can meet face-to-face with cross-national teams that work virtually and communicate asynchronously (Hinds et al., 2011). In other words, the existing multicultural team literature treats time context as a function of geography, or place, which is an element of space context. This prior literature shows that coordination around scheduling, managing pace and effort, and allocating resources (McGrath, 1991) becomes challenging in multicultural teams where members are in different time zones.

The communication context of time and space for multicultural teams includes more than just time zones and virtuality, which will be discussed in Chap. 9 (Virtual Communication). Time context refers to approaches to time that are more clock versus event-oriented, whereas space context refers to how people share and fill physical space during communication (Adair et al., 2016). Effective multicultural team communication across the time context occurs when low-context team members with a clock-time orientation are not distracted or frustrated with high-context team members who are more flexible with time, and high-context team members are able to meet low-context deadlines and temporal expectations for the team. Effective communication across the space context occurs when all team members are able to contribute equally and correctly interpret nonverbal facial and body language. How multicultural team members share communication space through interruptions, turn-taking, and body language and the impact on communication effectiveness are areas ripe for future research.

The Language of Time

Time context refers to how people communicate through time, in other words, how they attach meaning to meeting start and end times, deadlines, and lateness (Adair et al., 2016). The way we move through time communicates meaning; for example, taking time for a non-work-related check-in at the start of a meeting communicates flexibility and the importance of interpersonal connections. In high-context cultures where time is more fluid and defined by how events unfold naturally, people communicate attention and respect by allowing team meetings to begin when everyone has arrived and end when the business at hand naturally comes to a close (Hall, 1973). There are also cultural differences in time expression, with doing a task "right now" meaning "immediately" in some cultures and "at one's next available free moment during working hours" in other cultures. In contrast, in low-context cultures where clock time reigns, starting and ending team meetings according to schedule respects team members' time and lateness is considered rude (Hall, 1973). A shared understanding of time-related language and common expectations for time management is important for multicultural teams where members move and communicate through time differently.

For co-located culturally diverse teams, punctuality and lateness are common problems for team members socialized differently to event time and clock time (Adair et al., 2016). Cultural variation around what time a meeting scheduled for 9:00 am will actually start (Hall, 1973) makes coordination challenging. Multicultural team managers regularly encounter misunderstandings when team members set deadlines or use time-related phrases like "end of day" or "on time" that have different meanings in different parts of the world (Behfar et al., 2006; Sogancilar & Ors, 2018). To coordinate schedules and timelines, teams must develop shared expectations for the length of a "lunch break" (or "siesta") and realistic timelines (Behfar et al., 2006). Multicultural team managers also report cultural differences in how to separate work and social time, for example, how to bill a meal with clients that lasts all afternoon (Behfar et al., 2006).

Temporal Coordination Across Time Zones

For globally dispersed teams, asynchronous communication means responses can be slow and feedback infrequent (McGrath, 1991; Montoya-Weiss et al., 2001). When using text-based communication, such as email, messages lack tone of voice and nonverbal cues that make temporal coordination challenging (McGrath, 1991). When team members reside in different time zones but have overlapping work hours, they report fewer coordination problems and more convergence communication, which facilitates collective information processing (Cummings et al., 2009; Dennis et al., 2008).

Research on temporal brokerage has found that team members whose workday overlaps with subgroups that do not have any temporal overlap assume a greater role in managing team communication and coordination (Mell et al., 2021). The temporal overlap creates opportunities for synchronous, convergence communication that facilitates understanding shared goals and creating shared mental models (Kirkman & Mathieu, 2005; Maynard & Gilson, 2014). Asynchronous communication also has some benefits in that it gives time for thoughtful message interpretation and expression (Maynard & Gilson, 2014). Effective temporal brokers facilitate communication across individuals and subgroups that do not have temporal overlap, promoting participation and coordination that can be particularly tricky for virtual teams (Gibbs et al., 2021). Women and team members with multicultural backgrounds are particularly effective in temporal brokerage positions by promoting collaboration and participation from all team members (Jang, 2017; Mell et al., 2021). Now that research has identified temporal brokers as a central coordination role in virtual teams, it is worth looking more closely at roles and team structures that facilitate multicultural team effectiveness (Humphrey et al., 2009; Mell et al., 2021). Process interventions that guide virtual teams through key project stages are a top-down approach to standardize the time context (Montoya-Weiss et al., 2001). Like other standardization methods, this approach may decrease misunderstanding and conflict, but it may be at the expense of the potential synergistic benefits of cultural diversity in teams.

The Language of Space

In multicultural teams, cultural norms that stress respect through communication distance often conflict with cultural norms that show engagement through sharing communication space. In expressive high-context cultures, communicators share space with gesticulating arms, expressive voice, frequent interruptions, and physical closeness, whereas in reserved high-context cultures the space between communicators is unoccupied by words and bodies, remaining reserved for respectful listening and thoughtful pauses (Hall, 1976; Adair et al., 2016).

Interruptions and Turn-Taking

Multicultural team managers report that different norms for interruptions are challenging to manage (Behfar et al., 2006). An overlapping conversational style may be engaged, spontaneous, and energetic, but can be perceived as aggressive and dominant (Rehling, 2004). In contrast, a turn-taking style may be more calm, considerate, and formal but can leave team members feeling unheard (Rehling, 2004).

In a multi-method, multi-study paper on conflict in culturally heterogeneous teams, Ayoko et al. (2002) found that when group members engaged in interruptions and talking over, which are culturally normative in expressive high-context cultures, their groups were more likely to experience destructive conflict, defined as conflict that breaks down team process and impedes performance. In contrast, when group members engaged in humor, smiling, and long pauses, which are culturally normative in low-context cultures and reserved high-context cultures, groups experienced more constructive conflict, defined by healthy debate and problem-solving. The authors note that when some group members engage in divergent communication, a leader can refocus on convergent processes by engaging in discourse management, such as enforcing turn-taking or checking understanding (Ayoko et al., 2002).

Body Language and Emotion Display

Differences in how low- and high-context team members communicate through space can create discomfort, tension, and even misunderstanding for face-to-face teams. When high-context expressive team members take up shared communication space with dramatic voice and gestures, it can be interpreted as aggressive and dominating by high-context reserved team members, for whom silence and personal space communicate respect (Hall, 1973; Trompenaars & Hampden-Turner, 2011). A rigid posture may signal negative affect in one culture and attentiveness in another; for example, negotiators from China may maintain a respectful rigid body posture but spread their work materials across a shared workspace as an expression of power (Adair & Semnani-Azad, 2011). Norms around eating and drinking also involve communicating through space, and managers report that eating during meetings may be an efficient use of time in some cultures. Still, in other cultures, it is disrespectful and unpleasant for everyone (Behfar et al., 2006).

Display rules refer to the cultural appropriateness of showing positive and negative emotions in facial expressions (Matsumoto, 1991). In general, negative emotion is more likely to be evident in the facial expression of team members from individualistic and low power distance cultures than in collectivistic and high power distance cultures (Matsumoto, 1991; Matsumoto et al., 2008). However, in highly affective or emotive cultures, expressive and dramatic communication styles demonstrate norms for amplifying emotional displays (Matsumoto et al., 2008). When positive affect toward one's counterpart was manipulated, negotiators from Canada, a moderately expressive culture, had a faster speech rate and more expressiveness in their voice in comparison to Chinese negotiators, who remained calm and neutral (Semnani-Azad & Adair, 2013).

Managing emotion in multicultural teams is complex not only because of different emotion display rules but also due to the implicit language-based power structure, the challenges of constructive communication when emotions are intense, and different values for the practice of "talking it out" (Von Glinow et al., 2004). Interestingly, when working virtually, the influence of national culture on display norms is weakened, and display rules call for more positive emotion expression and negative emotion suppression in multicultural teams than in culturally homogenous teams (Glikson & Erez, 2013).

Future Directions

Moving forward, a key area for researchers is asking how global teams can develop an inclusive communication climate and full engagement without necessarily adopting direct, low-context communication norms. Expecting high-context team members to adapt direct, low-context communication styles and engage in Western modes of meaningful participation is not consistent with goals to maximize inclusivity or diversity. With the inclusive communication construct, Lisak and colleagues recognize that both low- and high-context communicators need to adjust and adapt to promote equal and equitable communication participation (Lisak et al., 2016), a sentiment echoed in models of third culture building in multicultural teams and multiparty negotiations (Adair et al., 2006; Adair & Liu, 2011). But to improve understanding, and ultimately collaboration, in multicultural teams, we propose that increased attention to implicit messaging and effort decoding it will improve global team processes, including participation, engagement, and understanding.

Proposition 1: In global teams comprised of both low- and high-context communicators, attention to implicit, nonverbal messaging through engaged listening will increase team members' participation and engagement while decreasing misunderstanding.

How can multicultural teams develop an inclusive communication climate when language use (e.g., native speaker, team's lingua franca) and minority status (e.g., visible minority, cultural minority) impact power and ascribed status, limiting who speaks up and who gets seen and heard? Researchers have yet to define the steps needed to make room for high-context and marginalized team members to speak up and be heard using communication styles and norms that best serve them. For consideration, turn-taking starting with the least fluent speaker might be a fruitful practice. Building strong interpersonal connections and trust should help reduce relational communication barriers (e.g., fixed networks, lack of openness) while allowing active and respectful communication across diverse styles (e.g., both open and reserved).

Proposition 2: In global teams comprising both low- and high-context communicators, nurturing interpersonal connections and team cohesion will decrease perceived power differences and increase team members' active participation using their own culturally normative communication styles.

We also suggest that high-context team members who are more flexible with time will be effective temporal brokers because they are able to fluidly move between different members' temporal styles. They have the facility to manage processes when low-context team members' strict clock- and calendar- time conflicts with high-context team members' flexible event time. Researchers can also examine whether this effect is amplified when team members are located in a time zone that overlaps with other members.

Proposition 3: In global teams, high-context members who move and communicate through flexible time will be more likely than low-context members who move and communicate through structured clock time to a) be temporal brokers and b) fill coordination roles.

Because cultural variation in communication across space is physical, it can create enormous discomfort and frustration in multicultural teams where some high-context members engage through sharing communication space and other high-context members show respect through giving space. Researchers need to investigate more closely how multicultural team members interpret and make attributions about distinct communication patterns across the space context and how these cognitions influence team process and performance.

Proposition 4: In global teams comprised of both low- and high-context communicators, proactively explaining culture-based meanings associated with spatial cues (e.g., silence means I'm listening vs silence means I probably disagree; interruption means I'm excited and engaged vs interruption means I'm getting frustrated) will increase team members' participation and engagement while decreasing misunderstanding and misattribution.

References

Adair, W. L., & Ganai, O. (2013). Unpacking four forms of emergent third culture in multicultural teams. In M. Yuki & M. Brewer (Eds.), *Culture and group processes* (pp. 195–216). Oxford University Press.

Adair, W. L., & Liu, L. A. (2011). Building multiculturally shared mental models (MSMM) in multiparty negotiations: A three-stage process model. In *Negotiation and groups* (pp. 57–78). Emerald Group Publishing Limited.

Adair, W. L., & Semnani-Azad, Z. (2011). The display of "dominant" nonverbal cues in negotiation: The role of culture and gender. *International Negotiation, 16*(3), 451–479.

Adair, W. L., Tinsley, C. H., & Taylor, M. (2006). Managing the intercultural interface: Third cultures, antecedents, and consequences. In *National culture and groups* (Vol. 9, pp. 205–232). Emerald Group Publishing Limited.

Adair, W. L., Buchan, N. R., Chen, X. P., & Liu, D. (2016). A model of communication context and measure of context dependence. *Academy of Management Discoveries, 2*(2), 198–217.

Adair, W. L., Liang, L. H., & Hideg, I. (2017). Buffering against the detrimental effects of demographic faultlines: The curious case of intragroup conflict in small work groups. *Negotiation and Conflict Management Research, 10*(1), 28–45.

Ayoko, O. B., Härtel, C. E., & Callan, V. J. (2002). Resolving the puzzle of productive and destructive conflict in culturally heterogeneous workgroups: A communication accommodation theory approach. *International Journal of Conflict Management, 13*(2), 165–195.

Behfar, K., Kern, M., & Brett, J. (2006). Managing challenges in multicultural teams. In Y. R. Chen (Ed.), *National culture and groups* (pp. 233–262). Emerald Group Publishing Limited.

Bezrukova, K., Jehn, K. A., Zanutto, E. L., & Thatcher, S. M. (2009). Do workgroup faultlines help or hurt? A moderated model of faultlines, team identification, and group performance. *Organization Science, 20*(1), 35–50.

Brett, J., Behfar, K., & Kern, M. C. (2006). Managing multicultural teams. *Harvard Business Review, 84*(11), 84–91.

Bui, H., Chau, V. S., Degl'Innocenti, M., Leone, L., & Vicentini, F. (2019). The resilient organisation: A meta-analysis of the effect of communication on team diversity and team performance. *Applied Psychology: An International Review, 68*, 621–657.

Carton, A. M., & Cummings, J. N. (2013). The impact of subgroup type and subgroup configurational properties on work team performance. *Journal of Applied Psychology, 98*(5), 732–758. https://doi.org/10.1037/a0033593

Cohen, S. G., & Bailey, D. E. (1997). What makes teams work: Group effectiveness research from the shop floor to the executive suite. *Journal of Management, 23*(3), 239–290.

Cummings, J. N., Espinosa, J. A., & Pickering, C. K. (2009). Crossing spatial and temporal boundaries in globally distributed projects: A relational model of coordination delay. *Information Systems Research, 20*(3), 420–439.

Dennis, A. R., Fuller, R. M., & Valacich, J. S. (2008). Media, tasks, and communication processes: A theory of media synchronicity. *MIS Quarterly, 32*, 575–600.

Devine, D. J. (2002). A review and integration of classification systems relevant to teams in organizations. *Group Dynamics: Theory, Research, and Practice, 6*(4), 291–310.

DiStefano, J. J., & Maznevski, M. L. (2000). Creating value with diverse teams in global management. *Organizational Dynamics, 29*(1), 45–63.

Earley, C. P., & Mosakowski, E. (2000). Creating hybrid team cultures: An empirical test of transnational team functioning. *Academy of Management Journal, 43*(1), 26–49.

Ely, R. J., & Thomas, D. A. (2001). Cultural diversity at work: The effects of diversity perspectives on work group processes and outcomes. *Administrative Science Quarterly, 46*(2), 229–273.

Gelfand, M. (2019). *Rule makers, rule breakers: Tight and loose cultures and the secret signals that direct our lives*. Scribner.

Gibbs, J. L., Gibson, C. B., Grushina, S. V., & Dunlop, P. D. (2021). Understanding orientations to participation: Overcoming status differences to foster engagement in global teams. *European Journal of Work and Organizational Psychology, 30*(5), 653–671.

Gibson, C. B., & Gibbs, J. L. (2006). Unpacking the concept of virtuality: The effects of geographic dispersion, electronic dependence, dynamic structure, and national diversity on team innovation. *Administrative Science Quarterly, 51*(3), 451–495.

Gibson, C., & Vermeulen, F. (2003). A healthy divide: Subgroups as a stimulus for team learning behavior. *Administrative Science Quarterly, 48*(2), 202–239.

Gibson, C., & Zellmer-Bruhn, M. (2001). Metaphors and meaning: An in[illegible]ultural analysis of the concept of teamwork. *Administrative Science Quarterly, 46*(2), 27[illegible] https://doi.org/10.2307/2667088

Gibson, C. B., Huang, L., Kirkman, B. L., & Shapiro, D. L. (2014). Where global [illegible] virtual meet: The value of examining the intersection of these elements in twenty-first-century teams. *Annual Review of Organizational Psychology and. Organizational Behavior, 1*(1), 217–244.

Glikson, E., & Erez, M. (2013). Emotion display norms in virtual teams. *Journal of Personnel Psychology, 12*(1), 22–32.

Glikson, E., & Erez, M. (2020). The emergence of a communication climate in global virtual teams. *Journal of World Business, 55*(6), 101001.

Hackman, J. R. (2002). *Leading teams: Setting the stage for great performances*. Harvard Business Press.

Hall, E. T. (1973). *The silent language*. Anchor.

Hall, E. T. (1976). *Beyond culture*. Anchor Press.

Harzing, A. W., Köster, K., & Magner, U. (2011). Babel in business: The language barrier and its solutions in the HQ-subsidiary relationship. *Journal of World Business, 46*(3), 279–287.

Hinds, P., & Mortensen, M. (2005). Understanding conflict in geographically distributed teams: The moderating effects of shared identity, shared context, and spontaneous communication. *Organization Science, 16*(3), 290–307.

Hinds, P., Liu, L., & Lyon, J. (2011). Putting the global in global work: An intercultural lens on the practice of cross-national collaboration. *Academy of Management Annals, 5*(1), 135–188.

Hinds, P. J., Neeley, T. B., & Cramton, C. D. (2014). Language as a lightning rod: Power contests, emotion regulation, and subgroup dynamics in global teams. *Journal of International Business Studies, 45*(5), 536–561.

Humphrey, S. E., Morgeson, F. P., & Mannor, M. J. (2009). Developing a theory of the strategic core of teams: A role composition model of team performance. *Journal of Applied Psychology, 94*(1), 48–61.

Jang, S. (2017). Cultural brokerage and creative performance in multicultural teams. *Organization Science, 28*(6), 993–1009.

Janssens, M., & Brett, J. M. (2006). Cultural intelligence in global teams: A fusion model of collaboration. *Group & Organization Management, 31*(1), 124–153.

Jiang, Y., Jackson, S. E., Shaw, J. B., & Chung, Y. (2012). The consequences of educational specialty and nationality faultlines for project teams. *Small Group Research, 43*(5), 613–644.

Jimenez, A., Boehe, D. M., Taras, V., & Caprar, D. V. (2017). Working across boundaries: Current and future perspectives on global virtual teams. *Journal of International Management, 23*(4), 341–349.

Kalra, K., & Szymanski, M. (2023). Alike yet distinct: The effect of language diversity on interpersonal relationships within national and multinational project teams. *Management and Organization Review, 19*, 1–28.

Keyton, J. (2000). Introduction: The relational side of groups. *Small Group Research, 31*(4), 387–396. https://doi.org/10.1177/104649640003100401

Kirkman, B. L., & Mathieu, J. E. (2005). The dimensions and antecedents of team virtuality. *Journal of Management, 31*(5), 700–718.

Lau, D. C., & Murnighan, J. K. (1998). Demographic diversity and faultlines: The compositional dynamics of organizational groups. *Academy of Management Review, 23*(2), 325–340.

Lau, D. C., & Murnighan, J. K. (2005). Interactions within groups and subgroups: The effects of demographic faultlines. *Academy of Management Journal, 48*(4), 645–659.

Lauring, J., & Klitmøller, A. (2015). Corporate language-based communication avoidance in MNCs: A multi-sited ethnography approach. *Journal of World Business, 50*(1), 46–55.

Lisak, A., Erez, M., Sui, Y., & Lee, C. (2016). The positive role of global leaders in enhancing multicultural team innovation. *Journal of International Business Studies, 47*(6), 655–673.

Mariam, M., & Chen, X. P. (2022). Implicit preference for communication directness in the United States. In *Academy of management proceedings* (Vol. 2022, No. 1, p. 13794). Academy of Manageme[illegible]

Marlow, [illegible]cerenza, C. N., & Salas, E. (2017). Communication in virtual teams: A conceptual f[illegible]ork and research agenda. *Human Resource Management Review, 27*(4), 575–589. https:[illegible]oi.org/10.1016/j.hrmr.2016.12.005

Matsumoto, D. (1991). Cultural influences on facial expressions of emotion. *Southern Journal of Communication, 56*(2), 128–137.

Matsumoto, D., Yoo, S. H., & Fontaine, J. (2008). Mapping expressive differences around the world: The relationship between emotional display rules and individualism versus collectivism. *Journal of Cross-Cultural Psychology, 39*(1), 55–74.

Maynard, M. T., & Gilson, L. L. (2014). The role of shared mental model development in understanding virtual team effectiveness. *Group & Organization Management, 39*(1), 3–32.

McGrath, J. E. (1984). *Groups: Interaction and performance*. Prentice-Hall.

McGrath, J. (1991). Time, interaction, and performance (TIP): A theory of groups. *Small Group Research, 22*(2), 147–174.

Mell, J. N., Jang, S., & Chai, S. (2021). Bridging temporal divides: Temporal brokerage in global teams and its impact on individual performance. *Organization Science, 32*(3), 731–751.

Meyer, B., Glenz, A., Antino, M., Rico, R., & González-Romá, V. (2014). Faultlines and subgroups: A meta-review and measurement guide. *Small Group Research, 45*(6), 633–670. https://doi.org/10.1177/1046496414552195

Montoya-Weiss, M. M., Massey, A. P., & Song, M. (2001). Getting it together: Temporal coordination and conflict management in global virtual teams. *Academy of Management Journal, 44*(6), 1251–1262.

Neeley, T. B. (2013). Language matters: Status loss and achieved status distinctions in global organizations. *Organization Science, 24*(2), 476–497.

Neeley, T. B., & Dumas, T. L. (2016). Unearned status gain: Evidence from a global language mandate. *Academy of Management Journal, 59*(1), 14–43.

Neeley, T. B., Hinds, P. J., & Cramton, C. D. (2012). The (un)hidden turmoil of language in global collaboration. *Organizational Dynamics, 41*, 236–244. https://doi.org/10.1016/j.orgdyn.2012.03.008

O'Leary, M. B., & Cummings, J. N. (2007). The spatial, temporal, and configurational characteristics of geographic dispersion in teams. *MIS Quarterly, 31*, 433–452.

Rehling, L. (2004). Improving teamwork through awareness of conversational styles. *Business Communication Quarterly, 67*(4), 475–482.

Sanchez-Burks, J. (2002). Protestant relational ideology and (in)attention to relational cues in work settings. *Journal of Personality and Social Psychology, 83*(4), 919–929. https://doi.org/10.1037/0022-3514.83.4.919

Sanchez-Burks, J., Nisbett, R. E., & Ybarra, O. (2000). Cultural styles, relationship schemas, and prejudice against out-groups. *Journal of Personality and Social Psychology, 79*(2), 174–189. https://doi.org/10.1037/0022-3514.79.2.174

Semnani-Azad, Z., & Adair, W. L. (2013). Watch your tone… relational paralinguistic messages in negotiation: The case of East and West. *International Studies of Management & Organization, 43*(4), 64–89.

Shan, J., Konishi, M., Pullin, P., & Lupina-Wegener, A. (2021). Effects of cultural intelligence on multicultural team effectiveness: The chain mediation role of common ingroup identity and communication quality. *Journal of Theoretical Social Psychology, 5*(4), 519–529.

Sogancilar, N., & Ors, H. (2018). Understanding the challenges of multicultural team management. *Journal of Business Economics and Finance, 7*(3), 259–268.

Stahl, G. K., & Maznevski, M. L. (2021). Unraveling the effects of cultural diversity in teams: A retrospective of research on multicultural work groups and an agenda for future research. *Journal of International Business Studies, 52*(1), 4–22.

Stahl, G. K., Maznevski, M. L., Voigt, A., & Jonsen, K. (2010). Unraveling the effects of cultural diversity in teams: A meta-analysis of research on multicultural work groups. *Journal of International Business Studies, 41*(4), 690–709.

Tenzer, H., & Pudelko, M. (2017). The influence of language differences on power dynamics in multinational teams. *Journal of World Business, 52*(1), 45–61. https://doi.org/10.1016/J.JWB.2016.11.002

Tenzer, H., Pudelko, M., & Harzing, A.-W. (2014). The impact of language barriers on trust formation in multinational teams. *Journal of International Business Studies, 45*(5), 508–535. https://doi.org/10.1057/jibs.2013.64

Ting-Toomey, S. (2005). The matrix of face: An updated face-negotiation theory. In W. B. Gudykunst (Ed.), *Theorizing about intercultural communication* (pp. 71–92). Sage.

Trompenaars, F., & Hampden-Turner, C. (2011). *Riding the waves of culture: Understanding diversity in global business* (2nd ed.). McGraw Hill.

Van Knippenberg, D., De Dreu, C. K., & Homan, A. C. (2004). Work group diversity and group performance: An integrative model and research agenda. *Journal of Applied Psychology, 89*(6), 1008–1022.

Volk, S., Köhler, T., & Pudelko, M. (2014). Brain drain: The cognitive neuroscience of foreign language processing in multinational corporations. *Journal of International Business Studies, 45*, 862–885. https://doi.org/10.1057/jibs.2014.26

Von Glinow, M. A., Shapiro, D. L., & Brett, J. M. (2004). Can we talk, and should we? Managing emotional conflict in multicultural teams. *Academy of Management Review, 29*(4), 578–592.

Wang, J., Cheng, G. H. L., Chen, T., & Leung, K. (2019). Team creativity/innovation in culturally diverse teams: A meta-analysis. *Journal of Organizational Behavior, 40*(6), 693–708.

Wu, C. P., & Ng, K. Y. (2021). Cultural intelligence and language competence: Synergistic effects on avoidance, task performance, and voice behaviors in multicultural teams. *Applied Psychology: An International Review, 70*(4), 1512–1542.

Zakaria, N. (2017). Emergent patterns of switching behaviors and intercultural communication styles of global virtual teams during distributed decision making. *Journal of International Management, 23*(4), 350–366.

Chapter 5
Beyond Silence: How Context Communicates in Cross-Cultural Negotiation

The art of negotiation is the art of hearing what is not said.

– Peter Drucker (1967)

Compared to other forms of communication, negotiation is an intensive interaction where two or more parties must make decisions together. Negotiation is regularly perceived with a competitive mindset, which makes it especially critical for the parties to communicate effectively to reach desirable outcomes (Thompson & Hastie, 1990). In buyer-seller or deal-making negotiations, parties come to the table with a reasonable expectation of reaching a deal that is better than their alternative (Fisher et al., 2011). In dispute contexts, where one party has made a claim and the other party has rejected it, the conflict typically involves blame, negative emotion, and low expectations for resolution, leading to even more competitive mindsets (Ury et al., 1988). Resolving conflict with a mutually satisfactory solution requires communicating, signaling, and enacting a cooperative strategy, which is particularly challenging in a cross-cultural setting where parties have different communication norms.

Recent reviews have covered topics on cultural differences in negotiation strategies and outcomes (Brett & Thompson, 2016), as well as the evolution of culture in negotiation research from a static influence on descriptive behaviors to its dynamic interactions with negotiator characteristics, motivations, and situation, to culture as a potential source for competency development and constructive solutions (Liu & Adair, 2017; Sharma & Liu, 2023). In this chapter, we analyze communication in cross-cultural negotiations from a holistic perspective that addresses the message, relationship, temporal, and spatial contexts, wherein high-context communicators send and receive information that is not contained in verbal messages (Adair et al., 2016; Hall, 1976). We propose new directions in research on communication in cross-cultural negotiations and discuss implications for navigating conflict and negotiating in a globally connected world.

W. L. Adair et al., *What Isn't Being Said*, Springer Series in Emerging Cultural Perspectives in Work, Organizational, and Personnel Studies,
https://doi.org/10.1007/978-3-031-53645-8_5

Communication in Cross-Cultural Negotiations and Conflict Management

The cross-cultural negotiation and conflict management literature has largely examined how cultural values and verbal communication norms create challenges for cross-cultural negotiation and conflict management. There is a need to bring nonverbal communication norms and behaviors into the conversation and explore implications for misunderstanding, information exchange, quality of communication, and trust in cross-cultural negotiations. Verbal communication refers to the use of spoken or written words to convey information, ideas, thoughts, and emotions in a transmitted message (Matsumoto & Hwang, 2013). Nonverbal communication, on the other hand, encompasses all forms of communication that do not use words and includes informative cues in the contexts of message, relationship, time, and space (Adair et al., 2016). To negotiators from direct, low-context cultures, counterparts from high-context cultures, who rely heavily on nonverbal communication, may seem difficult to read. Richard Lewis (2006) illustrates such a scene when he was interpreting for a low-context German team presentating to high-context representatives of a company in Madrid:

> The Germans had a slick presentation lasting 30 minutes, with slides, graphs, diagrams and video. The six Spanish managers facing them hardly watched the presentation at all. They were watching the salesmen. Were these the type of people they wanted to do business with? Did they like them? .... After the session was over the breathless Germans waited for the response. The Spaniards took them for lunch, which lasted until 4:00 pm. After that everybody took a siesta. The deal was done three days later. (p. 271)

Research to date suggests that to effectively exchange information and reach an understanding, more flexible high-context negotiators may adopt a more direct, low-context style (Adair et al., 2001). In fact, Cohen (1997) describes the high-context Japanese negotiation style as "adaptive" and characterizes the high-context negotiation style in general as follows:

> In contrast to the results-oriented American model, it declines to view the immediate issue in isolation; lays particular stress on long-term and affective aspects of the relationship between the parties; is preoccupied with considerations of symbolism, status, and face, and draws on highly developed communication strategies for evading confrontation. (p. 217)

Message Context

When negotiators rely entirely on words to convey meaning, their communication is context free. When words only express part of a message, receivers are expected to extract meaning from what is not said, from the context surrounding a verbal message (Hall, 1976). In intercultural communication settings, disputants from different cultures may experience misunderstanding or an overreading of cues in the message context due to cultural variations in norms for directness of expression and interpretation (Adair et al., 2016; Sanchez-Burks et al., 2003). Brett et al. (2014)

highlighted that culture membership equips individuals to communicate and react to conflict in manners consistent with their dominant cultural norms and behavioral practices. Empirically, Ting-Toomey and Kurogi (1998) argued that East Asians, such as Japanese, interpret direct messages as a threat and would react more competitively in conflict situations. Adair et al. (2007) found that US negotiators expressed preferences and priorities directly. In contrast, Japanese negotiators avoided direct questions that could be threatening, instead exchanging information indirectly through tracking changes in offers over time (see also Adair et al., 2001). In another study, Adair et al., (2004) found that US and Brazilian negotiators were more likely to share information directly than negotiators from Japan, Hong Kong, Russia, or Thailand.

The meaning and function of specific words, or the lack of words, across cultures is another potential trap for misunderstanding. To illustrate, we commonly refer to Japanese negotiators' reluctance to say "yes" or "no" in negotiation. Expressions such as "it will be difficult" and "we will do our best" are socially appropriate ways of saying "no" that save face for both parties but will be misunderstood if taken literally. In describing indirect ways of saying yes and no in Japan, Mexico, and Egypt, Cohen (1997) asks how one is to know when consent is genuine.

> If one's antennae were sufficiently attuned to accompanying verbal and nonverbal signals, it might be possible to read between the lines. Otherwise, the true message became clear only in retrospect. If nothing happened, then one had been the victim of the "social affirmative." (p. 143)

Research has touched on several aspects of message context in cross-cultural negotiation. The use of the pronoun "you" was shown to decrease social distance and increase joint gains in intercultural US-Korean negotiations where the Korean participants were bicultural (Kern et al., 2012). Researchers have noted that silence in Japan can indicate respect and listening as a harmonious relationship unfolds, and it can also indicate an impasse (Hodgson et al., 2008). Liu et al. (2010) found an asymmetrical pattern in the quality of communication experience between United States and Chinese negotiators while communicating in English: US Americans experience more comfort due to their confidence in communicating in their native language while Chinese experience more clarity due to the low context and explicit messages expressed by their US counterparts. They also showed that clarity, responsiveness, and comfort experienced by negotiators while communicating with counterparts are consequential in their intra- or intercultural negotiation economic outcomes. Zhang et al. (2021) found that cross-cultural negotiators' strategic communication could be mapped on messages based on their cultural profiles. Although both US and Chinese negotiators would communicate messages about cooperation and competition, US Americans tend to discuss economic interests and open dialogue more, while Chinese negotiators focus their messages on power and relationships.

Weingart et al. (2015) proposed that directness and intensity of conflict expressions are consequential to conflict escalation and management. The authors conceptualized that conflict expression includes directness of opposition and oppositional intensity. Directness in opposition is related to the degree of straightforwardness and clarity of the message. For example, one disputing party's expression has a higher degree of directness when it is pointed toward clear differences with the other party. On the other hand, the message's intensity is related to a party's entrenchment in positions and subversiveness of actions (Weingart et al., 2015). These scholars suggest that message combinations of high oppositional intensity and low directness, such as an expression of aggression that is not pointed to the focal party, would lead to unpleasant emotional reactions in the other parties and the inference of salient oppositions, thus further escalating the conflicts (Weingart et al., 2015). Meanwhile, the combinations of low oppositional intensity and either high or low directness can offer clear information availability and opportunities for conflict de-escalation and collaboration between the parties (Weingart et al., 2015). How these predictions play out across cultures will depend on parties' message context dependence, or norms for explicit expression, literal interpretation, and direct confrontation.

Successful negotiators and conflict managers are effective listeners. Although low-context communication norms are dominated by explicit and direct messages, listening is an integral part of the message context for high-context communicators (Hall, 1976; Adair et al., 2016). Figure 5.1 shows that the Chinese verb "to listen" involves a holistic set of faculties, including the perception of the other party, the focal communicator's ears, eyes, heart, and undivided attention. The holistic approach to listening also implies that negotiators detect implicit and indirect messages between the lines or beyond what is explicitly expressed, which could be especially critical in intercultural negotiations.

An important feature of listening in communication and negotiation is interpreting and responding to emotions expressed by the other parties. Lange et al. (2022) showed that emotional expressions and interpretations play significant roles in social coordination by directing inferences for contextual cues surrounding the expresser, the situation, and the observer. Such social coordination then would enable adaptive behaviors. Fang et al. (2021) show that there are cultural differences in perceiving emotional facial expressions, with Chinese participants being more sensitive to contrast effects (e.g., from happiness to sadness) in emotional transitions than participants from Canada or the Netherlands, an effect explained by

Fig. 5.1 The holistic meaning of the Chinese verb "to listen". (Wild, 2014)

cultural differences in perception and context sensitivity. Thus, engaged listening can be instrumental for negotiators to discover implicit and indirect messages as well as emotional expressions by other parties in cross-cultural negotiations.

Persuasion is another integral element in negotiation and conflict management. Yukl and Tracey (1992) found a wide repertoire of influence tactics used in workplace negotiations among subordinates, peers, and superiors, including rational persuasion, inspirational appeal, consultation, ingratiation, exchange, personal appeal, coalition, legitimizing, and pressure. When negotiating or resolving conflicts, power is a function of alternatives one has outside the current negotiation or conflict (Lewicki et al., 2020). Perceptions of power would then shape the content of messages individuals employ in the bargaining process, as well as their intentions to cooperate or compete with other parties. Cultural differences in power distance and uncertainty avoidance, as well as communication styles, further complicate preferences for persuasion strategies and the corresponding messages exchanged in cross-cultural interactions, with cultural variation reported in how negotiators respond to arguments framed logically (vs normatively) and appealing to power (vs. interests) (Adair & Brett, 2004; Adair et al., 2013; Beune et al., 2011; Tinsley, 2001). For example, Adair et al., (2004) found distinct patterns of persuasion used by negotiators from Russia and Japan (more informational arguments with or without implicit threats) in comparison to negotiators from the United States, Hong Kong, Brazil, and Thailand. In another study, researchers found that negotiators from China used more indirect persuasion than negotiators from Qatar, followed by the least indirect persuasion expressed by US negotiators (Aslani et al., 2016). Beyond influence strategies, other cultural communication norms related to message context include direct expression of disagreement and approaching conflict, which are more common for low- than high-context negotiators (Adair et al., 2016).

Relationship Context

Relationship context in negotiation and conflict management is where individual expectations and perceptions about how parties are interconnected reside. Lewicki et al. (1994) described five sources of power in negotiation that suggest various dynamics in the relationship context of cross-cultural negotiations. Information and expert powers refer to relative knowledge, technology, and know-how differences between and among the parties. Legitimate power reflects the variation in interparty authority and experience. Location in structure is a source of power because a party's position and centrality in various social networks can be important indicators that signal their bargaining leverage over other parties. Personal power indicates individual characteristics that can project strength or energy in relationship to others during social interaction. Together, these sources of power define the often complex relational dynamics among various parties that could make a difference in their bargaining positions, interests, alternatives, as well as potential tendencies in building coalitions. Negotiation research examining culture in context (see also Chap. 3, dynamic constructivist perspectives) finds that the negotiator role (buyer or seller) also impacts communication and verbal adaptive strategies (Cai et al., 2000). Furthermore, the degree to which parties adjust their communication content and style based on their attention to power and role cues often varies by culture (Adair et al., 2016).

In cross-cultural negotiation and conflict settings, the most saliently activated relationship context depends on the specific network of relationships among the negotiating or disputing parties. For example, Friedman et al. (2006) found that when in disagreement with a supervisor, both US and Chinese subordinates tried to avoid direct confrontation, even though Chinese worry more about the negative relational consequences than US Americans. In international business, foreign firms must often navigate complex social networks in host countries. These networks can be particularly convoluted, especially in emerging markets (e.g., Liu et al., 2014). Liu et al. (2014) showed that negotiators may use different strategies to navigate these networks depending on the types of professional, purposeful, and personal relationships. For example, professional relationships are those connections that occur with first-time business partners of choice. Purposeful relationships occur among individuals and organizations out of necessity, such as an entrepreneur requesting a business license from a government agency. Negotiators in first-time exchanges with those in professional or purposeful relationships might only use formal messages that are different from the informal messages in personal relationships, and these patterns should be more pronounced for high-context negotiators who attend closely to relationship context.

Liu et al. (2021) elucidated that relational schemata at the individual and organizational levels can be malleable and transformed due to internal motivation or external events. A case in point is the relational transformation between long-term partners from purely transactional to more communal over time. However, critical events or crises can trigger the relationship in other directions. Accordingly, the message content and encoding by the partners would vary based on the nature of their relationships at a given time. In cultures that value strong, long-term relationships, building trust helps define the relationship context. Researchers found that negotiators in India, a low trust culture, use questions and answers to get to know their counterpart, in comparison to negotiators in the United States, a high trust culture, who get down to business making and substantiating offers (Gunia et al., 2011).

Low-context communicators prefer to address conflict directly and high-context communicators may prefer more indirect approaches, for example, through a third party, which is another example of communicating through a relationship context. Tinsley and Weldon (2003) found that US managers preferred direct confrontation, and Chinese managers preferred indirect confrontation in a conflict scenario, such as using silence or passive-aggressive acts in the message context. Indirect confrontation is also an implicit way to address the relationship context, convey respect, and limit the loss of face for more high-context communicators (Brett et al., 2014).

The relationship context is also salient in international mediation and arbitration settings. Due to their cost efficiency and timely manner, mediation and arbitration are often used by international business and government organizations (e.g., Cavusgil et al., 2021). Leung (1987, 1997) showed evidence of cross-cultural variations in preferences for mediation, as Chinese prefer the mediator to be someone familiar, while US Americans prefer the mediator to be a stranger who is supposed to be more neutral.

How a communicator perceives the relationship among negotiating or disputing parties can influence how they express or formulate their messages. For example, a low-context communicator might use a threat or direct argument regardless of who the counterpart is. However, a high-context communicator may not use a threat if their counterpart has a higher status or has a personal network connection. In that case they might use a different, more indirect strategy. Negotiators from low- and high-context cultures communicate differently not only to build trust but also as a function of different levels of trust.

Time Context

The time context in cross-cultural negotiations and conflict management includes the scheduling and agenda setting before the negotiation, bargaining on single issues sequentially or using multiple-offer packages during the negotiation, and settlement implementation in the post-negotiation phase. Since there are cultural differences in time orientation (Hall, 1976; Adair et al., 2016), mismatched expectations on time could cause potential misunderstandings or cultural clashes. For example, a higher context communicator may choose to arrive late to a negotiation to signal status or project power, while lower context communicators would perceive the late arrival as disrespectful or unprofessional. This misunderstanding could increase competitiveness among negotiators. Similarly, one may take a call during a negotiation to signal power and status. In contrast, others in the same session would not be affected by the "power play" but regard the interruption as unprofessional (Zhang et al., 2021). Interculturally, more low-context communicators may want to get down to business with direct offers right away while more high-context communicators would need time to build trust to open opportunities for negotiating long-term relationships (Alon & Brett, 2007). The language of time is also captured in culture-specific idioms; for example, US employees "spend" and "waste" time, reflecting the saying "time is money," whereas in Italy "time settles everything" and in Western African nations "Hurry, hurry has no blessing," (Buchan et al., 2011).

Temporal context is also evident throughout a negotiation or conflict resolution, as expectations may differ regarding when to begin exchanging offers or for how long posturing is appropriate. In describing observations of a Mexican marketplace, Hall noted, "Unfolding before my very eyes was a perpetual ballet. Each culture, of course, was choreographed in its own way with its beat, tempo, and rhythm. Beyond this, there were individual performances, pairs dancing out their own dramas" (Hall, 1983, p. 155). Adair and Brett (2005) tested this idea of culturally specific negotiation dances and indeed found similar negotiation stages (posturing, information exchange, influence, and offers) across eight cultures, but found variation in low- and high-context negotiators' specific strategies and less coordinated communication in cross-cultural dyads. As noted above, the timing of different negotiation strategies can depend on the relationship context but also the function of the communication (Adair et al., 2004). For example, US negotiators were found to gather information before making offers, whereas Japanese negotiators were found to gather information from offers throughout the course of a negotiation (Adair et al., 2007). Natlandsmyr and Rognes (1995) similarly found different functions of single- versus multi-issue offers, with Norwegian negotiators making increasingly more complex offers over time on their path to high joint gain agreements, in comparison to Mexican negotiators who stuck with single-issue, win-lost offers and less cooperative agreements. In other words, when a particular strategy is enacted may carry meaning associated with an actor's construal of time.

In the workplace, scholars have found that individual temporal schemas can be socially constructed, adjustable, and anchored by other parties and organizational factors (Blount & Leroy, 2007). In groups, status differences could influence how members pace and align their activities over time (Chen et al., 2004). This subjective experience of time can lead individuals to entrain or resist various patterns of interaction with other parties and eventually create a temporal structure for social interactions (Shipp & Richardson, 2021). Therefore, we suggest cross-cultural negotiators engage proactive and prudent due diligence in their preparation with culturally different others, adjust and manage time expectations, and explicitly communicate time-related messages.

Space Context

At the individual level, the space context of communication suggests modes of exchange through nonverbal cues such as eye contact, silence, and physical movements. For example, Semnani-Azad and Adair (2011) found that European Canadian negotiators were more likely to signal power by displaying relaxed poses or negative emotions, while Chinese negotiators showed power by occupying more physical spaces at the negotiation table with paper and documents. A loud tone of voice could be interpreted as positive excitement by more low-context communicators or an aggressive attack by more high-context communicators. Interruptions could be considered either positive, as showing enthusiasm, or negative, as suggesting rudeness. Silence can also indicate disinterest in more low-context or respect in more high-context cultures. All these cultural differences in the meaning of nonverbal cues in the space context can cause misunderstanding that unintentionally derails negotiations.

The space domain of communication context also includes all senses of nonverbal cues in negotiation, including physical contact such as touching and hugs, and conveys information differently across cultures (Hall, 1976; Morrison & Conaway, 2006). For example, Barnlund (1975) showed that Japanese and US Americans prefer different areas of physical touch with friends of the same or opposite sexes and parents. In negotiation, high-context expressive Brazilians use more direct eye contact and physical connection than high-context reserved Japanese (Requejo & Graham, 2008). High-context Japanese negotiators will seat their most senior team member in the largest chair and furthest from the door (Hodgson et al., 2008). Culturally appropriate greetings through handshakes, hugs, or kisses could start a cross-cultural negotiation on the right foot, start things off on rocky ground, or even risk perceptions of threat or harassment, causing additional conflicts or misunderstandings.

In addition to touching, our senses of hearing, smelling, and tasting are all integral to our interaction with the world, including our negotiation partners (Hall, 1976). These senses enable us to recognize the facial expressions of a counterpart, to smell the air of tension or ease, or even to detect a physical or metaphorical storm coming through a sudden decrease in air pressure. Humans are now believed to possess up to fifty-three senses, and we are still learning more about their vast array (Rubin, 2023; Ward, 2023). Physical arrangements for negotiation settings could also potentially influence negotiators' mood and unconscious mind state. For instance, disgusting smells could make individuals unconsciously more judgmental and prejudiced (Ward, 2023). On the other hand, effective communicators could potentially arrange for pleasant smells, chilled drinking water for US Americans, sparkling water for West Europeans, and warm water for East Asians, comfortable chairs, soft lighting, and relaxing music in a conference room that might facilitate calm and rational exchanges in an upcoming negotiation. Similarly, the physical setting could also project impressions and images of power or domination.

At a broader or situational level, the space context of communication in negotiation can refer to the location or setting where negotiations occur, as physical settings can dictate the process and outcomes of intercultural interactions. As Herdeg (1983) reported, in 1968, during the Paris peace talks between the United States, South Vietnam, North Vietnam, and the National Liberation Front (NLF), the conference table's shape became a contentious issue. North Vietnam and the NLF favored a square table for equality, while the United States and South Vietnam suggested a rectangular one (Michaels, 2017). After several proposals and a ten-week deadlock, they ended up using a large round table with two smaller rectangular tables on opposite sides. Historians and both sides acknowledge the political symbolism in the table shapes and the impact on international negotiation.

Other cross-cultural negotiations, such as trade negotiations, peace negotiations, or negotiations at global organizations like the United Nations, the European Union, or the African Union, occur at the country level, although they are still executed by individuals as proxies. Therefore, the nonverbal signaling and circumstantial settings must be deliberately prepared and executed with due diligence to avoid cultural faux pas and ensure messages are received as intended.

Future Directions

Based on our discussion above, we propose that in addition to clear expressions to avoid misunderstanding, negotiation and conflict management scholars might investigate more high-context strategies including engaged listening, contextualized persuasion strategies, and sensitivity to time and space domains of communication context to overcome cultural barriers.

> Proposition 1: In cross-cultural interactions, engaged listening and contextualized persuasion strategies that tune in to both the explicit and implicit verbal and emotional expressions by other parties can facilitate mutual understanding of interests and strategies.

> Proposition 2: Perceptions of the relationship context by negotiators and disputants in cross-cultural settings can vary depending on the type of relationships and their centrality in the most salient networks. The more negotiators and conflict disputants actively adjust and manage the relationship context with the other party, the more likely they will be able to build a shared understanding and reach mutually beneficial outcomes.

> Proposition 3: Cross-cultural negotiators and conflict managers who actively manage the time context of communication by proactive and mutual adjustments of their time orientations in events planning, scheduling, task structure, and deadlines will reduce misunderstanding related to temporal cues.

> Proposition 4: The more negotiators conduct due diligence in cross-cultural interactions related to the space context that involves understanding nonverbal cues and planning situational settings, the more they can clearly signal prudent deliberation and respect for other parties, which could lead to more constructive outcomes.

References

Adair, W. L., & Brett, J. M. (2004). Culture and negotiation processes. In M. J. Gelfand & J. M. Brett (Eds.), *The handbook of negotiation and culture* (pp. 158–176). Stanford University Press.

Adair, W. L., & Brett, J. M. (2005). The negotiation dance: Time, culture, and behavioral sequences in negotiation. *Organization Science, 16*(1), 33–51.

Adair, W. L., Okumura, T., & Brett, J. M. (2001). Negotiation behaviors when cultures collide: The US and Japan. *Journal of Applied Psychology, 86*(3), 371–385. https://doi.org/10.1037/0021-9010.86.3.371

Adair, W. L., Brett, J. M., Lempereur, A., Okumura, T., Shikhirev, P., Tinsley, C., & Lytle, A. (2004). Culture and negotiation strategy. *Negotiation Journal, 20*(1), 87–111.

Adair, W. L., Weingart, L., & Brett, J. (2007). The timing and function of offers in US and Japanese negotiations. *Journal of Applied Psychology, 92*(4), 1056–1068.

Adair, W. L., Taylor, M., Chu, J., Ethier, N., Xiong, T., Okumura, T., & Brett, J. (2013). Effective influence in negotiation: The role of culture and framing. *International Studies of Management and Organization, 43*(4), 6–25.

Adair, W. L., Buchan, N., Chen, X.-P., & Liu, D. (2016). A model of communication context and measure of context dependence. *Academy of Management Discovery, 2*(2), 198–217. https://doi.org/10.5465/amd.2014.0018

Alon, I., & Brett, J. M. (2007). Perceptions of time and their impact on negotiations in the Arabic-speaking Islamic world. *Negotiation Journal, 23*(1), 55–73.

Aslani, S., Ramirez-Marin, J., Brett, J., Yao, J., Semnani-Azad, Z., Zhang, Z. X., & Adair, W. (2016). Dignity, face, and honor cultures: A study of negotiation strategy and outcomes in three cultures. *Journal of Organizational Behavior, 37*(8), 1178–1201.

Barnlund. (1975). Reprinted in Triandis, H. C. (1995). *Individualism and collectivism.* Westview Press.

Beune, K., Giebels, E., Adair, W. L., Fennis, B. M., & Van Der Zee, K. I. (2011). Criminal justice and. *Criminal Justice and Behavior, 38*(9), 934–954.

Blount, S., & Leroy, S. (2007). Individual temporality in the workplace: How individuals perceive and value time at work. In B. A. Rubin (Ed.), *Workplace temporalities* (Research in the sociology of work, Vol. 17, pp. 147–177). Emerald Group Publishing Limited. https://doi.org/10.1016/S0277-2833(07)17005-9

Brett, J. M., & Thompson, L. (2016). Negotiation. *Organizational Behavior and Human Decision Processes, 136*, 68–79.

Brett, J., Behfar, K., & Sanchez-Burks, J. (2014). Managing cross-culture conflicts: A close look at the implication of direct versus indirect confrontation. In *Handbook of conflict management research* (pp. 136–154). Edward Elgar Publishing.

Buchan, N. R., Adair, W. L., & Chen, X. P. (2011). Navigating international negotiations: A communications and social interaction style (CSIS) framework. In M. Benoliel (Ed.), *Negotiation excellence: Successful deal making* (pp. 271–292). World Scientific.

Cai, D. A., Wilson, S. R., & Drake, L. E. (2000). Culture in the context of intercultural negotiation: Individualism-collectivism and paths to integrative agreements. *Human Communication Research, 26*(4), 591–617.

Cavusgil, S. T., Ghauri, P., & Liu, L. A. (2021). *Doing business in emerging markets* (3rd ed.). Sage.

Chen, Y.-R., Blount, S., & Sanchez-Burks, J. (2004). The role of status differentials in group synchronization. In S. Blount (Ed.), *Time in groups* (Research on managing groups and teams, Vol. 6, pp. 111–133). Emerald Group Publishing Limited.

Cohen, R. A. (1997). *Negotiating across cultures: International communication in an interdependent world.* US Institute of Peace Press.

Drucker, P. (1967). *The effective executive: The definitive guide to getting the right things done.* Harper Collins.

Fang, X., Van Kleef, G. A., Kawakami, K., & Sauter, D. A. (2021). Cultural differences in perceiving transitions in emotional facial expressions: Easterners show greater contrast effects than Westerners. *Journal of Experimental Social Psychology, 95*(104143), 1–11.

Fisher, R., Ury, W. L., & Patton, B. (2011). *Getting to yes: Negotiating agreement without giving in*. Penguin.

Friedman, R. A., Chi, S.-C., & Liu, L. A. (2006). An expectancy model of Chinese American differences in conflict avoiding. *Journal of International Business Studies, 37*(1), 76–91.

Gunia, B. C., Brett, J. M., Nandkeolyar, A. K., & Kamdar, D. (2011). Paying a price: Culture, trust, and negotiation consequences. *Journal of Applied Psychology, 96*(4), 774–789.

Hall, E. T. (1976). *Beyond culture*. Anchor Press.

Hall, E. T. (1983). *The dance of life: The other dimension of time*. Anchor Press/Doubleday.

Herdeg, K. (1983). *The decorated diagram: Harvard architecture and the failure of the Bauhaus legacy*. MIT Press.

Hodgson, J. D., Sano, Y., & Graham, J. L. (2008). *Doing business with the new Japan: Succeeding in America's richest international market*. Rowman & Littlefield.

Kern, M. C., Lee, S., Aytug, Z. G., & Brett, J. M. (2012). Bridging social distance in intercultural negotiations: "You" and the bi-cultural negotiator. *International Journal of Conflict Management, 23*(2), 173–191.

Lange, J., Heerdink, M. W., & van Kleef, G. A. (2022). Reading emotions, reading people: Emotion perception and inferences drawn from perceived emotions. *Current Opinion in Psychology, 43*, 85–90. https://doi.org/10.1016/j.copsyc.2021.06.008

Leung, K. (1987). Some determinants of reactions to procedural models for conflict resolution: A cross-national study. *Journal of Personality and Social Psychology, 53*(5), 898–908. https://doi.org/10.1037/0022-3514.53.5.898
Leung, K. (1997). *Negotiation and reward allocations across cultures*. New Lexington Press/ Jossey-Bass Publishers.
Lewicki, R. J., Litterer, J., Minton, J., & Saunders, D. (1994). *Negotiation*. Irwin.
Lewicki, R. J., Barry, B., & Saunders, D. M. (2020). *Negotiation* (8th ed.). McGraw Hill.
Lewis, R. D. (2006). *When cultures collide: Leading across cultures* (3rd ed.). Nicholas Brealey International.
Liu, L. A., & Adair, W. L. (2017). Intercultural communication in international negotiation. In Y. Y. Kim & K. McKay-Semmler (Eds.), *The international encyclopedia of intercultural communication*. Wiley-Blackwell. https://doi.org/10.1002/9781118783665.ieicc0048
Liu, L. A., Chua, C. H., & Stahl, G. (2010). Quality of communication experience: Definition, measurement, and implications for intercultural negotiations. *Journal of Applied Psychology, 95*(3), 469–487. https://doi.org/10.1037/a0019094
Liu, L. A., Loch, K. D., & Bruce, D. C. (2014). Cultivating political wisdom like consiglieri in China and beyond. In J. Miles (Ed.), *New directions in management and organization theory* (pp. 339–352). Cambridge Scholars Publishing.
Liu, L. A., Chiu, C. Y., & Zhang, Z.-X. (2021). Dynamic transformation of communal and exchange schemata in multicultural relationships. *Cross Cultural & Strategic Management, 28*(2), 368–383.
Matsumoto, D., & Hwang, H. C. (2013). Culture and nonverbal communication. In J. Hall & M. Knapp (Eds.), *Handbook of nonverbal communication* (pp. 697–727). Mouton de Gruyter.
Michaels, J. (2017). *Stuck in endless preliminaries: Vietnam and the battle of the Paris peace table, November 1968-January 1969*. https://defenceindepth.co/2017/05/19/stuck-in-endless-preliminaries-vietnam-and-the-battle-of-the-paris-peace-table-november-1968-january-1969/
Morrison, T. & Conaway, W. A. (2006). *Kiss, bow, or shake hands*. Adams Media.
Natlandsmyr, J. H., & Rognes, J. (1995). Culture, behavior, and negotiation outcomes: A comparative and cross-cultural study of Mexican and Norwegian negotiators. *International Journal of Conflict Management, 6*(1), 5–29.
Requejo, W. H., & Graham, J. L. (2008). *Global negotiation: The new rules*. Macmillan.
Rubin, G. (2023). *Life in five senses: How exploring the senses got me out of my head and into the world*. Random House.
Sanchez-Burks, J., Lee, F., Choi, I., Nisbett, R., Zhao, S., & Jasook, K. (2003). Conversing across cultures: East-West communication styles in work and non-work contexts. *Journal of Personality and Social Psychology, 85*(2), 363–372.
Semnani-Azad, Z., & Adair, W. L. (2011). The display of "dominant" nonverbal cues in negotiation: The role of culture and gender. *International Negotiation, 16*(3), 451–479. https://doi.org/10.1163/157180611x592950
Sharma, S., & Liu, L. A. (2023). Culture and communication. In M. J. Gelfand & M. Erez (Eds.), *Oxford handbook of cross-cultural organizational behavior*. Oxford University Press.
Shipp, A. J., & Richardson, H. A. (2021). The impact of temporal schemata: Understanding when individuals entrain versus resist or create temporal structure. *Academy of Management Review, 46*(2), 299–319.
Thompson, L., & Hastie, R. (1990). Social perception in negotiation. *Organizational Behavior and Human Decision Processes, 47*(1), 98–123.
Ting-Toomey, S., & Kurogi, A. (1998). Facework competence in intercultural conflict: An updated face-negotiation theory. *International Journal of Intercultural Relations, 22*(2), 187–225.
Tinsley, C. H. (2001). How negotiators get to yes: Predicting the constellation of strategies used across cultures to negotiate conflict. *Journal of Applied Psychology, 86*(4), 583–593.

Tinsley, C. H., & Weldon, E. (2003). Responses to a normative conflict among American and Chinese managers. *International Journal of Cross Cultural Management, 3*(2), 183–194.

Ury, W. L., Brett, J. M., & Goldberg, S. B. (1988). *Getting disputes resolved: Designing systems to cut the costs of conflict*. Jossey-Bass.

Ward, A. (2023). *Sensational: A new story of our senses*. Profile Books.

Weingart, L., Behfar, K., Bendersky, C., Todorova, T., & Jehn, K. (2015). The directness of oppositional intensity in conflict expressions. *Academy of Management Review, 40*(2), 235–262.

Wild, R. (2014, January 19). *The Chinese symbol for listening*. The Leadership Blog. https://rwwleadership.wordpress.com/2014/01/19/the-chinese-symbol-for-listening/

Yukl, G., & Tracey, J. B. (1992). Consequences of influence tactics used with subordinates, peers, and the boss. *Journal of Applied Psychology, 77*(4), 525–535. https://doi.org/10.1037/0021-9010.77.4.525

Zhang, Z.-X., Liu, L. A., & Ma, L. (2021). Negotiation beliefs: Comparing Americans and Chinese. *International Business Review, 30*(5), 101849. https://doi.org/10.1016/j.ibusrev.2021.101849

Chapter 6
Translating What Is and Isn't Said: Voice, Gossip, and Feedback in a Global Workplace

Gossip is the art of saying nothing in a way that leaves nothing unsaid.

– Walter Winchell

The tongue weighs practically nothing but so few people can hold it.

– Anonymous

Employees within and across organizational levels connect through formal and informal communication channels that embody message, relationship, time, and space context. Employee voice is defined as prosocial discretionary behavior to instill change (Morrison, 2023). Workplace gossip is a communication act between employees about a non-present other (Foster, 2004; Peters & Kashima, 2007). Feedback is a core job characteristic that conveys knowledge of results and work effectiveness (Hackman & Oldham, 1976). These mostly dyadic or small group workplace communication interactions, which can be upward, downward, or lateral, are difficult to manage for employees and managers from diverse cultural backgrounds with different communication styles.

How do preferences for direct, explicit communication in low-context cultures and indirect, implicit communication in high-context cultures (Hall, 1976) influence voice, gossip, and feedback at work? Brett gives an example of how bicycle distributors in the United States, a low-context culture, delivered feedback about a faulty part to their suppliers in China, a high-context culture. Instead of making a direct statement of fact (e.g., the bikes are faulty), they used a face-saving question, "Is this part supposed to rattle?" to convey the problem indirectly (Brett, 2007). Without directly answering the question, the Chinese counterparts sent a new shipment of bicycles that did not rattle. Here both the feedback and response were handled with indirect messaging and attention to relationship context.

As university faculty, we have noticed that among our diverse groups of graduate students, North American students tend to gossip in larger groups and in the presence of faculty. In contrast, students from East and South Asia tend to approach faculty privately to convey overheard student gossip (personal observations). Recognizing the distinct role of space relationship contexts is necessary to

W. L. Adair et al., *What Isn't Being Said*, Springer Series in Emerging Cultural Perspectives in Work, Organizational, and Personnel Studies,
https://doi.org/10.1007/978-3-031-53645-8_6

understand that the formal, private channels utilized by high-context students do not diminish the importance of the message.

Below, we review the literature on employee voice, gossip, and feedback, highlighting the often unrecognized implicit sources of messaging present in the communication contexts surrounding the words (message context), interlocutors' relationships (relationship context), and the temporal (time context), and sensory (space context) domains. We suggest that nonverbal communication in voice, gossip, and feedback behavior has been overlooked in the literature and offer avenues for future research.

Voice and Silence

Organizations and employees benefit when workers raise concerns and make suggestions for improvement and when those voices are heard (Van Dyne & LePine, 1998; Morrison, 2011). Speaking up, or voice, is defined as informal communication with the intent of helping to achieve a work goal (Klaas et al., 2012). Employee voice may support (forms include promotive, supportive, or constructive) or criticize (forms include prohibitive, defensive, or destructive) how things are being done in an organization (Liang et al., 2012; Maynes & Podaskoff, 2014), but the assumed goal is to improve organizational processes and performance. Indeed, several studies show that employee voice improves team and organizational performance (Van Dyne & LePine, 1998).

Silence refers to an employee's conscious decision not to speak up in situations that may involve managerial errors, unfair treatment, or moral violations (Knoll & van Dick, 2013). Employee silence may be acquiescent, meaning an employee assumes that speaking up won't change anything, or quiescent, when an employee fears negative repercussions of speaking up (Knoll et al., 2021). The third form of silence is prosocial and occurs when employees avoid speaking up so as not to embarrass others (Knoll et al., 2021). When an employee remains silent, their underlying motivations remain unknown, as does the unspoken organizational message; thus, compared to voice, employee silence is more likely to be misunderstood, and misattributions may lead to unintended consequences for the employee (Van Dyne et al., 2003).

Voice is an extra-role behavior that entails risk (e.g., loss of face, punishment) for employees who speak up (Burris, 2012; Detert & Burris, 2007). Many individual, cultural, and situational variables influence who is likely to speak up, who is likely to remain silent, and who is likely to be heard (see Morrison, 2011 for a review). Recent research conceptualizes constructive voice as a dyadic process of communication and social exchange between employee and manager wherein a manager interprets the voice expressed by an employee as a positive or negative action, which then informs the manager's response (Kim et al., 2023). Just as in the process model of communication (see Chap. 2, this volume), this loop of reciprocal communication exchange occurs not only verbally but also nonverbally across communication context in sending, receiving, and responding stages. Because voice is speaking up, the messaging may be more direct or indirect due to employees' low- or high-context communication style. Because silence is not speaking up, the messaging may be extremely challenging for more low-context communicators to understand.

Voice, Silence, and Message Context

Some cultures value verbal communication for social connection (e.g., Mexico), information exchange (e.g., the United States), or problem analysis (e.g., France), while in other cultures, these same functions are fulfilled more through listening and silent reflection (e.g., Japan) (Hall, 1976). It is not surprising that in low-context cultures where people use more explicit, verbal forms of communication, it has been found that employees are more likely to speak up at work than in high-context cultures (Thomas & Au, 2002).

Ward et al. (2016) investigated the role of individual norms for low/high context communication in predicting employee voice. Using a culturally diverse sample of university professors and a gender-diverse sample of manufacturing employees, they found that more high-context communicators were less likely than more low-context communicators to engage in prohibitive voice, pointing out problems with existing practices, but not promotive voice, making improvement suggestions. This effect was more prominent when the employee-supervisor relationship quality (Leader-Member-Exchange, LMX) was lower, suggesting that employees who have a stronger relationship with their supervisor, a function of relationship context, are less likely to stay silent (Milliken et al., 2003).

Employees may choose to speak up more directly for clarity or more indirectly to avoid challenging superiors, and managerial endorsement of employee concerns voiced in different ways may vary culturally (Lam et al., 2019). Multiple studies have found that US and Chinese managers are more likely to endorse employee concerns when expressed more directly and respectfully, suggesting communication clarity is paramount in employee voice (Krenz et al., 2019; Lam et al., 2019). Direct voice is explicit and clear, ensuring the manager understands the concerns raised (Brett et al., 2014; Weingart et al., 2015). In contrast to direct voice, indirect voice would be characterized by asking questions or making hints (Brett, 2000). Although directness led to managerial response in both the United States and China, societal values explaining this effect depend on employees being perceived as credible in the United States and as polite in China (Lam et al., 2019). Thus, directness is socially construed differently in the United States and China.

In the United States, politically correct language, defined by words and tactics that seemingly avoid offending marginalized groups, is an example of indirect messaging that may lack clarity (Hunter, 2005) and even stifle open communication (Avery & Steingard, 2008; Barker, 1994). It has also been found that political correctness at work is more common among employees with a strong other-orientation, which requires awareness of and attention to social cues in one's environment

(Koopman et al., 2023). Employees with high context communication norms may be particularly prone to political correctness, which might impact communication clarity and effectiveness.

The other side of the coin for voice is being heard (Burris et al., 2013). Research had found that a promotive voice was more likely to be heard when employees had low (vs high) context communication norms, when LMX was high, and when the voice was perceived to be constructive (Ward et al., 2016). For example, an indirect, high-context employee may believe they engaged in a promotive voice by making a change suggestion in the form of a question, but their direct, low-context supervisor might not have understood because they interpreted the question as a request for information, not as a voice behavior.

The message context is one source of the many potential misinterpretations and misattributions of voice and silence in diverse, multicultural workplaces. Low-context employees are likely to speak up with direct, explicit suggestions, communication that high-context managers may attribute to employees being arrogant and questioning authority. To avoid such attributions, high-context employees may stay silent or express voice with implicit messages that low-context managers do not fully understand.

Voice, Silence, and Relationship Context

The nature and quality of the relationship between manager and employee is an example of relationship context. Research has found that relationship impacts the likelihood of voice more in high power distance cultures than low power distance cultures (Botero & Van Dyne, 2009). For example, in a high power distance culture where the leader and managerial role is conferred with greater status, authority, and decision-making power than the subordinate role, employees tend to fear negative repercussions and criticism for speaking up (Morrison, 2011), whereas in low power distance cultures, people are more willing to speak up (Wei et al., 2015; Song et al., 2019). Power distance also increases the negative effect of the authoritarian leadership style on voice behavior (Li & Sun, 2015). Meanwhile, power distance values have been shown to influence different forms of silence, primarily acquiescent silence (Rhee et al., 2014). In a study of silence motives in 33 countries, Knoll et al. (2021) found that power distance was positively related to staying silent for fear of reprisal (quiescent silence), not wanting to harm others (prosocial silence), and holding onto the information as power (opportunistic silence). However, that study did not find any effect of power distance on acquiescent silence (resignation). Beyond power distance, cultural values for collectivism and in-group harmony are related to preferences for conflict avoidance (Leung et al., 2002) and were found to predict lower levels of employee voice and decreased the positive effect of LMX on employee voice in Korea, but not in the United States (Park & Nawakitphaitoon, 2018).

Ren et al. (2022) propose a model of implicit voice that accounts for employee and supervisor face concerns. Face is defined as one's status in the eyes of others, and cross-cultural communication scholars show cultural variation in self-face maintenance and other-face maintenance as motivations driving communication (Ting-Toomey & Kurogi, 1998). Implicit voice delivery raises concerns using indirect channels or implicit language to avoid potentially embarrassing or causing loss of face for one's supervisor (Ren et al., 2022). This form of voice is high-context because it relies less on words and more on the listener to infer meaning in the message domain (Hall, 1976), as illustrated by this sample item from the Implicit Voice Delivery scale: "I asked my supervisor questions, the answers to which imply better ways of getting things done" (Ren et al., 2022). In addition, employees who use implicit voice adjust what they say and how they say it within the relationship domain to preserve face and relational harmony (Adair et al., 2016). In a multi-wave study of employees and their supervisors in North China, Ren et al. (2022) confirmed the role of employee other-face concern and supervisor self-face concern in predicting implicit voice delivery and that supervisors with high-context interpretation norms were more likely to endorse implicit voice.

Voice behavior has also been studied as a function of face concern, which is stronger in collectivist and high relationship context cultures (Ting-Toomey, 2005; Adair et al., 2016). Isaakyan et al. (2021) proposed that voice in a public setting is more threatening to managers' image than voice expressed in a private one-on-one conversation. Over a series of studies, they found support for this face management argument (Brown & Levinson, 1987), such that managers were less likely to endorse voice expressed in public (vs private), and this effect was explained through image threat. The effect was greater when LMX was low (Isaakyan et al., 2021).

Affinity groups as informal social mechanisms for minority group members in organizations have been found to provide networks, feedback mechanisms, and opportunities for voice (Colgan & McKearney, 2012; Syed, 2014). Employee resource groups (ERGs) are informal groups for employees and allies based on minority group status (McNulty et al., 2018). ERGs and affinity groups may be a source of voice and engagement for cultural minority employees who typically report lower psychological safety and verbal behavior than their host national counterparts on a team (Farley et al., 2022; see also Chap. 4, this volume).

Voice and Silence in the Time and Space Contexts

The time domain of communication context is evident in employee voice when frequency, timing, and length of voice messages convey implicit meaning. By frequency, we refer not to how often an employee speaks up but to how many times an employee speaks up with the same message. When an employee voices the same concern multiple times to the same manager or multiple managers, the repetition may signal urgency and the employee's feelings of not being heard. In low-context cultures that run on clock time, employee voice is more likely to be scheduled on the agenda of a regular meeting. In contrast, in high-context cultures that run on event time, employee voice may occur more spontaneously as the need or opportunity arises. Similarly, expressing voice as "one more thing" at the end of an already long meeting would be more common for higher- than lower-context communicators. This is because more low-context communicators equate staying on schedule with professionalism and respect for others' time (Lewis, 2018).

Voice across the space domain manifests in where an employee speaks up, for example, in private or public, and how an employee speaks up, for example, with dramatic expression or physical closeness. Interrupting one's manager to express concerns may signal more urgency in low-context cultures where interruptions are considered rude, or less urgency in expressive high-context cultures where interruptions can be a form of shared communication space and relational engagement (Adair et al., 2016). For example, an employee speaking over their manager (entering their auditory space) to say "yes, and also I think…" might signal active engagement in the conversation as a dyadic process of information sharing and meaning-making. Likewise, outwardly expressing emotions like frustration and anger in voice (entering the general sensory space of one's interlocutor) is more likely in expressive high-context cultures, like Spain, where dramatic expression is a way of connecting with others (Hall, 1960). In reserved high-context cultures, like Japan, managers would expect voice to be shared in private with respectful physical and sensory distance and passive expression. In low-context cultures, direct messaging in the workplace typically lacks socio-emotional content (Sanchez-Burks et al., 2003).

Expressing voice can be direct or indirect, creating challenges for interpretation in a multicultural workplace. Low-context managers who expect direct messages may perceive implicit, indirect voice as unimportant or passive-aggressive. High-context managers who prefer indirect, private, and passive expression may react negatively to low-context employees who raise explicit concerns in team meetings.

> In our view, gossip is a potentially powerful and efficient means of transmitting information about the rules, norms, and other guidelines for living in a culture. (Baumeister et al., 2004, p. 113)

Gossip

Gossip is a form of social communication from one individual (the gossiper) to another (the audience) about a non-present other(s) (Foster, 2004; Peters & Kashima, 2007). Gossip is a universal human behavior in all societies and cultures (Dunbar, 2004; Brady et al., 2017). While early research treats gossip as a communicative act with malicious intent (Foster, 2004), scholars have expanded the scope of gossip research to define gossip as communication about a non-present other regarding their non-normative behaviors, which can be either negative or positive (Brady et al., 2017; Sun et al., 2023). Brady et al. (2017) found that people gossip about co-workers and supervisors in the United States as well as in China. The types of gossip and measurement scales were also cross-culturally valid, including negative gossip (e.g., "questioned a co-worker's abilities") and positive gossip (e.g., "complimented a co-worker's actions"). Note that the gossip scale developed in this study mainly reflects its content rather than the context through which it is transmitted. This broad categorization of gossip has enabled researchers to discover a wide range of functions and outcomes related to gossip. At the individual or interpersonal level, gossip helps bond people together and maintain social relationships or social network positions (Bosson et al., 2006; Martinescu et al., 2019). At the group level, gossip is a means of conveying information that involves codes of conduct and moral rules, socializing and culturizing people to conform to rules and norms (Beersma & Van Kleef, 2012; Brady et al., 2017). It is this function of gossip that we consider in detail as related to the context of culture and communication.

Gossip as Cultural Learning and Norm Transmission

In the article "Gossip as Cultural Learning," Baumeister et al. (2004) argue that gossip can convey valuable information about culture and society to the hearer. It is "a potentially powerful and efficient means of transmitting information about the rules, norms, and other guidelines for living in a culture" (p. 115). Because norms are embedded in culture (see Chap. 2, this volume) and gossip is a communication act, this perspective opens an avenue for cross-cultural research on differences in the pervasiveness of gossip and the role of the four domains of communication context in gossip form and effectiveness. Although gossip happens everywhere, the extent to which gossip is relied upon to transmit rule- and- norm-related information differs across cultures and organizations with different communication norms.

Gossip and Communication Context

In low-context cultures, people engage in straight talk, express meaning clearly using explicit, coded messages, and say what they mean and mean what they say (Hall, 1976). Gossip expressed directly should be more effective in low-context cultures, and gossip comprising stories and anecdotes should be more effective in high-context cultures. As a subtle message leaves much room for interpretation, people with low-context communication norms may not understand the underlying meaning of gossip conveyed through stories and anecdotes. Thus, we expect that in low-context cultures, gossip will be less pervasive as a means of norm transmission because codified written rules and norms are clearly articulated using words (verbal or written), conveyed directly to the audience. In US organizations where communication norms are generally low-context, organizational values, rules, norms, processes, and criteria are often clearly documented. Furthermore, meeting minutes are often carefully recorded and kept on record. These files and documents are explicitly transmitted to different levels of the organization, where employees follow and use them as guidelines when encountering relevant situations.

In contrast, people in high-context cultures might feel more comfortable using gossip to transmit rules and norms because informal communication fits well with two distinct characteristics of high-context communication. One is the implicitness of the meaning in the gossip, as the norms embedded in stories and anecdotes are not explicitly spelled out. The other characteristic of high-context communication is indirectness because the norms embedded in the gossip are not directly conveyed to the audience but through a story or anecdote about a non-present other. Although the majority of the research on gossip has been conducted in low-context cultures, we expect that gossip will be more pervasive in high-context cultures. Because people in high-context cultures tend to be more concerned about relationship harmony (thus more conflict-avoidant) than those in low-context cultures (Gudykunst, 2005; Triandis, 1994), conveying rules and norms via gossip can also serve these purposes.

Meanwhile, the *relationship* domain of communication context can also influence gossip. There are several types of relationship in this case, one is the relationship between the gossiper and the audience, another is between the audience and the non-present other, and yet another is the relationship between the gossiper and the non-present other. Research has shown how hierarchical power relationships shape individuals' gossip motives and behaviors. Martinescu et al. (2019) made a distinction between downward gossip, upward gossip (gossip between people of different statuses), and lateral gossip (gossip between people of equal status). They found that downward gossip was less frequent and elaborate than upward and lateral interactions. Moreover, upward gossip was more functional for exerting informational influence and seeking instrumental support than lateral gossip, which was more functional for seeking information and expressing social support. Although this was not a cross-cultural study, the significant role of status (e.g., upward vs downward communication) suggests that gossip frequency and content may differ in cultures with distinct power distance values and context dependence norms. Lewis (2006) describes how gossip is intertwined with the relationship and time context in many cultures:

> In Spain, Italy, Brazil, and Japan, gossip quickly updates and bypasses facts and statistics, provides political background to commercial decisions and facilitates invaluable debate between people who do not meet officially. The cafes of Madrid and Lisbon overflow with businesspeople, and the whole of Central and South America "networks" merrily until one or two in the morning. (p. 6)

Regarding the time domain of communication context, it is conceivable that gossip at an earlier time will be more effective than at a later time in instilling rules and norms because early gossip may have the inception effect (Cole et al., 2022) – planting a seed in people's mind, which will bloom on its own with time. In this case, since the rules and norms are implicitly and indirectly embedded in the gossip, representing the highest form of inception (Cole et al., 2022), the gossip will encounter the least resistance for people to accept it. However, since there is often a time lag between accepting an idea and implementing or enacting it, early gossip will be more effective in achieving the goal than later gossip.

The space domain of communication context describes how gossip is conveyed in several respects. First is the physical space or the location where gossip is conveyed. Because gossip is informal social communication, we maintain that in low-context and expressive high-context cultures, gossip outside one's formal workspace (e.g., office), will be more effective because the atmosphere there (e.g., café, restaurant, home) will be more relaxed than at work, which enables the gossiper to tell the story/anecdote more freely. Second is the physical distance between the gossiper and the audience. Are they standing/sitting close or distant? When the gossip is transmitted, is there touching (if yes, which body parts) between the people? Is the voice loud or soft? Is the facial expression animated? Is there laughter? Although no existing empirical studies answer these questions, we suggest future research examine the role of spatial cues in gossip in low- and high-context cultures.

Feedback and Communication Context

Feedback is the provision of information about an employee's work effectiveness to motivate and direct performance improvement (Hackman & Oldham, 1976). Ashford and Cummings (1983) delineate five factors in the realm of feedback seeking. The method factor includes feedback seeking through observation, comparison, direct, or indirect inquiry, drawing parallels to the directness/indirectness elements of the message context. A second factor, target, defines the relationship with the feedback source, supervisor, or peer. Two factors, frequency – how often feedback is sought, and timing – immediate or with delay, are related to the temporal context of communication. Lastly, the feedback topic includes both the content of feedback and also the presentation style, the latter of which involves spatial and sensory context (Ashford & Cummings, 1983; Ashford et al., 2003). Although they do not explicitly discuss low/high context communication, these authors emphasize the role of cultural norms in feedback seeking.

> While a culturally diverse setting increases the instrumental need for feedback, the adjacent intercultural communication differences are likely to increase the effort costs of feedback seeking. There may also be differences between Western and non-Western cultures about whether feedback-seeking behavior is respectful or appropriate. (Ashford et al., 2003, p. 784)

Whereas feedback seeking is upward directed search for performance-related information that can fulfill image, ego, and instrumental needs (Ashford & Cummings, 1983), feedback delivery is downward communication directed to the employee (Larson, 1989). Feedback delivery is a form of performance appraisal that can occur in formal, standardized, informal, and unprompted formats (Larson, 1984). Cross-cultural empirical research in both literatures has been limited, and while most scholars allude to communication style, the overwhelming approach has been value-based.

Sully De Luque and Sommer (2000) proposed that in more holistic and high-context cultures, feedback would be sought more indirectly than in specific, low-context cultures. These authors also proposed that employees in high power distance cultures would be more likely to seek and value feedback from supervisors and high-status organizational members than employees in low power distance cultures (Sully de Luque & Sommer, 2000; Patel et al., 2019). A study by MacDonald et al. (2013) found support for a complex pattern of preferences for feedback source (peer vs supervisor) and setting (public vs private) that they predicted based on cultural values for egalitarianism and power distance and related feedback motives for Canadian and Chinese employees. Another study found that low power distance values along with self-assertiveness explained a greater likelihood of new employees seeking feedback in the United States compared to China (Morrison et al., 2004).

We would expect feedback seeking in more high-context cultures to occur through more indirect channels, for example, via observation, indirect questions, or a third party, than in more low-context cultures. Sully de Luque recently offered a typology of feedback-seeking behaviors that clearly illustrates more direct versus more indirect approaches (Sully de Luque et al., 2019). They define direct inquiry as a "direct and explicit request for feedback from a supervisor" and indirect inquiry as "indirect discussions with the information source, manifested as hypothetical inquiries, third-party inquiries, inquiries about comparable peers, or disguised questions to seek information in the workplace" (Sully de Luque et al., 2019, p. 123). Careful monitoring and observation for cues in the environment is another indirect strategy that occurs in both the message and space domains of communication context and that we would expect to be more common in high-context than in low-context cultures.

In performance appraisal, researchers have proposed examining how culture influences the content, style, and purpose of feedback (Fletcher & Perry, 2001). Chiang and Birtch (2010) noted that the existing appraisal literature is largely rooted in US values and notions of procedural justice. They examined appraisal related to cultural values for assertiveness, uncertainty avoidance, power distance, and in-group collectivism in seven countries categorized into Anglo (Canada, the United Kingdom, the United States), Confucian (Hong Kong, Singapore), and Nordic European (Finland, Sweden) clusters (House et al., 2004). They found that highly formalized, top-down, infrequent, and solo-source appraisal was more common in Confucian than Nordic European and Anglo cultures, reflecting contextualized communication based on relationship norms in Hong Kong and Singapore (Chiang & Birtch, 2010). The frequency of appraisal, which was highest in the Anglo cluster, could be related to low temporal context dependence in these cultures, which have rules and systems for feedback on a regular, calendar-oriented schedule.

In addition to these research areas, the culture and communication context should be relevant for feedback topics and targets as manifested in the relationship domain. In more high-context cultures, feedback may cover a broad range of tasks and socio-emotional facets of work, while in more low-context cultures the feedback is more likely to be focused directly on performance indicators. Also in high-context cultures, feedback is more likely to be downward, from manager to employee, than in low-context cultures, where peer-to-peer feedback and even employee-supervisor feedback (see above section on employee voice) is common.

Future Directions

We have discussed how communication context in the domains of message, relationship, time, and space would influence the forms and functions of voice, silence, gossip, and feedback in the workplace of different cultures that vary in value orientations and communication norms. Our review and discussion indicate that cross-cultural research on these topics is limited, and many opportunities exist to explore their manifestation, underlying mechanisms, and practical implications in future research. On that note, and taking together our discussion so far, we propose the following propositions.

> Proposition 1: Voice, silence, gossip, and feedback behaviors expressed indirectly by high-context communicators are more likely to be interpreted as passive aggressiveness by low-context than high-context communicators. Voice and gossip expressed directly by low context communicators are more likely to be interpreted as inappropriate by high-context than low-context communicators.

> Proposition 2: High-context employees are more likely than low-context employees to modify their voice, silence, gossip, and feedback behaviors based on their relationship with their counterparts. Furthermore, paying attention to relationship cues will be positively related to the correct interpretation of voice, silence, feedback seeking, and gossip in cross-cultural interactions.

> Proposition 3: Across cultures, voice, silence, gossip, and feedback will be more effective when they are transmitted at an earlier time than a later time and/or transmitted multiple times than a single time. In low-context cultures, voice and feedback are more likely to occur at regularly scheduled times than in high-context cultures. In high-context cultures, voice and feedback are more likely to occur spontaneously and outside of scheduled meetings than in low-context cultures.

> Proposition 4: Voice, silence, gossip, and feedback accompanied by dramatic expression and physical closeness signaling conversational engagement will be considered more appropriate in expressive high-context cultures than in reserved high-context or low-context cultures. Voice, silence, gossip, and feedback accompanied by neutral emotional expression will be considered more appropriate in reserved high-context cultures than in expressive high-context or low-context cultures.

References

Adair, W. L., Buchan, N. R., Chen, X. P., & Liu, D. (2016). A model of communication context and measure of context dependence. *Academy of Management Discoveries, 2*(2), 198–217.

Ashford, S. J., & Cummings, L. L. (1983). Feedback as an individual resource: Personal strategies of creating information. *Organizational Behavior and Human Performance, 32*(3), 370–398.

Ashford, S. J., Blatt, R., & VandeWalle, D. (2003). Reflections on the looking glass: A review of research on feedback-seeking behavior in organizations. *Journal of Management, 29*(6), 773–799.

Avery, D. R., & Steingard, D. S. (2008). Achieving political trans-correctness: Integrating sensitivity and authenticity in diversity management education. *Journal of Management Education, 32*(3), 269–293.

Barker, K. (1994). The be PC or not to be?: A social psychological inquiry into political correctness. *Journal of Social Behavior and Personality, 9*(2), 271–281.

Baumeister, R. F., Zhang, L., & Vohs, K. D. (2004). Gossip as cultural learning. *Review of General Psychology, 8*(2), 111–121.

Beersma, B., & Van Kleef, G. A. (2012). Why people gossip: An empirical analysis of social motives, antecedents, and consequences. *Journal of Applied Social Psychology, 42*(11), 2640–2670.

Bosson, J. K., Johnson, A. B., Niederhoffer, K., & Swann, W. (2006). Interpersonal chemistry through negativity: Bonding by sharing negative attitudes about others. *Personal Relationships, 13*, 135–150.

Botero, I. C., & Van Dyne, L. (2009). Employee voice behavior: Interactive effects of LMX and power distance in the United States and Colombia. *Management Communication Quarterly, 23*(1), 84–104.

Brady, D. L., Brown, D. J., & Liang, L. H. (2017). Moving beyond assumptions of deviance: The reconceptualization and measurement of workplace gossip. *Journal of Applied Psychology, 102*(1), 1–25.

Brett, J. M. (2000). Culture and negotiation. *International Journal of Psychology, 35*(2), 97–104.

Brett, J. M. (2007). *Negotiating globally: How to negotiate deals, resolve disputes, and make decisions across cultural boundaries*. Wiley.

Brett, J., Behfar, K., & Sanchez-Burks, J. (2014). Managing cross-culture conflicts: A close look at the implication of direct versus indirect confrontation. In *Handbook of conflict management research* (pp. 136–154). Edward Elgar Publishing.

Brown, P., & Levinson, S. C. (1987). *Politeness: Some universals in language usage* (Vol. 4). Cambridge University Press.

Burris, E. R. (2012). The risks and rewards of speaking up: Managerial responses to employee voice. *Academy of Management Journal, 55*(4), 851–875.

Burris, E. R., Detert, J. R., & Romney, A. C. (2013). Speaking up vs. being heard: The disagreement around and outcomes of employee voice. *Organization Science, 24*, 22–38. https://doi.org/10.1287/orsc.1110.0732

Chiang, F. F., & Birtch, T. A. (2010). Appraising performance across borders: An empirical examination of the purposes and practices of performance appraisal in a multi-country context. *Journal of Management Studies, 47*(7), 1365–1393.

Cole, B. M., Chen, X. P., & He, W. (2022). *Planting your idea in another's head: Inception and the veil of agency*. Working Paper.

Colgan, F., & McKearney, A. (2012). Visibility and voice in organisations: Lesbian, gay, bisexual and transgendered employee networks. *Equality, Diversity and Inclusion: An International Journal, 31*(4), 359–378.

Detert, J. R., & Burris, E. R. (2007). Leadership behavior and employee voice: Is the door really open?. *Academy of Management Journal, 50*(4), 869–884.

Dunbar, R. I. (2004). Gossip in evolutionary perspective. *Review of General Psychology, 8*(2), 100–110.

Farley, S., Dawson, J., Greenaway, T., Meade, K., & Hernández Ibar, D. (2022). Does international status affect competence ratings in newly formed multinational teams? The role of psychological safety growth and verbal behavior. *Journal of Cross-Cultural Psychology, 53*(10), 1277–1299.

Fletcher, C., & Perry, E. (2001). *Performance appraisal and feedback: A consideration of national culture and a review of contemporary research and future trends* (Vols. 1–2). Sage.

Foster, E. K. (2004). Research on gossip: Taxonomy, methods, and future directions. *Review of General Psychology, 8*(2), 78–99.

Gudykunst, W. B. (2005). An anxiety/uncertainty management (AUM) theory of strangers' intercultural adjustment. In W. B. Gudykunst (Ed.), *Theorizing about intercultural communication* (pp. 419–457). Sage.

Hackman, J. R., & Oldham, G. R. (1976). Motivation through the design of work: Test of a theory. *Organizational Behavior and Human Performance, 16*(2), 250–279.

Hall, E. T. (1960). The silent language in overseas business. *Harvard Business Review, 38*(3), 87–96.

Hall, E. T. (1976). *Beyond culture*. Anchor Press.

House, R., Hanges, P. J., Javidan, M., Dorfman, P. W., & Gupta, V. (2004). *Culture, leadership and organizations: The GLOBE study of 62 societies*. Sage.

Hunter, P. (2005). Is political correctness damaging science? Peer pressure and mainstream thinking may discourage novelty and innovation. *EMBO Reports, 6*(5), 405–407.

Isaakyan, S., Sherf, E. N., Tangirala, S., & Guenter, H. (2021). Keeping it between us: Managerial endorsement of public versus private voice. *Journal of Applied Psychology, 106*(7), 1049.

Kim, Y. J., Lam, C. F., Oh, J., & Sohn, W. (2023). Employee constructive voice: An integrative review and a dyadic approach. *Journal of Management, 49*(1), 430–473.

Klaas, B. S., Olson-Buchanan, J. B., & Ward, A. K. (2012). The determinants of alternative forms of workplace voice: An integrative perspective. *Journal of Management, 38*(1), 314–345.

Knoll, M., & Van Dick, R. (2013). Do I hear the whistle…? A first attempt to measure four forms of employee silence and their correlates. *Journal of Business Ethics, 113*, 349–362.

Knoll, M., Götz, M., Adriasola, E., Al-Atwi, A. A., Arenas, A., Atitsogbe, K. A., et al. (2021). International differences in employee silence motives: Scale validation, prevalence, and relationships with culture characteristics across 33 countries. *Journal of Organizational Behavior, 42*(5), 619–648.

Koopman, J., Lanaj, K., Lee, Y. E., Alterman, V., Bradley, C., & Stoverink, A. C. (2023). Walking on eggshells: A self-control perspective on workplace political correctness. *Journal of Applied Psychology, 108*(3), 425–445.

Krenz, H. L., Burtscher, M. J., & Kolbe, M. (2019). *"Not only hard to make but also hard to take": Team leaders' reactions to voice*. Gruppe. Interaktion. Organisation. Zeitschrift für Angewandte Organisationspsychologie (GIO).

Lam, C. F., Lee, C., & Sui, Y. (2019). Say it as it is: Consequences of voice directness, voice politeness, and voicer credibility on voice endorsement. *Journal of Applied Psychology, 104*(5), 642–658.

Larson, J. R., Jr. (1984). The performance feedback process: A preliminary model. *Organizational Behavior and Human Performance, 33*(1), 42–76.

Larson, J. R., Jr. (1989). The dynamic interplay between employees' feedback-seeking strategies and supervisors' delivery of performance feedback. *Academy of Management Review, 14*(3), 408–422.

Leung, K., Koch, P. T., & Lu, L. (2002). A dualistic model of harmony and its implications for conflict management in Asia. *Asia Pacific Journal of Management, 19*, 201–220.

Lewis, R. D. (2006). *When cultures collide: Leading across cultures* (3rd ed.). Nicholas Brealey International.

Lewis, R. D. (2018). *When cultures collide: Leading across cultures* (4th ed.). Nicholas Brealey International.

Li, Y., & Sun, J. M. (2015). Traditional Chinese leadership and employee voice behavior: A cross-level examination. *The Leadership Quarterly, 26*(2), 172–189.

Liang, J., Farh, C. I., & Farh, J. L. (2012). Psychological antecedents of promotive and prohibitive voice: A two-wave examination. *Academy of Management Journal, 55*(1), 71–92.

MacDonald, H. A., Sulsky, L. M., Spence, J. R., & Brown, D. J. (2013). Cultural differences in the motivation to seek performance feedback: A comparative policy-capturing study. *Human Performance, 26*, 211–235.

Martinescu, E., Janssen, O., & Nijstad, B. A. (2019). Gossip as a resource: How and why power relationships shape gossip behavior. *Organizational Behavior and Human Decision Processes, 153*, 89–102.

Maynes, T. D., & Podsakoff, P. M. (2014). Speaking more broadly: An examination of the nature, antecedents, and consequences of an expanded set of employee voice behaviors. *Journal of Applied Psychology, 99*(1), 87–112.

McNulty, Y., McPhail, R., Inversi, C., Dundon, T., & Nechanska, E. (2018). Employee voice mechanisms for lesbian, gay, bisexual and transgender expatriation: The role of Employee-Resource Groups (ERGs) and allies. *The International Journal of Human Resource Management, 29*(5), 829–856.

Milliken, F. J., Morrison, E. W., & Hewlin, P. F. (2003). An exploratory study of employee silence: Issues that employees don't communicate upward and why. *Journal of Management Studies, 40*, 1453–1476. https://doi.org/10.1111/1467-6486.00387

Morrison, E. W. (2011). Employee voice behavior: Integration and directions for future research. *The Academy of Management Annals, 5*, 373–412. https://doi.org/10.1080/19416520.2011.574506

Morrison, E. W. (2023). Employee voice and silence: Taking stock a decade later. *Annual Review of Organizational Psychology and Organizational Behavior, 10*, 79–107.

Morrison, E. W., Chen, Y. R., & Salgado, S. R. (2004). Cultural differences in newcomer feedback seeking: A comparison of the United States and Hong Kong. *Applied Psychology. An International Review, 53*, 1–22.

Park, J. Y., & Nawakitphaitoon, K. (2018). The cross-cultural study of LMX and individual employee voice: The moderating role of conflict avoidance. *Human Resource Management Journal, 28*(1), 14–30.

Patel, K. R., Silva, R. A., & Dahling, J. J. (2019). Leveraging feedback orientation in the workplace: Directions for research and practice. In L. A. Steelman & J. R. Williams (Eds.), *Feedback at work* (pp. 97–11). Springer.

Peters, K., & Kashima, Y. (2007). From social talk to social action: Shaping the social triad with emotion sharing. *Journal of Personality and Social Psychology, 93*(5), 780–797.

Ren, R., Ma, L., Wang, H., & Ju, D. (2022). Implicit voice delivery: Its antecedents, consequences, and boundary conditions. *Management and Organization Review, 18*(1), 43–72.

Rhee, J., Dedahnov, A., & Lee, D. (2014). Relationships among power distance, collectivism, punishment, and acquiescent, defensive, or prosocial silence. *Social Behavior and Personality, 42*, 705–720. https://doi.org/10.2224/sbp.2014.42.5.705

Sanchez-Burks, J., Lee, F., Choi, I., Nisbett, R., Zhao, S., & Koo, J. (2003). Conversing across cultures: East-West communication styles in work and nonwork contexts. *Journal of Personality and Social Psychology, 85*(2), 363–372.

Song, J., Gu, J., Wu, J., & Xu, S. (2019). Differential promotive voice–prohibitive voice relationships with employee performance: Power distance orientation as a moderator. *Asia Pacific Journal of Management, 36*, 1053–1077.

Sully De Luque, M. F., & Sommer, S. M. (2000). The impact of culture on feedback-seeking behavior: An integrated model and propositions. *Academy of Management Review, 25*(4), 829–849.

Sully de Luque, M. F., Wollan, M. L., & Boyi, V. (2019). Beyond the strategies of feedback seeking: A review and initial conceptualization of feedback-seeking styles. In L. A. Steelman & J. R. Williams (Eds.), *Feedback at work* (pp. 113–139). Springer.

Sun, T., Schilpzand, P., & Liu, Y. (2023). Workplace gossip: An integrative review of its antecedents, functions, and consequences. *Journal of Organizational Behavior, 44*(2), 311–334.

Syed, J. (2014). Diversity management and missing voices. In A. Wilkinson, J. Donaghey, T. Dundon, & R. Freeman (Eds.), *Handbook of research on employee voice* (pp. 421–438). Edward Elgar.

Thomas, D. C., & Au, K. (2002). The effect of cultural differences on behavioral responses to low job satisfaction. *Journal of International Business Studies, 33*(2), 309–326.

Ting-Toomey, S. (2005). The matrix of face: An updated face-negotiation theory. In W. B. Gudykunst (Ed.), *Theorizing about intercultural communication* (pp. 71–92). Sage.

Ting-Toomey, S., & Kurogi, A. (1998). Facework competence in intercultural conflict: An updated face-negotiation theory. *International Journal of Intercultural Relations, 22*(2), 187–225.

Triandis, H. C. (1994). *Culture and social behavior*. Mcgraw-Hill Book Company.
Van Dyne, L., & LePine, J. A. (1998). Helping and voice extra-role behaviors: Evidence of construct and predictive validity. *Academy of Management Journal, 41*(1), 108–119. https://doi.org/10.2307/256902
Van Dyne, L., Ang, S., & Botero, I. C. (2003). Conceptualizing employee silence and employee voice as multidimensional constructs. *Journal of Management Studies, 40*(6), 1359–1392.
Ward, A. K., Ravlin, E. C., Klaas, B. S., Ployhart, R. E., & Buchan, N. R. (2016). When do high-context communicators speak up? Exploring contextual communication orientation and employee voice. *Journal of Applied Psychology, 101*(10), 1498–1511.
Wei, X., Zhang, Z., & Chen, X. (2015). I will speak up if my voice is socially desirable: A moderated mediating process of promotive versus prohibitive voice. *Journal of Applied Psychology, 100*, 1641–1652. https://doi.org/10.1037/a0039046
Weingart, L. R., Behfar, K. J., Bendersky, C., Todorova, G., & Jehn, K. A. (2015). The directness and oppositional intensity of conflict expression. *Academy of Management Review, 40*(2), 235–262.

Chapter 7
Leading Through Nonverbal Communication Across Cultures

> *All leadership communication is intercultural... What an organizational leader says can be an important message, but equally and sometimes more important, is what a leader does not say, how a leader responds to what others say, or how he or she fails to respond.*
>
> – *Ruben and Gigliotti (2017)*

While leadership is studied extensively in management, and its definition is diverse across perspectives (e.g., the intrapersonal, interpersonal, team, or organizational level), scholars generally agree on the following three important characteristics. First, leadership is a process of social influence that advances a task or goal. Second, leadership creates and manages meaning. Third, leadership is an attribution made by followers or observers (Conger, 1991; Fairhurst, 2008; Smircich & Morgan, 1982). Taken together, leadership can be defined as a "process whereby an individual influences a group of individuals to achieve a common goal" (Northouse, 2007, p. 3).

Social influence often occurs in human interactions, and communication plays a central role; what is communicated and how it is communicated determine the breadth and depth of leadership effectiveness. By adopting a communication perspective to study cross-cultural leadership, we view the leadership phenomenon as *a process of social influence informed by and shaped by verbal and nonverbal communication*. Notably, this treatment of the leadership phenomenon departs from the majority of the existing literature that focuses on values and belief systems in studying leadership across cultures, such as the GLOBE project (House et al., 2002). In this chapter we will extrapolate the role of communication in the social influence process of leader emergence, followed by a detailed discussion of how the four domains of communication context manifest in different cultures to achieve leadership effectiveness.

W. L. Adair et al., *What Isn't Being Said*, Springer Series in Emerging Cultural Perspectives in Work, Organizational, and Personnel Studies,
https://doi.org/10.1007/978-3-031-53645-8_7

The Role of Communication in Discursive Leadership

As flat structures, self-management teams, and distributive leadership become increasingly popular in modern organizations, what managers communicate and how they communicate their messages to yield influence are important research questions to explore. Several articles endeavored to answer these questions in a special issue on "Leadership and Communication" published in the International Journal of Business Communication in 2017. In particular, Ruben and Gigliotti (2017) introduced a system view whereby communication is viewed as a basic life process rather than an exchange of information or meaning between people because not all messages are intentionally created, although all impart meanings. For example, a leader's annual letter to stakeholders is constructed to achieve specific influence goals, while casual conversation before the start of a meeting may be created unconsciously with no specific intention in mind. Moreover, a leader's speech can be written in a way to convey a specific intention. Yet, speech delivery (e.g., tone of voice, facial expressions, body movement) may be unconsciously enacted without such intention. However, all communications, especially communication style, can influence people's perception of leadership potential.

Mariam and Chen (2022) showed how communication style, direct or indirect communication, in particular, influenced people's judgment about others' leadership potential in the United States. They conducted five studies adopting different research methods – word association test, implicit association test, vignette-based experiment, and survey study using a recall paradigm, and found consistent results. First, people associate more positive attributes (e.g., competence, honesty) with direct rather than indirect communicators, and they associate more negative attributes (e.g., incompetence, dishonesty) with indirect rather than direct communicators. Second, they relied on the attributes inferred from communication style to judge the communicator's fit with a leadership prototype and select this person to take on a leadership position. Finally, when factual information on competence and honesty was made salient, the communication style effects on leadership potential were mitigated. They thus labeled this phenomenon as implicit bias against indirect communicators.

These findings seem to explain the "bamboo ceiling effects" demonstrated by a series of studies that compared East Asian Americans (e.g., Chinese) with South Asian Americans (e.g., Indian) who work or study in the United States (Lu et al., 2020, 2022). The authors found that East Asians were less likely than South Asians and Whites to attain leadership positions in US organizations, whereas South Asians were more likely than Whites to do so (Lu et al., 2020). They also found that East Asians underperformed South Asians and Whites in US law schools and business schools despite performing well on admission tests (Lu et al., 2022), and that the non-consulting salary gap between East/Southeast and South Asians was estimated to be $4002/year (Lu, 2023). More remarkable is that in all these studies, the success of South Asians in obtaining leadership positions is not because they are more motivated than East Asians or because there is less prejudice against them than East Asians, but because they are more verbally assertive in their communication.

Along the same line, cultures generally seem to shape prototypical leadership attributes (Javidan et al., 2006). Implicit leadership theories (Lord & Maher, 1991) suggest that people make implicit associations linking certain attributes with effective leadership. In the United States, an individualistic culture that is task-oriented and values individual attributes, empirical studies show that intelligence (knowledgeable, intellectual), strength (commanding, assertive), and masculinity (male, tall) have appeared consistently among the top attributes needed for leadership in the past two decades (Offermann & Coats, 2017). However, Aritz and Walker (2014) found that East Asians prefer different attributes. In a cross-cultural comparison of communication-based leadership styles, they found that in the United States, people's first choice of leader is the one with a "decisive and task-oriented" communication style. In contrast, in China and Japan, people's first choice of leader is someone with a "status-conscious and procedural" communication style but ranked "decisive and task-oriented" as the third choice.

Meanwhile, East Asians viewed the directive style as too aggressive and were more willing to contribute and participate in teamwork when leaders exhibited a cooperative style (considerate and respectful). Similarly, in a study that included participants in the United States and Hungary, Gaal found that nonverbal behaviors such as tone of voice, eye contact, and natural hand movements influenced people's perception of charisma. Participants from Hungary perceived aggressive hand and arm gestures as charismatic, while those from the United States did not.

Leadership Influence via Nonverbal Communication

Once a person is in a leadership position, the power accompanied by that position is likely to augment the person's influence in robust ways. As the quote at the beginning of this chapter put it, "What an organizational leader says can be an important message, but equally and sometimes more important, is what a leader does not say, how a leader responds to what others say, or how he or she fails to respond." (Ruben & Gigliotti, 2017, p. 25). Accumulated research in cross-cultural communication has indicated that there are significant norms in different cultures guiding whether expressing agreement or disagreement is appropriate (e.g., Smith, 2011), the extent to which information related to power and status is considered in communication, how time is construed and the meaning of lateness implied (Allen et al., 2018; Levine, 2008; van Eerde & Buengeler, 2015), and what are considered as appropriate physical distance, touching, facial, and body expressions in social interactions (Hall, 1960; Lewis, 2018). Next, we will articulate how each of the four domains of communication context may determine leadership influence.

Leading via Message Context

How a message is expressed or interpreted comprises the message domain of communication context, with more low-context communicators using more direct and explicit forms and more high-context communicators using more indirect and implicit forms (Adair et al., 2016). How leaders convey disagreement across cultures is likely related to the appropriateness of expressing agreement/disagreement and response extremity (Smith, 2011). Research has shown that Chinese are more likely to choose the middle point in their response to a question/statement using 5-point or 7-point Likert scales due to their tendency to present a modest self (Chiu & Yang, 1987). Conceptualizing communication styles as a dimension of culture, Smith (2011) examined how response styles, i.e., agreement/disagreement and extremity-moderation differed across cultures. He found that countries can be categorized into four types of cultures: (a) moderate culture, where both agreement and disagreement are low (e.g., China, Singapore, Japan, Moldova), (b) dissent culture, where agreement is low but disagreement is high (e.g., Germany, the United Kingdom, Sweden, Greece, Azerbaijan), (c) consensus culture, where agreement is high but disagreement is low (e.g., Nigeria, Bangladesh, India, Vietnam, Puerto Rico), and (d) extremity culture, where both agreement and disagreement are high (e.g., Morocco, Iraq, Israel, Venezuela, Saudi Arabia). These findings provide an important lens to understand how agreement and disagreement are expressed (e.g., directly and explicitly or indirectly and implicitly) in different cultures, which would influence how employees react, which would be closely related to leadership effectiveness.

Another key element of the message domain is the emotional connotation of a message. A review of the leadership literature suggests that most leadership studies focus on leader behaviors rather than the emotional connotation underlying these behaviors. One exception is the research on transformational leadership (Bass & Riggio, 2006; Podsakoff et al., 1990), referring to leadership behaviors characterized by vision articulation, intellectual stimulation, fostering collaboration, high performance expectation, role modeling, and individualized consideration. As all these behaviors involve verbal and nonverbal communication, research has demonstrated that it is the positive emotions leaders exhibit in these communicative acts (Bono et al., 2007) that mediated the positive effects of transformational leadership on employee identification with the organization and their performing extra-role organization citizenship behaviors. These positive emotions are caught by the subordinates through unconscious mimicry during their interaction with the leader, which drives positive outcomes (Barsade, 2002). A recent study using a Chinese sample (Gong et al., in press) shows that CEO's passion for organizational development can inspire middle managers' transformational leadership behaviors via emotion contagion and social information processing, positively affecting front-line employee job creativity.

Leaders influencing employees through the emotional route are not restricted to transformational leadership behaviors. Authoritarian leadership, a leadership style that uses authority to control subordinates and demands unquestioning compliance and absolute obedience from subordinates (Chen et al., 2014; Schaubroeck et al., 2017), has been found to induce negative emotions such as fear and anger (Cheng et al., 2004), through which performance is affected. Research shows that employees under authoritarian leadership experience negative emotions and must regulate these emotions through suppression (Chiang et al., 2021; Yao et al., 2022) to avoid harsh punishment. This suppression leads to work-team emotional exhaustion, low performance (Chiang et al., 2021), and work-life conflict (Yao et al., 2022). Interestingly, these effects were weaker when leaders themselves freely expressed emotions, which was more likely to occur in low-context cultures such as the United States (e.g., Steve Jobs of Apple, Jeff Bezos of Amazon) than in reserved high-context cultures such as Japan and China (e.g., Dewang Cao of Fuyao). These findings suggest the power of nonverbal communication through emotions in moderating the leader's behavioral effects on employee experience at work.

Leading via Relationship Context

Viewing leadership from a communication perspective fits especially well with leader-member exchange theory (LMX, Graen & Ul-Bien, 1995), which defines leadership as a constant exchange process between a leader and a subordinate. Through this process, trust between leader and member is established. Such leader-member exchange often entails verbal and nonverbal communication. As Omilon-Hodges and Baker (2017, p. 119) put it, "leader-member relationships are produced by, and are a product of, communicative acts." As such, the communication process is at the forefront of LMX. A leader communication exchange scale was thus developed to identify the positive and negative exchanges that would lead to different quality of the relationship between a leader and member. The positive leader communication exchange included nonverbal communication as a key dimension, with sample items such as "my manager looks me in the eye when we communicate" and "my manager indicates through head gesture that he or she is listening to me." Similarly, nonverbal communication is also a key dimension in negative leader communication exchange, with sample items like, "my manager gives dirty looks" and "my manager sighs when I approach him/her." Moreover, a careful look at this scale suggests that even the dimension labeled "verbal communication" reflects how the message is delivered rather than the message itself. "My manager talks to me in an abrupt, rushed manner," "My manager is arrogant in our conversations," and "My manager interrupts me" are a few examples of how managers communicate through message, time, and space context. These findings illustrate the importance of the nonverbals surrounding a message in developing leader-member relationships.

As leaders have more power and higher status in the workplace, the nonverbal aspects surrounding a message can influence how leaders' communication is encoded and decoded (Adair et al., 2016). When interacting with subordinates, how often leaders speak (i.e., frequency) and how much they talk (i.e., length of communication) are likely to determine whether or not their power and status can be confirmed or sustained. Although there is limited research on the cultural differences in this regard, studies have shown some intriguing patterns.

Aritz and Walker (2014) established the relationship between communication and leadership style through detailed case studies in East Asian and US cultures. They operationalized leader communication behavior using five indicators: meaning of questions, links between turns, topic shifts, listening, and simultaneous speech and then described how each or combined indicators represent a different leadership style that would work more or less effectively with team members from different cultures. They identified three leadership styles: directive, cooperative, and collaborative. Adopting a case study method, the authors found that East Asian leaders took significantly fewer turns and spoke fewer words in a group decision-making meeting than US team leaders. Moreover, almost all US-born male leaders demonstrated a directive leadership style, resulting in lower satisfaction among East Asian members, who felt not as included, valued, or supported within their groups.

In a single culture study (the majority of participants identified as leaders were White and aged 25–35 years), Aritz et al. (2017) analyzed 28 transcribed videotaped recordings of small group decision-making meetings and found that the use of questions could help professionals construct authority and leadership. Questions are defined as utterances that (a) solicit information, confirmation, or action and (b) create an opportunity for the recipient to produce a responsive turn. The authors analyzed the questions leaders asked and discovered how they use questioning to make themselves appear authoritative and powerful. One finding is that leaders asked significantly more questions than non-leaders. Second, leaders asked more than twice the number of "yes or no" questions and three times as many content-related questions as non-leaders. Moreover, most questions were used to request confirmation or ask for information.

Du-Babcock and Tanaka (2017) selected a setting where English as lingua franca was used among Hong Kong and Japanese business professionals to study how different leadership styles affect the decision-making process and outcome in multicultural teams. In this study, the participants assumed the role of the board of directors (size ranged 5–8) in a simulated decision-making meeting between business professionals from Hong Kong and Japan. Adopting the turn-taking framework (Sacks et al., 1974) to content-analyze and assess communication and leadership, the authors found that linguistic and contextual factors discursively constructed different styles of leadership: cooperative, collaborative – with the length of speaking time and the volume of spoken words more evenly distributed among members, or directive – one person dominated. They found that cooperative and collaborative leadership resulted in decision consensus, whereas the final decision was split when a directive style dominated a group meeting. The authors thus conclude that "the mutually supportive and inclusive nature of cooperative and collaborative leadership may be more suitable for Asian business discourse where collective identity and linguistic constraints coexist" (Du-Babcock & Tanaka, 2017, p. 95).

Leading via Time Context

While leadership is an ongoing social influence process, the time component that is crucial to reveal the dynamic nature of influence is unfortunately missed in leadership research (Castillo & Trinh, 2018). In the limited studies reviewed in Castillo and Trinh (2018), all conceptualized time as standard clock time rather than psychological or event time (Mitchell & James, 2001). More shockingly, no studies on diversity and cross-cultural leadership, or power and influence, included time in the study design.

However, the time domain of communication context is different from studying the time effects on leadership emergence or development. Instead, it is about how leaders rely on time to convey what they want and interpret others' actions related to time. One's presence/absence or early/late arrival to a meeting can become the most influential message to all in attendance (van Eerde & Buengeler, 2015). Although meeting lateness is common across cultures (van Eerde & Buengeler, 2015), the meaning of lateness (e.g., how late is late?) differs significantly across cultures that view time as linear (clock time, monochronic) vs. nonlinear (event time, polychronic) (Bluedorn, 2002). In a linear monochronic culture, leaders arriving late to a meeting may be perceived negatively (e.g., disrespectful), but the same behavior may be interpreted as signaling power or status in a polychronic culture (Gell, 1992). Similarly, an employee not meeting a deadline is likely to be perceived negatively (e.g., incompetent or unmotivated) by a leader in a monochronic culture but may be perceived positively (e.g., making an extra effort) by a leader in a polychronic culture (Triandis, 1994).

In a cross-cultural study on lateness for meetings and appointments, van Eerde and Azar (2020) distinguished between clock time and event time cultures. They examined time norms related to lateness among South African, Dutch, and Pakistani respondents. They found that Pakistani respondents (from an event time culture) accepted larger time intervals of lateness than the other two groups (from clock time cultures). More importantly, they found that power and status mattered in lateness norms. Specifically, Dutch respondents did not allow longer waiting times for people with higher status, whereas South African and Pakistani respondents did.

In another cross-cultural study on leaders' lateness to meetings and attendee reactions (counterproductive behavior and co-worker trust), Allen et al. showed that in China, Germany, Italy, the Netherlands, and the United States, meeting lateness was generally related to perceptions of impaired meeting processes as well as negative meeting outcomes and group-related attitudes, demonstrating the convergence of negative consequences regarding meeting lateness. However, the five countries included in this study all fall into the "clock time" culture (Lewis, 2018). Therefore, the findings cannot lead to the conclusion that there are no cultural differences regarding the consequences of meeting lateness.

Richard Lewis (2018) described how leaders in Arab countries conduct their meetings according to event time. First, the Arab people have a loose conception of time, and it is certainly nonlinear. There is no clear beginning or end of a meeting, which can also be interrupted by any visitor who is an acquaintance of the leader. It is conceivable such treatment of a meeting will be perceived as chaotic, disorganized, and highly ineffective and inefficient by leaders in countries that value time and view time as commodity, such as Germany and Switzerland (Lewis, 2018).

The social norms of work time also differ across cultures. US Americans work the most hours in the world, and the United States is among the least generous developed countries regarding vacation time and public policies that support employed parents (Negrey, 2012). In China, "996" (work 9 h/day 6 days/wk) is becoming a new norm of work time for thousands of young employees in Internet companies. Leaders in such "live to work" cultures work long hours and expect their employees to do the same; otherwise, the employees will be judged as "lazy" or "not committed." On the other hand, working on weekends is against the law in France, and people take vacations for the entire month of August (Today, 2016). In Arab countries, the daily work time is 6 hours, with many small prayer breaks. In these "work to live" cultures, leaders work shorter hours, and if the workers do not follow the norm, they are likely to be judged as "workaholics" and "have no life." It is evident that how leaders use time significantly affects how organizations are structured and operated, how subordinates behave along the time dimension (when to go to work, how many hours to work, How regularly to work, How to experience work time, etc.), and the signals their temporal cues send.

Leading via Space Context

Hall referred to space as the "silent language" (Hall, 1960), through which complex meanings can be conveyed or interpreted. For example, a leader's open-door or closed-door office hour policies represent a nonverbal space message that may speak far more loudly than other carefully planned and scripted verbal messages (Lewis, 2018). Often, it is where a leader chooses to have a meeting with a subordinate rather than the meeting content itself that reveals the true intention of the leader. For example, when a performance evaluation meeting is conducted in the leader's office versus in the subordinate's office, in a conference room, in a coffee shop, or even at a dinner table, it can have very different meanings in the subordinate's mind. Meanwhile, meaning can be also conveyed through seating position, such as who is the most important person in a round table dinner, who sits in the middle when taking a photograph. Studies also show that some cultures prefer to sit side by side, while others prefer to sit face-to-face, which could result in different evaluations of a leader whose seating preference is aligned or misaligned with the specific cultural norm (Cline & Puhl, 1984).

The traditional 'open house' in Arab countries, where visitors (including strangers) may gain access to leaders at all times, has evolved into an 'open office' in the twenty-first century. Lewis (2018) described it vividly in his book *When Cultures Collide:*

> Open office' may sound friendly enough, but things can become chaotic if you have the first appointment. Northerners (westerners) expect to be guaranteed some kind of privacy while they discuss their business matters. In England or Germany, secretaries do not allow bosses to be disturbed by new arrivals during the course of a meeting. It can happen in Portugal, Spain, South America, or Sicily, but even there newcomers are often asked to wait. In Arab countries, they are shown straight into the office, according to the age-old tradition. (p. 338)

He continues,

> Recently I asked the Commercial Counsellor at one of the embassies in Abu Dhabi, how one solves this problem. He answered as follows: You have to maneuver your chair so that you are sitting right next to the man you are doing business with. On the other side of his desk is not close enough – you have to be no more than a foot away and nearer to him than anybody else. When you have secured this position, you then shout down his right or left ear, depending on which side you are on. You continue to pound his ear with your propositions until he agrees with them. (p. 339)

The space domain of communication context also includes facial expressions, hand gestures, body movement, eye contact, tone of voice, etc. (Hall, 1976; Adair et al., 2016). Along these lines, research in Western cultures suggests that vocal attractiveness (e.g., a strong and confident voice) can augment a leader's visionary message and strengthen the influence of verbal communication, which explains an additional 12% variance in leader effectiveness beyond leader charisma, motivation, and personality (e.g., DeGroot et al., 2011; Howell & Frost, 1989). Interestingly, the combination of a non-visionary message with a strong delivery (attentive, relaxed, friendly and dominant) is more effective than the combination of a visionary message with a weak delivery (inattentive, nervous, unfriendly, and timid) (Holladay & Coombs, 1994), demonstrating the extra power of nonverbals over verbal messages to influence people.

In addition, Western research suggests that nonverbals conveying liking and approach, such as genuine smiling and leaning towards another, that is, immediacy (Mehrabian, 1969), or automatic imitation of nonverbal cues, that is, mimicry, are important for promoting social influence (see Chartrand & Lakin, 2013, for a review). Immediacy and mimicry both help interacting partners develop a smooth, natural, and reciprocal pattern of exchanges (Bernieri & Rosenthal, 1991). Indeed, charismatic leaders' effectiveness increased when they effectively used immediacy or conveyed passion through animated body gestures and voice (Bono & Ilies, 2006; Frese et al., 2003; Towler, 2003; see also Babad, 2007).

One challenge related to leading via space in a cross-cultural setting is that appropriate nonverbals for subordinates are different in different cultures. For example, looking down conveys respect in some cultures (Kleinke, 1986), but leaders in low-context cultures would consider averted gaze as a lack of confidence or impolite. Touching is considered necessary to establish a friendly relationship in expressive high-contact cultures (e.g., South American countries), but touching in the workplace could cause confusion or problems for leaders in the United States. In general, when a person's nonverbal spatial behavior is inconsistent with an interacting partner's expectations, it is likely to cause interpersonal discomfort (e.g., Tiedens & Fragale, 2003). Thus, effective leadership requires one to be able to decode others' nonverbal behaviors in a given context and encode proper nonverbal behaviors in response (Remland, 1981).

Future Directions

This chapter views leadership as a social influence process wherein communication, especially nonverbal communication, plays a central role. We discussed how the message, relationship, time, and space domains of communication context manifest in leadership emergence and effectiveness in different cultures. In summary, we propose the following:

> Proposition 1: Cross-cultural leadership effectiveness is determined partly by the message context of communication, that is, how leaders deliver a message (directly/explicitly or indirectly/implicitly) and how such a message is interpreted by the recipient. When there is a greater overlap between the intention and interpretation, there will be better understanding and thus higher effectiveness.

> Proposition 2: Cross-cultural leadership effectiveness is highly related to the extent to which leaders pay attention to the relationship they have with the interlocuter in adapting their communication style in different cultures (e.g., a collaborative style is more effective with team members in East Asia whereas a directive style is more effective with team members in the United States).

> Proposition 3: Cross-cultural leadership effectiveness is influenced by the extent to which leaders and followers share the same view and understanding of time as linear or nonlinear, as commodity or non-commodity in their communication and interactions.

> Proposition 4: Cross-cultural leadership effectiveness is a function of the extent to which leaders and followers can understand the silent language – physical distance, facial expressions, eye contact, tone of voice, body movement – in a similar or expected manner.

References

Adair, W. L., Buchan, N. R., Chen, X. P., & Liu, D. (2016). A model of communication context and measure of context dependence. *Academy of Management Discoveries, 2*(2), 198–217.

Allen, J. A., Lehmann-Willenbrock, N., & Rogelberg, S. G. (2018). Let's get this meeting started: Meeting lateness and actual meeting outcomes. *Journal of Organizational Behavior, 39*(8), 1008–1021.

Aritz, J., & Walker, R. C. (2014). Leadership styles in multicultural groups: Americans and East Asians working together. *International Journal of Business Communication, 51*, 72–92.

Aritz, J., Walker, R. C., Cardon, P., & Li, Z. (2017). Discourse of leadership: The power of questions in organizational decision making. *International Journal of Business Communication, 54*(2), 161–181.

Babad, E. (2007). Teachers' nonverbal behavior and its effects on students. In R. P. Perry & J. C. Smart (Eds.), *The scholarship of teaching and learning in higher education: An evidence-based perspective*. Springer.

Barsade, S. G. (2002). The ripple effect: Emotional contagion and its influence on group behavior. *Administrative Science Quarterly, 47*(4), 644–675.

Bass, B. M., & Riggio, R. E. (2006). *Transformational leadership*. Taylor Francis Publishing.

Bernieri, F. J., & Rosenthal, R. (1991). Interpersonal coordination: Behavior matching and interactional synchrony. In R. S. Feldman & B. Rimé (Eds.), *Fundamentals of nonverbal behavior* (pp. 401–432). Cambridge University Press.

Bluedorn, A. C. (2002). *The human organization of time: Temporal realities and experience*. Stanford University Press.

Bono, J. E., & Ilies, R. (2006). Charisma, positive emotions and mood contagion. *The Leadership Quarterly, 17*(4), 317–334.

Bono, J. E., Foldes, H. J., Vinson, G., & Muros, J. P. (2007). Workplace emotions: The role of supervision and leadership. *Journal of Applied Psychology, 92*(5), 1357–1367.

Castillo, E. A., & Trinh, M. P. (2018). In search of missing time: A review of the study of time in leadership research. *The Leadership Quarterly, Volume 29* (1), 165–178.

Chartrand, T. L., & Lakin, J. L. (2013). The antecedents and consequences of human behavioral mimicry. *Annual Review of Psychology, 64*, 285–230.

Chen, X. P., Eberly, M., Chiang, T-J., Farh, J. L., & Cheng, B. S. (2014). Affective trust in Chinese leaders: Linking paternalistic leadership to employee performance. *Journal of Management, 40*(3), 796–819.

Cheng, B. S., Chou, L. F., Wu, T. Y., Huang, M. P., & Farh, J. L. (2004). Paternalistic leadership and subordinate responses: Establishing a leadership model in Chinese organizations. *Asian Journal of Social Psychology, 7*(1), 89–117.

Chiang, T. J., Chen, X. P., Liu, H., Akutsu, S., & Wang, Z. (2021). We have emotions but can't show them! Authoritarian leadership, emotion suppression climate, and team performance. *Human Relations, 74*(7), 1082–1111.

Chiu, C., & Yang, C. F. (1987). Chinese subjects' dilemmas: Humility and cognitive laziness as problems in using rating scales. *Bulletin of the Hong Kong Psychological Society, 18*(1), 39–50.

Cline, R. J., & Puhl, C. A. (1984). Gender, culture, and geography: A comparison of seating arrangements in the United States and Taiwan. *International Journal of Intercultural Relations, 8*, 199–219.

Conger, J. A. (1991). Inspiring others: The language of leadership. *Academy of Management Perspectives, 5*(3), 31–45.

DeGroot, T., Aime, F., Johnson, S. G., & Kluemper, D. (2011). Does talking the talk help walking the walk? An examination of the effect of vocal attractiveness in leader effectiveness. *The Leadership Quarterly, 22*, 680–689.

Du-Babcock, B., & Tanaka, H. (2017). Leadership construction in intra-Asian English as Lingua Franca decision-making meetings. *International Journal of Business Communication, 54*(1), 83–98.

Fairhurst, G. T. (2008). Discursive leadership: A communication alternative to leadership psychology. *Management Communication Quarterly, 21*(4), 510–521.

Frese, M., Beimel, S., & Schoenborn, S. (2003). Action training for charismatic leadership: Two evaluations of studies of a commercial training module on inspirational communication of a vision. *Personnel Psychology, 56*(3), 671–698.

Gell, A. (1992). *The anthropology of time: Cultural constructions of temporal maps and images*. Routledge.

Gong, Q., Liu, D., Chen, X. P., Chen, G. Q., & Jiang, C. Y. (in press). The fire to inspire: How CEO passion affects employee job creativity. *Journal of Management Studies*.

Graen, G. B., & Uhl-Bien, M. (1995). The relationship-based approach to leadership: Development of LMX theory of leadership over 25 years: Applying a multi-level, multidomain perspective. *The Leadership Quarterly, 6*, 219–247.

Hall, E. T. (1960). The silent language in overseas business. *Harvard Business Review, 38*(3), 87–96.

Hall, E. T. (1976). *Beyond cultures*. Doubleday.

Holladay, S. J., & Coombs, W. T. (1994). Speaking of visions and visions being spoken: An exploration of the effects of content and delivery on perceptions of leader charisma. *Management Communication Quarterly, 8*, 165–189.

House, R., Javidan, M., Hanges, P., & Dorfman, P. (2002). Understanding cultures and implicit leadership theories across the globe: An introduction to project GLOBE. *Journal of World Business, 37*(1), 3–10.

Howell, J. M., & Frost, P. J. (1989). A laboratory study of charismatic leadership. *Organizational Behavior and Human Decision Processes, 43*(2), 243–269.

Javidan, M., House, R., Dorfman, P., et al. (2006). Conceptualizing and measuring cultures and their consequences: A comparative review of GLOBE's and Hofstede's approaches. *Journal of International Business Studies, 37*, 897–914.

Kleinke, C. L. (1986). *Meeting and understanding people*. WH Freeman.

Levine, R. V. (2008). *A geography of time: On tempo, culture, and the pace of life*. Basic Books.

Lewis, R. (2018). *When cultures collide: Leading across cultures* (4th ed.). Nicholas Brealey Publishing.

Lord, R. G., & Maher, K. J. (1991). Cognitive theory in industrial and organizational psychology. In *Handbook of industrial and organizational psychology* (Vol. 2, pp. 1–62). Consulting Psychological Press.

Lu, J. G. (2023). Asians don't ask? Relational concerns, negotiation propensity, and starting salaries. *Journal of Applied Psychology, 108*(2), 273–290.

Lu, J. G., Nisbett, R. E., & Morris, M. W. (2020). Why East Asians but not South Asians are underrepresented in leadership positions in the United States. *Proceedings of the National Academy of Sciences, 117*(9), 4590–4600.

Lu, J. G., Nisbett, R. E., & Morris, M. W. (2022). The surprising underperformance of East Asians in US law and business schools: The liability of low assertiveness and the ameliorative potential of online classrooms. *National Academy of Sciences of the United States of America, 119*(13), e2118244119.

Mariam, M., & Chen, X. P. (2022). *Implicit preference for communication directness in the United States*. Annual meeting of the Academy of Management, Seattle.

Mehrabian, A. (1969). Significance of posture and position in the communication of attitude and status relationships. *Psychological Bulletin, 71*(5), 359–372.

Mitchell, T. R., & James, L. R. (2001). Building better theory: Time and the specification of when things happen. *Academy of Management Review, 26*, 530–547.

Negrey, C. L. (2012). *Work time: Conflict, control, and change*. Polity Press.

Northouse, P. (2007). *Leadership theory and practice*. Sage.

Offermann, L. R., & Coats, M. R. (2017). Implicit theories of leadership: Stability and change over two decades. *The Leadership Quarterly, 29*(4), 512–533.

Omilion-Hodges, L. M., & Baker, C. R. (2017). Communicating leader-member requalition quality: The development of lader communication exchange scales to measure relationship building and maintenance through the exchange of communication-based goods. *International Journal of Business Communication, 54*(2), 115–145.

Podsakoff, P. M., MacKenzie, S. B., Moorman, R. H., & Fetter, R. (1990). Transformational leader behaviors and their effects on followers' trust in leader, satisfaction, and organizational citizenship behaviors. *The Leadership Quarterly, 1*, 107–142.

Remland, M. (1981). Developing leadership skills in nonverbal communication: A situational perspective. *The Journal of Business Communication (1973), 18*(3), 17–29.

Ruben, B. D., & Gigliotti, R. A. (2017). Communication: Sine qua non of organizational leadership theory and practice. *International Journal of Business Communication*, 1–19. https://doi.org/10.1177/2329488416675447

Sacks, H., Schegloff, E. A., & Jefferson, G. (1974). A simplest systematics for the organization of turn taking for conversation. *Language, 50*(4), 696–735.

Schaubroeck, J. M., Shen, Y., & Chong, S. (2017). A dual-stage moderated mediation model linking authoritarian leadership to follower outcomes. *Journal of Applied Psychology, 102*(2), 203–214.

Smircich, L., & Morgan, G. (1982). Leadership: The management of meaning. *The Journal of Applied Behavioral Science, 18*, 257–273.

Smith, P. B. (2011). Communication styles as dimensions of national culture. *Journal of Cross-Cultural Psychology, 42*(2), 216–233.

Stump, S. (2016). *Today*. Retrieved from https://www.today.com/money/french-law-makes-weekend-work-emails-illegal-grants-right-disconnect-t94886

Tiedens, L. Z., & Fragale, A. R. (2003). Power moves: Complementarity in dominant and submissive nonverbal behavior. *Journal of Personality and Social Psychology, 84*(3), 558–568.

Towler, A. J. (2003). Effects of charismatic influence training on attitudes, behavior, and performance. *Personnel Psychology, 56*, 363–381.

Triandis, H. C. (1994). *Culture and social behavior*. Mcgraw-Hill Book Company.

van Eerde, W., & Azar, S. (2020). Too late? What do you mean? Cultural norms regarding lateness for meetings and appointments. *Cross-Cultural Research, 54*(2–3), 111–129.

van Eerde, W., & Buengeler, C. (2015). Meetings all over the world: Structural and psychological characteristics of meetings in different countries. In *The Cambridge handbook of meeting science* (pp. 177–202). Cambridge University Press.

Yao, L., Chen, X. P., & Wei, H. (2022). How do authoritarian and benevolent leadership affect employee work–family conflict? An emotional regulation perspective. *Asia Pacific Journal of Management*. https://doi.org/10.1007/s10490-022-09824-x

Chapter 8
How Much Is Nonverbal? Exploring Workplace Incivility Across Cultures

People may hear your words, but they feel your attitude.
– John C. Maxwell

Workplace incivility refers to "low-intensity deviant behavior with ambiguous intent to harm the target, in violation of workplace norms for mutual respect. Uncivil behaviors are characteristically rude and discourteous, displaying a lack of regard for others." (Andersson & Pearson, 1999, p. 547). Typical examples of workplace incivility include using condescending tone, making demeaning comments to others, paying little attention to others' opinions, and failing to show appreciation for others' contributions (Andersson & Pearson, 1999; Pearson et al., 2001; Porath & Pearson, 2010). As such, workplace incivility is essentially a communicative act, with both components of verbal (e.g., words) and nonverbal (e.g., tone of voice) messaging. Although there are many manifestations of incivility in the workplace, in this chapter, we focus on five specific forms of incivility to explore their cultural differences. In particular, we discuss covert forms of incivility, represented by ostracism or social exclusion, and direct forms of incivility, including abusive supervision, microaggression, and bullying. We embed our discussion in the four domains of communication context – message, relationship, time, and space – to understand the meaning and manifestation of incivility in different cultures and make propositions to reduce incivility and to create an inclusive workplace.

Ostracism, Silent Treatment, and Social Exclusion

Ostracism is defined as ignoring and excluding individuals or groups by individuals or groups; it is also referred to as social exclusion (Williams, 1997). Ostracism in the workplace occurs when an individual or group omits taking actions to engage another organizational member when it would be socially appropriate to include them (Robinson et al., 2013). Social exclusion is communicated via silence (no speaking/talking) and nonverbal cues indicating avoidance or retreat; thus, scholars

W. L. Adair et al., *What Isn't Being Said*, Springer Series in Emerging Cultural Perspectives in Work, Organizational, and Personnel Studies,
https://doi.org/10.1007/978-3-031-53645-8_8

often use ostracism, silent treatment, and social exclusion interchangeably to describe this incivility. More concretely, Ferris et al. (2008) developed self-report items to measure the extent to which a person is the target of ostracism, including: "Others ignored me at work," "Others left the area when I entered," and "My greetings have gone unanswered at work."

The above definition and situations of ostracism highlight two unique characteristics. First, this social exclusion emerges from *inaction* rather than action, which involves more ambiguity and uncertainty than more overt types of incivility, causing the target of ostracism to ruminate about why it happened or whether it even happened at all. Second, ostracism is closely related to what others do or do not do, or what's socially appropriate or not, which implies that it is the existing workplace social norm that determines the meaning and impact of the inaction in question (Robinson et al., 2013). In other words, what constitutes a social exclusion act depends on construal expectations around social situations in a specific organization or culture (Rudert & Greifeneder, 2016).

Ostracism is nonverbal in nature and primarily related to the space domain of communication, indicating *not engaging* in a social interaction. As we know that the norms guiding nonverbal interaction differ across cultures, it is important to consider whether certain nonverbals that are often described as social exclusion acts in the United States or Canada, such as avoiding eye contact or not waving back, may not be considered social exclusion in East Asian cultures like Japan or China. In East Asian cultures, people are physically reserved in communication and are also highly conscious of power and status differentiation that determine appropriate communication acts (Hofstede, 1991; Lewis, 2018).

People in East Asian cultures also pay close attention to the relational context when choosing their verbal and nonverbal communication styles. When a subordinate avoids eye contact in the hallway while their manager walks by, this could be a sign of respect, or fear, or simply nervousness rather than an intent to ignore or socially exclude the supervisor. Similarly, when meeting in a superior's office to show respect, the subordinate often looks down and avoids eye contact (thus involving the visual sense of space context), and busily takes notes, but these acts are not construed as social exclusion. In contrast, looking directly into the eyes of the boss may imply that the subordinate is disrespectful and resentful. Now, imagine a US American boss working in a Japanese office for the first time. It is quite likely that they may feel socially isolated because subordinates may not respond to their high-five greetings, initiate a conversation with them, or invite them to any social gatherings. The misunderstanding may also arise from the social norm for buying lunch in China, where the most senior person or the person with the highest power/status should pay for the entire group. So if a newly arrived US expatriate only pays for their own lunch in a group lunch setting (involving the time and relationship contexts), it would be perceived as violating social inclusion norms.

If being excluded is interpreted as a violation of an inclusion norm, ostracism will trigger identity threats and negative effects because the desire to be accepted by others is one of the most basic and pervasive human drives (Baumeister & Leary, 1995). Targets of social exclusion experience decrements in physical health and increases in stress and anxiety (Williams, 2001), exhibit more aggression (Kirkpatrick et al., 2002; Leary et al., 2003; Twenge et al., 2001) and self-defeating behavior (Twenge et al., 2002), experience declines in self-esteem (Leary et al., 1995), and even inner numbness (Baumeister & Twenge, 2014).

Culture and Response to Ostracism

While all consequences of social exclusion are negative, some are more severe than others for people in one culture compared to another. In a review paper, Uskul and Over (2017) found that although people from collectivistic cultures that emphasize social interdependence (e.g., Japan, Korea) had higher rejection sensitivity than those from individualistic cultures (e.g., Western Europe, the United States) (Garris et al., 2011; Sato et al., 2014; Yamaguchi et al., 1995); individuals from highly interdependent communities (e.g., Turkey, China, India) were less negatively affected by ostracism than those from individualistic cultural groups (e.g., Germany, the United States) (Graupmann et al., 2016; Pfundmair et al., 2015). These findings suggest that having strong social connections has protective effects against ostracism. The authors then offered several explanations for the protective effect of social interdependence, all highly related to communication with high context dependence in the relationship domain. One explanation is that people in cultures with high social interdependence are likely to seek help from friends and relatives when being ostracized. They are likely to talk about it, share emotions with one another, and receive comfort. This strategy is effective because socially interdependent people have more chronic cognitive accessibility to positive social representations that can serve as a buffer against the negative consequences of ostracism than do people in low social interdependent cultures (Gardner et al., 2005; Knowles, 2014; Over & Uskul, 2016). Another explanation is that individuals with a strong sense of social interdependence might not perceive ostracism as especially threatening because they tend to focus on belonging securely and trust more narrowly (primarily in-group members, see Yamagishi, 1988).

Cultural differences in responses to social exclusion are also related to how ostracism is culturally understood. When being excluded is consistent with the prevailing cultural norms, then the exclusion may not be interpreted as threatening, and thus, there will be less negative reflexive reactions to ostracism. For example, in a library or in an elevator, the implicit prevailing norm may be that people do not make eye contact or greet one another, and then being ignored is not as threatening as in a social gathering or company party (Rudert & Greifeneder, 2016).

A more recent study (He et al., 2021) relies on emotion regulation as a strategy to deal with the pain caused by ostracism. The authors reason that individual emotion regulation capabilities could help deal with negative emotions caused by ostracism. They distinguish between ostracism from people of the same-race and other-race for White and East Asian participants and find that all participants express greater negative emotion and engage in stronger emotion regulation when facing own-race than other-race social exclusion. However, Whites were more capable of regulating the exclusion-induced negative emotions than East Asians, suggesting that less social interdependence in a society might be related to more individual capacity in regulating negative emotions.

The role of social interdependence in buffering the negative impact of ostracism may also be relevant for linguistic ostracism, defined as any situation in which people converse in a language that others cannot understand (Dotan-Eliaz et al., 2009; Hitlan et al., 2006). Empirical studies show that linguistic ostracism (operationalized with coworkers excluding while speaking in Spanish) had more negative effects than ostracism alone (operationalized with coworkers excluding while speaking in English), including lower workgroup commitment, higher symbolic threat, and increased prejudice among English-speaking participants (Hitlan et al., 2006). Moreover, Dotan-Eliaz et al. (2009) found that participants who experienced linguistic ostracism in Russian felt more rejection and anger, less attraction to coworkers, and lower team potency than those without such linguistic ostracism. However, they also identified one important moderator –social self-efficacy, which can reverse the effect. Specifically, those high in social self-efficacy when linguistically ostracized, actually performed better than those linguistically included, but those low in social self-efficacy performed worse. Because social self-efficacy reflects one's confidence in social capabilities, including building relationships with others and earning trust, it is highly related to social interdependence.

To summarize, ostracism is nonverbal in nature. It involves physical distance, body orientation, eye contact, silence, and the cues in the space domain of communication context (which include space as perceived by all the senses), which are highly culturally bound. Meanwhile, the consequences of social exclusion are painful across all cultures, but cultural characteristics related to social interdependence seem to reduce its negative effects.

Abusive Supervision, Bullying, and Microaggression

If ostracism, silent treatment, and social exclusion are implicit/indirect ways of expressing incivility in the workplace, then abusive supervision, bullying, and microaggressions are more direct and explicit forms of incivility. Abusive supervision refers to supervisors' non-physical "sustained display of hostile verbal and nonverbal behaviors" (Tepper, 2000, p. 178) and is often manifested in unfriendly words or behaviors toward employees at work. Bullying is deliberate and repeated verbal, physical, or cyber aggression, intending to cause harm and distress to the victim (Einarsen et al., 1994; Salin et al., 2019). Bullying includes work-related bullying, represented by behaviors such as giving unreasonable tasks, deadlines, or workload, as well as physically intimidating bullying behaviors, such as shouting, spontaneous anger, or physical aggression like grabbing or pushing (Power et al., 2013). Microaggressions are subtle verbal, behavioral, and situational indignities that express hostility, derogatory, or insults to the target person or group (Pierce, 1970; Sue et al., 2007; Sue & Spanierman, 2020).

Directly expressed incivility, communicated both verbally and nonverbally, often results in negative and complex emotional, cognitive, and behavioral outcomes for individuals and organizations, including deviance, exhaustion, turnover, low performance, and withdrawal (Barling et al., 2009; Gallegos et al., 2022; Tepper et al., 2006, 2009, 2017). In addition to creating and reinforcing norms for hostile work environments, these forms of incivility further reduce psychological safety, defined as team members' belief that one can speak up, take risks, and admit mistakes without fear of negative consequences (Edmondson & Lei, 2014), especially for minority and underrepresented groups based on race, ethnicity, sexual orientation, religious affiliation, physical capabilities, among others (Williams, 2020; Budge et al., 2013; Galupo & Resnick, 2016; Resnick & Galupo, 2019).

Culture and Abusive Supervision, Bullying, and Microaggression

Despite the lack of cross-cultural research and theory building in the wider field of psychology studying human aggression (Bond, 2004; Li & Lim, 2017), there are theoretical speculations as well as limited comparative and culture-specific studies that provide insights, especially in abusive supervision and bullying. Irani and Oswald (2009) theorized that human aggression and workplace incivility are related to cultural values through learned behaviors, internalized expectation, and behavioral modeling. For example, they suggest that members of highly collectivist and power distant cultures (Hofstede, 1980, 2001) would be more likely to tolerate incivility than members of cultures low in collectivism and power distance, especially when the source of incivility holds more structural authority. Likewise, Jacobson et al. (2014) theorized that the GLOBE dimensions (House et al., 2004) of assertiveness, power distance, and in-group collectivism would be positively related to the prevalence of workplace bullying. Empirically, a meta-analysis (Mackey et al., 2013) found that abusive supervision occurred more frequently in East Asian countries such as China, South Korea, and Japan, where collectivism and power distance are high. Other literature shows cross-cultural construct and scale validity for direct forms of incivility (Hu et al., 2011; Ahmad, 2018; Salin et al., 2019; Severance et al., 2013), suggesting that cultural differences lay in the normative construal of the behaviors.

Anglo and Confucian cultural clusters show normative differences in the acceptability of abusive supervision, where it elicits stronger negative reactions and injustice perceptions for those in Anglo cultures than those in Confucian cultures (Vogel et al., 2015). Other scholars studied culture-specific forms of workplace incivility. For example, studies conducted in East Asia (Hon & Lu, 2016; Liu & Wang, 2013; Rotundo & Xie, 2008; Seo et al., 2012) found that the Confucian virtues of being patient despite unreasonable situations have promoted tolerance and acceptance of counterproductive behaviors such as abusive supervision and bullying among Chinese, Korean, and Taiwanese employees. Giorgi et al. (2015) studied how Italians tolerate bullying and speculated that Latin European countries have relatively low humane orientation (House et al., 2004), meaning individuals do not expect compassion in the workplace and, therefore, would moderately tolerate bullying. In South Africa, Motsei and Nkomo (2016) found that victims and bystanders of bullying linked the negative dynamics to social identities and their status of being in-group or out-group. Microaggressions are subtle everyday slights against a person's minority identity that may be intentional or unintentional and by definition depend on the victim's decoding of the message as an insult (Sue et al., 2007). In other words, microaggressions inherently rely on the context in which they occur to be fully understood. As a result, reported cultural differences and comparative studies are rare (Stambaugh & Ford, 2015; Sue et al., 2007; Sue & Spanierman, 2020).

In summary, overt workplace incivilities of abusive supervision, bullying, and microaggressions are communicated both verbally and nonverbally. Although there are similarities in the factor structures and conceptual categories of abusive supervision and bullying, the interpersonal dynamics, prevailing patterns of behaviors, and the cultural reasons for the expression and responses of these behaviors still differ.

Strategies for Coping and Understanding Workplace Incivility from the Four Domains of Communication Context

Below we analyze these uncivil behaviors through the lenses of the four domains of communication context and propose how understanding and navigating the communication contexts around explicit incivility might offer opportunities to discover new coping strategies. Given that the verbal and physical expressions of abusive and bullying behaviors are culture-specific (Severance et al., 2013), culture and situation-specific messages and interpretations will be needed to cope with abusive supervision and bullying.

Message Context

The message context of communication encompasses nonverbal cues that imply and infer meanings of verbal expressions. Research has delved into the multifaceted expressions of harmful and oppressive practices in professional spheres (Ghayas & Jabeen, 2020; Martinko et al., 2013). These hostile interactions can often take the form of "petty tyranny, shouting, and demeaning conduct" (Ashforth, 1994), carrying implications of arbitrariness, self-promotion, disregard for others, and unjustified punishment. Other examples of abusive supervision include superiors taking undue credit (Keashly et al., 1994) and scapegoating (Girard, 1989).

Studies have identified that harmful verbal and nonverbal communications, such as mockery, dishonesty, or social undermining (Farh & Chen, 2014; Raver & Gelfand, 2005), perceived and exhibited interpersonal aggression, pervasive harassment regularly displayed in the workplace (Raver & Gelfand, 2005), and overt depreciation from colleagues can precipitate intensified cycles of abuse or adverse outcomes, such as increased employee turnover and diminished productivity (Chen et al., 2011).

Because abusive supervision and bullying can take so many forms, each of which can be expressed and interpreted more directly or more indirectly, the potential negative impacts and misunderstandings are amplified in multicultural workplaces with both low- and high-context employees. Stambaugh and Ford (2015) found that pathologizing cultural values and communication styles of a marginalized minority seems to be one of the major manifestations of microaggression. In other words, the offenders of microaggression assume the communication style of the dominant culture is the ideal means of expression (i.e., ethnocentrism) and expect cultural minorities to use the dominant culture lens to interpret meaning and the dominant culture style in their own communication. Cultural minority group members who don't adapt their communication style are likely to perceive verbal and nonverbal microaggressions, suggesting they are second-class citizens. For example, those speaking with a strong accent could be laughed at or ostracized in the workplace.

Some multicultural organizations have taken a proactive approach to manage the message context in the workplace by introducing a common professional language such as English. For example, using English in airplane cockpits or in multinational companies has reduced hierarchy-related verbal abuse in Korean and Japanese organizations (Gladwell, 2008; Neely, 2019). On the other hand, as mentioned in the social exclusion section of this chapter and elsewhere in this book, those with lower English proficiency could be susceptible to new types of challenges in terms of power dynamics and direct or indirect mistreatment (Tenzer & Pudelko, 2017). Therefore, efforts to standardize the message context to reduce misperceptions and misunderstanding should be considered with caution.

Relationship Context

The relationship context of communication refers to the extent to which interlocutors adjust what they say and how they say it based on their relationship with their counterparts. Even within culture, mismatched interpretations of a certain relationship can affect the verbal and nonverbal messages exchanged by individuals and cause incivility such as interpersonal attacks or bullying, aggravated abuse in rudeness, silent treatment, blaming, or expressed anger (Tepper et al., 2004), and consequentially lead to other negative consequences such as employee departure or turnover (Chen et al., 2011; Hu et al., 2011). Baillien et al. (2016) found that frequent and turbulent employee relationships intensified incivility such as bullying. Harris et al. found that leaders who experience relationship conflict with peers subsequently abuse their subordinates.

In the cross-cultural context, mistreatment, such as abusive supervision, bullying, and microaggression, is sometimes linked to the victims' social identity, embedded in culture-specific social hierarchies and power structures (D'Cruz et al., 2021; Motsei & Nkomo, 2016). Similarly, cultures differ in the perception and acceptance of supervisors using abusive behaviors to signal dominance (Giorgi et al., 2015; Liu & Wang, 2013). Chi et al. (2019) further delineated that mistreatment from in-group members would elicit less revenge or negative emotions than mistreatment from out-group members among Taiwanese, while US Americans did not show in-group out-group differences.

Coping strategies to reduce microaggressions can include psychological mechanisms such as mindful attention to the victims to increase empathy and intentional discerning that separate intentional aggression from unintentional oversights (e.g., Washington et al., 2020). Similarly, communication strategies of disarming, defying, and building social connections can also help reduce microaggression (Washington et al., 2020; Williams, 2020). Liu et al., (2021a) suggest that relational mindsets or schemata can be malleable in multicultural situations, and globally competent communicators must be sensitive to monitor and adjust their messages to culturally different others. Initiating and maintaining personal and professional relationships are hallmarks of globally competent individuals (e.g., Corner et al., 2021). Actively managing the relationship context could potentially involve initiating a conversation and self-disclosure of one's own family or a mutual friend, which might resonate with the other party to build a social connection. Such social connections could highlight the interdependence between the parties, and potentially reduce the occurrences of incivility across various cultures. Similarly, victims of workplace incivility could diffuse and transform the negative impact of abusive behaviors or messages from the relational perspective by focusing on commonalities between the two parties so that they can build rapport for more amicable outcomes. If necessary, the involvement or intervention of a third party, whose demeanor is friendly to both the aggressor and the victim, may also help to connect common goals in their communication.

Space Context and Time Context

The space context of communication refers to cues in the physical environment that affect communicated expressions, such as nonverbal glances, gestures, interruptions, or physical contact in one's sensory space. The time context involves cues based on different temporal orientations regarding scheduling, task structures, and clock vs. event time, which would be conveyed in workplace exchanges. Several studies found that disruptive behaviors in shared spaces at work and the use of physical force, together with verbal abuse, are perceived as uncivil across cultures (Severance et al., 2013; Salin et al., 2019). The measures for physically intimidating behaviors in bullying (Einarsen et al., 2009) include finger-pointing, invasion of personal space, shoving, and blocking or barring the way, suggesting nonverbal communication and invasion of personal space. In addition to overt incivility, microaggressions may also be reflected in spatial cues such as interruption, words or music with profane or offensive lyrics, showing polarizing political views, or stipulating gender-conforming dress codes that can be experienced as a microaggression by some (Volokh, 1997). The time context of abusive supervision, bullying, and microaggression is closely related to the space context because physical interruptions or urgent demands directly impact how people allocate their time and schedule at work. When delivered with aggression and pressure by supervisors or coworkers, such interruptions would require the receivers to readjust their temporal orientation with stress, distraction, and lower levels of motivation and performance (Leroy et al., 2020).

Given that communication is a salient feature in abusive supervision, bullying, and microaggression, Tepper et al. (2007) found that direct upward maintenance communication, measured by adaptive and open communication with supervisors, can reduce the impact of abusive supervision on employee distress in the United States. Similarly, Liu et al., (2021b) found that open communication would neutralize the negative relationship between abusive supervision and voice behavior among Chinese. From the supervisors' perspective, downward communicative adaptability, which includes social composure, wit, appropriate disclosure, articulation, social experience, and social confirmation, seems to reduce downward abusive communication among a diverse group of US Americans (Sager et al., 2015). Additionally, relationships with family and friends can support open communications that might aid in coping with incivil treatments at the workplace.

The literature reviews of the coping strategies for mistreatment at the workplace have been centered on indirect communication via avoidance or direct confrontation (Tepper et al., 2007, 2017), which are temporary and not optimal solutions. Considerations of the time context and space context may provide new insights into understanding and reducing the negative consequences of abusive supervision, bullying, and microaggression. In the space domain, abusive behaviors are manifested not only in nonverbal cues, for example, the silent treatment, but also in verbal cues like interruption or negative emotional expressions that occur within the space domain. Therefore, understanding and communicating time orientation and space sensitivity creates space for mutual understanding and the co-creation of respectful solutions for managing abusive supervision.

In a multicultural workplace, incivility can be communicated consciously and non-consciously through multiple spatial cues, which might be interpreted and responded to in a variety of ways, thus leading to misunderstanding or escalation of conflicts. At the individual level, when faced with the silent treatment, interruptions, or negative emotions in the workplace, victims of incivility may need to use nonverbal cues to express mental toughness, calmness, and resolution, such as steady eye contact, upright posture, and a firm stance. Organizational leaders can design workspaces that cultivate inclusion and civil behaviors, such as identifying physical areas and online channels for individual reflections, open conversations, and emotional management. For example, relaxing music can be played in conference rooms where tensions are likely to occur.

Based on the above discussions on ostracism, social exclusion, abusive supervision, bullying, and microaggression, we make the following propositions about communication and incivility at the individual and organizational levels:

Proposition 1: The negative effect of ostracism on individual-felt pain will be moderated by the subjective perception of exclusion based on cultural norms for communication cues of time and space, such that cultural norm-congruent communicated ostracism is less threatening than cultural norm-incongruent communicated ostracism.

Proposition 2: Social interdependence at both cultural and individual levels can mitigate the negative effects of ostracism on individuals who feel pain because social interdependence increases a target person's resilience to overcome the adversity associated with social exclusion.

Proposition 3: The negative effects of overt incivility, including abusive supervision, bullying, and microaggression, can be alleviated by actively managing the relationship context. Specifically, victims of these incivilities can navigate the adverse situations by leveraging social connections that highlight the interdependence with the perpetrator in both personal and professional settings.

Proposition 4: Proactively managed communication through space and time may mitigate the negative effects of overt incivility, such as abusive supervision, bullying, and microaggression. Understanding, planning, and intentional signaling of nonverbal cues that limit interruption could communicate equality and inclusion in the workplace by both individuals and organizations. Flexibility and clarity in communicating scheduling, interaction frequency, and deadlines may reduce instances of misunderstanding and mistreatment in the workplace.

References

Ahmad, S. (2018). Can ethical leadership inhibit workplace bullying across East and West: Exploring cross-cultural interactional justice as a mediating mechanism. *European Management Journal, 36*(2), 223–234.

Andersson, L. M., & Pearson, C. M. (1999). Tit for tat? The spiraling effect of incivility in the workplace. *Academy of Management Review, 24*, 452–471.

Ashforth, B. (1994). Petty tyranny in organizations. *Human Relations, 47*(7), 755–778.

Baillien, E., Camps, J., Van den Broeck, A., Stouten, J., Godderis, L., Sercu, M., & De Witte, H. (2016). An eye for an eye will make the whole world blind: Conflict escalation into workplace bullying and the role of distributive conflict behavior. *Journal of Business Ethics, 137*(2), 415–429.

Barling, J., Dupré, K. E., & Kelloway, E. K. (2009). Predicting workplace aggression and violence. *Annual Review of Psychology, 60*, 671–692.

Baumeister, R. F., & Leary, M. R. (1995). The need to belong: Desire for interpersonal attachments as a fundamental human motivation. *Psychological Bulletin, 117*, 497–529.

Baumeister, R. F., & Twenge, J. M. (2014). The inner world of rejection. In J. P. Forgas & K. D. Williams (Eds.), *The social self: Cognitive, interpersonal and intergroup perspectives* (pp. 161–174). Psychology Press.

Bond, M. H. (2004). Culture and aggression: From context to coercion. *Personality and Social Psychology Review, 8*, 62–78.

Budge, S. L., Adelson, J. L., & Howard, K. A. S. (2013). Anxiety and depression in transgender individuals: The roles of transition status, loss, social support, and coping. *Journal of Consulting and Clinical Psychology, 81*(3), 545–557.

Chen, G., Sharma, P. N., Edinger, S. K., Shapiro, D. L., & Farh, J. L. (2011). Motivating and demotivating forces in teams: Cross-level influences of empowering leadership and relationship conflict. *Journal of Applied Psychology, 96*, 541–557.

Chi, S.-C. S., Friedman, R. A., Chu, C.-C., & Shih, H.-L. (2019). Chinese acceptance of mistreatment by in-relation offenders can be neutralized by triggering a "group" collectivism perspective. *European Journal of Work and Organizational Psychology, 28*(3), 384–398.

Corner, A. J., Liu, L. A., & Bird, A. (2021). Intercultural competencies for emerging markets: A contextualized approach. *International Business Review, 30*, 101792. https://doi.org/10.1016/j.ibusrev.2020.101792

D'Cruz, P., Noronha, E., Caponecchio, C., Escartin, J., Salin, D., & Tuckey, M. (2021). *Workplace bullying. Dignity and inclusion at work*. Springer.

Dotan-Eliaz, O., Sommer, K. L., & Rubin, Y. S. (2009). Multilingual groups: Effects of linguistic ostracism on felt rejection and anger, coworker attraction, perceived team potency, and creative performance. *Basic and Applied Social Psychology, 31*(4), 363–375.

Edmondson, A. C., & Lei, Z. (2014). Psychological safety: The history, renaissance, and future of an interpersonal construct. *The Annual Review of Organizational Psychology and Organizational Behavior, 1*(1), 23–43.

Einarsen, S., Rayknes, B. I., & Matthiesen, S. B. (1994). Bullying and harassment at work and their relationships to work environment quality: An exploratory study. *European Journal of Work and Organizational Psychology, 4*, 381–401.

Einarsen, S., Hoel, H., & Notelaersa, G. (2009). Measuring exposure to bullying and harassment at work: Validity, factor structure and psychometric properties of the Negative Acts Questionnaire-Revised. *Work and Stress, 23*, 24–44.

Farh, C. I. C., & Chen, Z. (2014). Beyond the individual victim: Multilevel consequences of abusive supervision in teams. *Journal of Applied Psychology, 99*(6), 1074–1095.

Ferris, D. L., Brown, D. J., Berry, J. W., & Lian, H. W. (2008). The development and validation of the workplace ostracism scale. *Journal of Applied Psychology, 93*(6), 1348–1366.

Gallegos, I., Guàrdia-Olmos, J., & Berger, R. (2022). Abusive supervision: A systematic review and new research approaches. *Frontiers in Communication, 6*, 640908. https://doi.org/10.3389/fcomm.2021.640908

Galupo, M. P., & Resnick, C. A. (2016). Experiences of LGBT microaggressions in the workplace: Implications for policy. In T. Kollen (Ed.), *Sexual orientation and transgender issues in organizations* (pp. 276–292). Springer. https://doi.org/10.1007/978-3-319-29623-4_16

Gardner, W. L., Pickett, C. L., & Knowles, M. (2005). Social snacking and shielding: Using social symbols, selves, and surrogates in the service of belonging needs. In K. D. Williams, J. P. Forgas, & W. Von Hippel (Eds.), *The social outcast: Ostracism, social exclusion, rejection, and bullying* (pp. 227–242). Psychology Press.

Garris, C. P., Ohbuchi, K. I., Oikawa, H., & Harris, M. J. (2011). Consequences of interpersonal rejection: A cross-cultural experimental study. *Journal of Cross-Cultural Psychology, 42*(6), 1066–1083.

Ghayas, M. M., & Jabeen, R. (2020). Abusive supervision: Dimensions and scale. *New Horizons, 14*(1), 107–130. https://doi.org/10.29270/NH.14.1(20).07

Giorgi, G., Leon-Perez, J., & Arenas, A. (2015). Are bullying behaviors tolerated in some cultures? Evidence for a curvilinear relationship between workplace bullying and job satisfaction among Italian workers. *Journal of Business Ethics, 131*(1), 227–237.

Girard, R. (1989). *The scapegoat*. Johns Hopkins University Press.

Gladwell, M. (2008). *Outliers: The story of success*. Little Brown.

Graupmann, V., Pfundmair, M., Matsoukas, P., & Erber, R. (2016). Rejection via video: The impact of observed group and individual rejection. *Social Psychology, 47*, 345–350. https://doi.org/10.1027/1864-9335/a000283

He, Z., Muhlert, N., & Elliott, R. (2021). Emotion regulation of social exclusion: A cross-cultural study. *Humanities and Social Sciences Communications, 8*, 173. https://doi.org/10.1057/s41599-021-00857-z

Hitlan, R. T., Kelly, K. M., Schepman, S., Schneider, K. T., & Zárate, M. A. (2006). Language exclusion and the consequences of perceived ostracism in the workplace. *Group Dynamics: Theory, Research, and Practice, 10*(1), 56–70.

Hofstede, G. H. (1980). *Culture's consequences: International differences in work-related values* (1st ed.). Sage.

Hofstede, G. (1991). *Cultures and organizations*. McGraw Hill.

Hofstede, G. H. (2001). *Culture's consequences: International differences in work-related values* (2nd ed.). Sage.

Hon, A. H. Y., & Lu, L. (2016). When will the trickle-down effect of abusive supervision be alleviated? The moderating roles of power distance and traditional cultures. *Cornell Hospitality Quarterly, 57*(4), 421–433.

House, R., Hanges, P. J., Javidan, M., Dorfman, P. W., & Gupta, V. (2004). *Culture, leadership and organizations: The GLOBE study of 62 societies*. Sage.

Hu, C., Wu, T.-Y., & Wang, Y.-H. (2011). Measurement equivalence/invariance of the abusive supervision measure across workers from Taiwan and the United States. *The Journal of Psychology: Interdisciplinary and Applied, 145*(2), 111–131.

Irani, F. S., & Oswald, S. L. (2009). Workplace aggression: Is national culture a factor? *Business Renaissance Quarterly, 4*(1), 63–89.

Jacobson, K. J., Hood, J. N., & Van Buren, H. J. (2014). Workplace bullying across cultures: A research agenda. *International Journal of Cross-Cultural Management, 14*(1), 47–65.

Keashly, L., Trott, V., & MacLean, L. M. (1994). Abusive behavior in the workplace: A preliminary investigation. *Violence and Victims, 9*, 341–341.

Kirkpatrick, L. A., Waugh, C. E., Valencia, A., & Webster, G. D. (2002). The functional domain specificity of self-esteem and the differential prediction of aggression. *Journal of Personality and Social Psychology, 82*, 756–767.

Knowles, M. L. (2014). Social rejection increases perspective taking. *Journal of Experimental Social Psychology, 55*, 126–132.

Leary, M. R., Tambor, E. S., Terdal, S. K., & Downs, D. L. (1995). Self-esteem as an interpersonal monitor: The sociometer hypothesis. *Journal of Personality and Social Psychology, 68*, 518–530.

Leary, M. R., Kowalski, R. M., Smith, L., & Phillips, S. (2003). Teasing, rejection, and violence: Case studies of the school shootings. *Aggressive Behavior, 29*, 202–214.

Leroy, S., Schmidt, M. A., & Madjar, N. (2020). Interruptions and task transitions: Understanding their characteristics, processes, and consequences. *Academy of Management Annals, 14*(2), 661–694. https://doi.org/10.5465/annals.2017.0146

Lewis, R. (2018). *When cultures collide: Leading across cultures* (4th ed.). Nicholas Brealey Publishing.

Li, X., & Lim, S. (2017). Cross-cultural differences in workplace aggression. In N. Bowling & M. S. Hershcovis (Eds.), *Research and theory on workplace aggression* (pp. 245–268). Cambridge University Press.

Liu, X.-Y., & Wang, J. (2013). Abusive supervision and organizational citizenship behaviour: Is supervisor–subordinate guanxi a mediator? *International Journal of Human Resource Management, 24*(7), 1471–1489.

Liu, L. A., Chiu, C. Y., & Zhang, Z.-X. (2021a). Dynamic transformation of communal and exchange schemata in multicultural relationships. *Cross Cultural & Strategic Management, 28*(2), 368–383.

Liu, C., Sun, S., & Dube, F. N. M. (2021b). The buffering effects of subordinates' forgiveness and communication openness on abusive supervision and voice behavior. *SAGE Open*, 1–17. https://doi.org/10.1177/2158244021104108

Mackey, J. D., Ellen, B. P., Hochwarter, W. A., & Ferris, G. R. (2013). Subordinate social adaptability and the consequences of abusive supervision perceptions in two samples. *The Leadership Quarterly, 24*, 732–746.

Martinko, M. J., Harvey, P., Brees, J. R., & Mackey, J. (2013). A review of abusive supervision research. *Journal of Organizational Behavior, 34*(1), 120–137.

Motsei, N., & Nkomo, S. M. (2016). Antecedents of bullying in the South African workplace: Societal context matters. *Africa Journal of Management, 2*(1), 50–72.

Neely, T. (2019). *The language of global success: How a common tongue transforms multinational organizations*. Princeton University Press.

Over, H., & Uskul, A. K. (2016). Culture moderates children's responses to ostracism situations. *Journal of Personality and Social Psychology, 110*(5), 710–724. https://doi.org/10.1037/pspi0000050

Pearson, C., Andersson, L., & Wegner, J. (2001). When workers flout convention: A study of workplace incivility. *Human Relations, 54*, 1387–1419.

Pfundmair, M., Aydin, N., Du, H., Yeung, S., Frey, D., & Graupmann, V. (2015). Exclude me if you can – Cultural effects on the outcomes of exclusion. *Journal of Cross-Cultural Psychology, 46*(4), 579–596.

Pierce, C. (1970). Offensive mechanisms. In F. B. Barbour (Ed.), *The black seventies* (pp. 265–282). Porter Sargent.

Porath, C. L., & Pearson, C. M. (2010). The cost of bad behavior. *Organizational Dynamics, 39*, 64–71. https://doi.org/10.1016/j.orgdyn.2009.10.006

Power, J. L., Brotheridge, C. M., Blenkinsopp, J., Bowes-Sperry, L., Bozionelos, N., Buzády, Z., Chuang, A., et al. (2013). Acceptability of workplace bullying: A comparative study on six continents. *Journal of Business Research, 66*(3), 374–380.

Raver, J. L., & Gelfand, M. J. (2005). Beyond the individual victim: Linking sexual harassment, team processes, and team performance. *Academy of Management Journal, 48*, 387–400.

Resnick, C. A., & Galupo, M. P. (2019). Assessing experiences with LGBT microaggressions in the workplace: Development and validation of the Microaggression Experiences at Work Scale. *Journal of Homosexuality, 66*(10), 1380–1403. https://doi.org/10.1080/00918369.2018.1542207

Robinson, S., O'Reiley, J., & Wang, W. (2013). Invisible at work: An integrated model of workplace ostracism. *Journal of Management, 39*(1), 203–231. https://doi.org/10.1177/0149206312466141

Rotundo, M., & Xie, J. L. (2008). Understanding the domain of counterproductive work behaviour in China. *International Journal of Human Resource Management, 19*(5), 856–877.

Rudert, S. C., & Greifeneder, R. (2016). When it's okay that I don't play: Social norms and the situated construal of social exclusion. *Personality and Social Psychology Bulletin, 42*(7), 955–969.

Sager, K. L., Wallace, E. A., Jarrett, B., & Richey, J. A. (2015). Exploring the role of communication competence in abusive supervision: A test of a mode linking downward communicative adaptability to downward abusive communication. *SAGE Open*, 1–8. https://doi.org/10.1177/2158244015604689

Salin, D., Cowan, R., Adewumi, O., Apospori, E., Bochantin, J., D'Cruz, P., Djurkovic, N., Durniat, K., Escartín, J., Guo, J., Išik, I., Koeszegi, S. T., McCormack, D., Monserrat, S. I., & Zedlacher, E. (2019). Workplace bullying across the globe: A cross-cultural comparison. *Personnel Review, 48*(1), 204–219.

Sato, K., Yuki, M., & Norasakkunkit, V. (2014). A socio-ecological approach to cross-cultural differences in the sensitivity to social rejection: The partially mediating role of relational mobility. *Journal of Cross-Cultural Psychology, 45*, 1549–1560.

Seo, Y. N., Leather, P., & Coyne, I. (2012). South Korean culture and history: The implications for workplace bullying. *Aggression and Violent Behavior, 17*(5), 419–422.

Severance, L., Bui-Wrzosinska, L., Gelfand, M. J., Lyons, S., Nowak, A., Borkowski, W., Soomro, N., Soomro, N., Rafaeli, A., Treister, D. E., Lin, C.-C., & Yamaguchi, S. (2013). The psychological structure of aggression across cultures. *Journal of Organizational Behavior, 34*(6), 835–865.

Stambaugh, T., & Ford, D. Y. (2015). Microaggressions, multiculturalism, and gifted individuals who are Black, Hispanic, or low income. *Journal of Counseling & Development, 93*(2), 192–201. https://doi.org/10.1002/j.1556-6676.2015.00195.x

Sue, D. W., & Spanierman, L. (2020). *Microaggressions in everyday life* (2nd ed.). Wiley.

Sue, D. W., Capodilupo, C. M., Torino, G. C., Bucceri, J. M., Holder, A. M. B., Nadal, K. L., & Esquilin, M. (2007). Racial microaggressions in everyday life: Implications for clinical practice. *American Psychologist, 62*(4), 271–286. https://doi.org/10.1037/0003-066X.62.4.271

Tenzer, H., & Pudelko, M. (2017). The influence of language differences on power dynamics in multinational teams. *Journal of World Business, 52*(1), 45–61.

Tepper, B. J. (2000). Consequences of abusive supervision. *Academy of Management Journal, 43*(2), 178–190.

Tepper, B. J., Duffy, M. K., Hoobler, J., & Ensley, M. D. (2004). Moderators of the relationships between coworkers' organizational citizenship behavior and fellow employees' attitudes. *Journal of Applied Psychology, 89*(3), 455–465.

Tepper, B. J., Duffy, M. K., Henle, C. A., & Lambert, L. S. (2006). Procedural injustice, victim precipitation, and abusive supervision. *Personnel Psychology, 59*(1), 101–123.

Tepper, B. J., Moss, S. E., Lockhart, D. E., & Carr, J. C. (2007). Abusive supervision, upward maintenance communication, and subordinates' psychological stress. *Academy of Management Journal, 50*(5), 1169–1180.

Tepper, B. J., Carr, J. C., Breaux, D. M., Geider, S., Hu, C., & Hua, W. (2009). Abusive supervision, intentions to quit, and employees' workplace deviance: A power/dependence analysis. *Organizational Behavior and Human Decision Processes, 109*(2), 156–167.

Tepper, B. J., Simon, L., & Park, H. (2017). Abusive supervision. *Annual Review of Organizational Psychology and Organizational Behavior, 4*, 123–152.

Twenge, J. M., Baumeister, R. F., Tice, D. M., & Stucke, T. S. (2001). If you can't join them, beat them: Effects of social exclusion on aggressive behavior. *Journal of Personality and Social Psychology, 81*, 1058–1069.

Twenge, J. M., Catanese, K. R., & Baumeister, R. F. (2002). Social exclusion causes self-defeating behavior. *Journal of Personality and Social Psychology, 83*, 606–615.

Uskul, A. K., & Over, H. (2017). Culture, social interdependence, and ostracism. *Current Directions in Psychological Science, 26*(4), 371–376.

Vogel, R. M., Mitchell, M. S., Tepper, B. J., Restobug, S. L. D., Hu, C., et al. (2015). A cross-cultural examination of subordinates' perceptions of and reactions to abusive supervision. *Journal of Organizational Behavior, 36*, 720–745.

Volokh, E. (1997). What speech does "hostile work environment" harassment law restrict? *Georgetown Law Journal, 627*. https://www2.law.ucla.edu/volokh/harass/breadth.htm

Washington, E. F., Birch, A. H., & Roberts, L. M. (2020, June 3). When and how to respond to microaggressions. *Harvard Business Review*.

Williams, K. D. (1997). Social ostracism. In R. M. Kowalski (Ed.), *Aversive interpersonal behaviors* (pp. 133–170). Plenum.

Williams, K. D. (2001). *Ostracism: The power of silence* (p. 282). Guilford.

Williams, M. (2020). Microaggressions: Clarification, evidence, and impact. *Perspectives on Psychological Science, 15*(1), 3–26. https://doi.org/10.1177/1745691619827499

Yamagishi, T. (1988). Exit from the group as an individualistic solution to the free rider problem in the United States and Japan. *Journal of Experimental Social Psychology, 24*(6), 530–542.

Yamaguchi, S., Kuhlman, D. M., & Sugimori, S. (1995). Personality correlates of socio-centric tendencies in individualistic and collectivistic cultures. *Journal of Cross-Cultural Psychology, 26*, 658–672.

Chapter 9
What's Not Being Said When Communications are Virtual?

In-person meetings provide a sense of intimacy, connection and empathy that is difficult to replicate via video. – Paul Axtell

Information and communication technology unlocks the value of time, allowing and enabling multi-tasking, multi-channels, multi-this and multi-that. – Li Ka-shing

Virtual interactions are characterized by the use of information technologies to facilitate cross-boundary communication to accomplish critical tasks (Wang et al., 2022; Gibson & Gibbs, 2006; Kirkman & Mathieu, 2005; Raghuram et al., 2019). A 2020 report by McKinsey & Company suggests that the pandemic accelerated the adoption of digital information technologies by several years and has led to a significant increase in the use of virtual communication (McKinsey & Company, 2023). Yet, virtual communication carries an even more daunting task than face-to-face communication; because much of non-verbal communication is hidden or hampered in virtual communication, what's not being said is even more difficult to decipher. In such environments the ability to decode and read implicit communications between the spoken or written lines – that is, whether communicators are higher or lower in communication contextualization – will influence the understanding and effectiveness of the interaction.

Over 15 years ago, Gibson and Gibbs accurately envisioned virtuality as it is often employed today: a higher-order construct comprising four characteristics – geographic dispersion, electronic dependence, dynamic structural arrangements, and national diversity (2006). Examining virtuality at the ground level, one might assess whether the information technologies employed allow for copresence, visibility, audibility, contemporality, simultaneity, and sequentiality (Purvanova, 2014). E-mail and chat, for example, are conducted from different geographic locations and, thus, lack copresence. The corresponders, dependent on electronic virtual communication, cannot see or hear one another and thus have no visibility and audibility. Due to the dynamic structural arrangements made and particularly if geographic and nationally diverse teams are interacting, people may not be available to communicate at the same time and lack contemporality. They may open or see the communications later than they were sent, and so lack simultaneity. Sequentiality may

W. L. Adair et al., *What Isn't Being Said*, Springer Series in Emerging Cultural Perspectives in Work, Organizational, and Personnel Studies,
https://doi.org/10.1007/978-3-031-53645-8_9

be absent because the flow of communication may be lost (Purvanova, 2014; Clark & Brennan, 1991).

Virtual meetings or video conferencing conducted by Zoom, Microsoft Teams or other means may compensate for some of these absences. Still, even so, the quality of the interlocutors' presence on screen, their visibility, and their audibility are often affected by technological failings, human intention, or error (e.g., weak internet, no use of camera, or failing to unmute). Consequently, with all modes of virtual communication, there is potential for the diminished understanding of written or verbal information exchange and the impeded encoding and decoding of nonverbal communication.

Much literature on virtual communication has focused on the dynamics and effectiveness of teams that employ it (e.g., Jarvenpaa & Leidner, 1999; Gibson & Gibbs, 2006; Mesmer-Magnus et al., 2011; Purvanova, 2014; Marlow et al., 2017; Rhymer, 2023). Central to these studies is a theory rooted in the engineering concept of communication bandwidth: how many channels of communication are used by a given medium at once and how much information can be effectively transmitted and understood at a given time. The general assumption common to these studies "is that face-to-face communication is superior to all other media, including computer-mediated communication, because it possesses the most communication channels and hence allows for the transmission of multiple information bits" (Purvanova, 2014, p. 5).

Media richness theory builds on the concept of communication bandwidth. It suggests that communication media vary in the amount of information they are able to transmit, the depth of detail articulated, and the richness of messages conveyed (Daft & Lengel, 1986). Information-rich nonverbal cues as to what is really being said (e.g., tone of voice, inflection, silence, volume, facial expressions, and gestures) are more easily expressed in face-to-face communication than in virtual communication if even they are transmitted virtually at all (Pitts et al., 2012; Rhymer, 2023; Burke & Chidambaram, 1999; Martins et al., 2004). The meaning of written text may be difficult to decipher without understanding the tone behind it, the inability to see a nod of confirmation or hear hesitation in someone's voice when reading an e-mail may result in misunderstanding or misattribution, the incapacity to witness the fidgeting movements of discomfort or distraction in a large meeting when able to see only small images of attendees in a Zoom window; these are all examples in which virtual communication hampers the richness of the information.

As virtual communication technology has evolved – from texts, chats, or e-mails to fully synchronous online virtual meetings – the capability to convey increasing levels of informational richness has also improved. Accordingly, current research suggests that there are situations when the effectiveness of communication via virtual means (particularly as applied to team settings) may equal or exceed the effectiveness of face-to-face interactions (e.g., Marlow et al., 2017; Rhymer, 2023). Status-and language-based communication barriers in multicultural teams can be reduced in virtual environments because e-mail is a lean medium in which the message is encoded in written words that lack paraverbal (e.g. [an authoritative or timid] tone of voice) and nonverbal (e.g. [an imposing or humble] posture) cues in comparison to more rich media (Daft & Lengel, 1986). Researchers have found that lean communication channels reduce culture and language-based cues, for example, accents, and give non-native speakers time to compose and comprehend messages that don't require nuanced interpretation (Klitmøller & Lauring, 2013; Klitmøller et al., 2015). In contrast, rich channels, e.g., face-to-face in-person or computer-mediated interactions, amplify culture and language differences, but they also make room for nonverbal cues that aid the expression and interpretation of non-standardized messages (Klitmøller & Lauring, 2013; Klitmøller et al., 2015). In other words, standardized computer-mediated communication has the potential to equalize language-based power in multicultural teams, but perhaps at the risk of losing the richness of meaning and expression that can be conveyed in face-to-face encounters.

Much of human communication depends on context – the unspoken, unformulated, inexplicit rules governing how information is handled and how people interact and relate. Communicators can draw upon or read cues in the context, be it the temporal or the spatial context, from the context of their relationship with the other person, or from the way the message itself is communicated. The more information-rich a communication medium is, the more context will be easily recognized and understood and the more nonverbal messages will be fluently encoded and decoded. For more high-context communicators, these nonverbal cues imbue the communication with meaning and, together with verbal messages, encompass the entire interaction. One Brazilian manager commenting on the exclusive use of virtual communication during the pandemic instead of more information-rich face-to-face interactions expressed that "nonverbal communication gave context and with remote work if felt like (we) were getting one piece of the puzzle at a time from each interaction" (Waight et al., 2022, p. 241).

In the following sections we discuss nonverbal communication in virtual interactions in each contextual domain of message, relationship, time, and space. The challenges of encoding and decoding nonverbal communication in each domain through a virtual medium are presented and possible ways to overcome the challenges. We end with propositions for future research based on the gaps in our understanding of the dynamics of virtual nonverbal communication.

Virtual Communication and Nonverbal Cues in the Message Context

There is likely no more complex situation to encode and decode nonverbal communication than when interacting cross-culturally by virtual means. Uncertainty may prevail regarding communication and social norms in that context; members may have access to different information or have differing worldviews (Gibson & Gibbs, 2006; Gibson et al., 2014; Glikson & Erez, 2020). Furthermore, language barriers create faultlines and status differences – often different than the status distinctions in the cultures themselves – leading to miscommunication, misinterpretation and perhaps conflict (Hinds & Mortensen, 2005; Hinds et al., 2014; Klitmøller et al., 2015; Neeley et al., 2012; Tenzer & Pudelko, 2017; Tenzer et al., 2014; Von Glinow et al., 2004). Yet given that interactions are virtual, the display and understanding of nonverbal contextual cues are inhibited, and crucial nuance is lost; as such, resolution of such conflict becomes more difficult (Daim et al., 2012; Johri, 2012; Klitmøller & Lauring, 2013; Kreijns et al., 2003; Marlow et al., 2017; Shapiro et al., 2002).

A myriad of differing and often implicit social norms across cultures regarding what is polite and appropriate in a given context complicates communication when conducted virtually (Glikson & Erez, 2020). Without the nuanced understanding of non-verbal contextual cues to avoid conflict and maintain harmony in Japan, for example – the word "no" is never spoken, but instead, several other polite responses will be offered – someone negotiating in a virtual meeting may not understand that an offer is being rejected even though their Japanese partner never verbally articulated "N" "O" (Gesteland, 2012). Without appreciation of social norms in the message context regarding directness and indirectness, a generally indirect communicator from Southeast Asia might regard the directness of someone raised in the Israeli culture as rude or offensive, while indirectness might be regarded as frustrating and intentionally confusing by the more direct speaker (Brew & Cairns, 2004; Katriel, 1986; Oetzel & Ting-Toomey, 2003). Without being able to feel the warmth being extended along with the words, the constant interruptions and finishing of sentences in a virtual meeting by a communicator from Latin America might be interpreted as rude by their foreign counterpart rather than as an intended means to build simpatia between them (Triandis et al., 1984).

A danger when communicating virtually with geographically distant partners from different countries or cultures is that in the absence of deeper information and understanding about the counterparts that often replaces initial social categorization in face-to-face encounters, in-group/out-group distinctions may be made solely based on easily accessible social categories such as ethnicity or nationality and not updated (Brewer & Kramer 1985; Whitener et al., 1998). These distinctions then often lead to stereotyping and distrust of the counterpart, exacerbating the difficulty of clear information exchange, whether verbal or nonverbal (Gibson & Gibbs, 2006). Diversity in the cultural backgrounds of the team members and the in-group/out-group identifications that may result "are likely to cause communication breakdowns (Kirkman & Shapiro, 1997; Gibson & Zellmer-Bruhn, 2001), making it difficult to aggregate and process information, particularly for knowledge that is uncodified (Nonaka & Takeuchi, 1995)" (Gibson & Gibbs, 2006, p. 460).

How might the challenges of understanding message context in virtual communication be overcome? As discussed by Pitts et al. (2012), one remedy lies in the development of emotional intelligence. Emotional intelligence (EI) refers to a person's ability to detect, understand and manage the emotions of others (Mayer et al., 2008). Research shows that relative to in-person interactions, communication via virtual teams yielded decreased social interaction, communication, and emotional expression (Jarvenpaa & Leidner, 1999). If highly emotionally intelligent communicators are shown to be effective at detecting and managing emotions in an information-lean virtual environment, training in emotional intelligence may be a key to unlocking the implicit, uncoded messages being transmitted, and communication might thus become clearer and better understood.

A second remedy lies in the development of cultural intelligence (CQ), or the capabilities that can enable someone to function effectively in culturally diverse environments (Earley & Ang, 2003). Data recently collected from 262 global virtual teams by Presbitero (2021) demonstrates that a member's CQ positively relates to their effectiveness in terms of synergy, or the processes of coordinating team efforts and resolving conflicts (Watson et al., 2003) and direction, or one's effectiveness in moving forward with the setting of goals and objectives (Watson et al., 2003). Furthermore, the communication accommodations of a virtual team member – the "adjustments individuals make to maintain or decrease the social distance in interaction" (Giles & Ogay, 2007, p. 293) – are influenced by CQ (Presbitero, 2021). A second recent study of 263 global virtual teams shows that an increase in the team's average motivational CQ, an individual's interest in experiencing global diversity (Van Dyne et al., 2012), will increase social integration – measured as cohesiveness, trust/morale and satisfaction with the team – and performance and that the motivational CQ of the team leader is a necessary condition for team social integration (Richter et al., 2021).

A third solution points to the importance of cross-cultural training for virtual communicators. The complexity of such communication can be encapsulated in the nonverbal expression of silence. Silence has multiple meanings depending on the cultural context of the communication and those communicating (Anawati & Craig, 2006). In East Asian and Nordic countries, silence is considered polite and can signify careful thought, agreement, or even disagreement in an effort to save face (Lewis, 2010). In the United States, silence is often unexpected and a confounding, frustrating, and/or embarrassing void to be filled (Graham & Requejo, 2009). Accordingly, "an important first step for leaders is to obtain information regarding members' cultural backgrounds, time constraints, terminology (e.g., slang, colloquialisms, jargon), and communication preferences, and …develop a training program that educates both the leader and followers about their respective cultures" (Earley & Peterson, 2004). A bonus in learning about other cultures and how they communicate, deepening one's understanding of cultural cues, and honing the ability to tend to them, is that in the process one's emotional intelligence is likely to be honed (Miao et al., 2012) and their cultural intelligence as well (Earley & Mosakowski, 2004).

Virtual Interactions and Nonverbal Cues in the Relationship Context

A deep literature on virtual teams suggests that as compared to face-to-face interactions, virtual teams communicate less information (Martins et al., 2004), develop relationships at a slower rate (Burke & Chidambaram, 1999; Pitts et al., 2012), and that trust development in particular, is quite challenging (Mesmer-Magnus & DeChurch, 2009; Marlow et al., 2017). Media richness theory implies that relatively information-lean virtual communication environments cannot convey nonverbal information such as warmth and will inhibit relationship development (Daft & Lengel, 1986). Yet Marlow et al. (2017) discuss studies indicating it is possible to strengthen affective states (Jarvenpaa & Leidner, 1999) and that virtual teams are able to share relationship-supportive information via virtual tools (Burke & Chidambaram, 1999; Walther, 2009). The question is, what information and which tools?

Mesmer-Magnus and DeChurch (2009) suggest that virtual communication has many advantages relative to face-to-face interaction, including "conversation which is less inhibited by social norms and group pressures, reduced potential for production blocking and evaluation apprehension, and more convenient/direct access to team members who have problem relevant information (e.g., via direct e-mails, instant messaging, phone calls)" (p. 216). Furthermore, compared to an in-person meeting, virtual interactions via e-mail or instant messaging offer a record of communication/decisions and more time to digest and consider information shared by team members (Mesmer-Magnus & DeChurch, 2009). These advantages are all likely to be more apparent when interacting virtually across cultures. In cultures where strong social norms regarding seniority and position at the table may inhibit speakers, junior parties may feel less encumbered by the positional norms in virtual contexts and less reluctant to share information. Communication might be done via e-mails, and such asynchronous interactions might prove more effective for the timely flow of information. Finally, non-native speakers of the language used in face-to-face interactions have a better chance of fully understanding the communications when there is more time to digest and consider them.

Mesmer-Magnus and DeChurch (2009) meta-analyzed the team information-sharing literature and found two different forms of information sharing, uniqueness, and openness, which have differing influences on team outcomes. Unique information sharing entails instrumental information specifically about the task at hand; open information sharing is information that promotes team members' relationship development (Glikson & Erez, 2020). The results of the meta-analysis demonstrated that unique information sharing links more to team problem-solving and task performance while open information sharing more strongly relates to team satisfaction and cohesion (Mesmer-Magnus & DeChurch, 2009; Rhymer, 2023).

In an information-rich face-to-face interaction, there are many ways to foster interpersonal team processes; in more information-lean virtual interactions, information exchange is the primary means to foster team dynamics (Mesmer-Magnus & DeChurch, 2009). Open sharing of information, which Glikson and Erez termed "relationally oriented" communication, includes both verbal and nonverbal messages that create the social fabric of the group, e.g., warmth or affiliation (2020). Wang et al. (2022) demonstrated that Chinese managers during the COVID-19 pandemic could increase leader-member psychological closeness, curb anxiety, and nurture social bonds with employees by using an information-rich virtual medium

(WeChat video conferencing); using this virtual medium, leaders could convey personal feelings via nonverbal cues in the relationship context.

Field studies of virtual teams using more information-rich communication media demonstrated performance levels that were on par with face-to-face teams, and familiarity likely mitigated the adverse effects of virtuality (Marlow et al., 2017; Purvanova, 2014). Open information sharing of personal information increases authentic familiarity with the individual, replacing superficial knowledge based on stereotypical categorizations (Johri, 2012; Glikson & Erez, 2020). Furthermore, individual-level empirical research has demonstrated that leader openness is a key factor that strongly influences employee perceptions of psychological safety, or people's perceptions of the consequences of taking interpersonal risks in a context such as the workplace (Detert & Burris, 2007), which in turn influences team information sharing, learning, and innovation (Newman et al., 2017).

Virtual Nonverbal Communication Cues in the Time Context

Timing is everything when communicating virtually. In groups residing in different time zones, trust development may be inhibited if a colleague does not receive a teammate's reply to a message in a manner considered "timely" (Marlow et al., 2017). Further, when there is little temporal overlap, interactions might include multi-hour or multi-day delays that can result in individual members being excluded from the decision process and a group's work becoming out of sync (Rhymer, 2023). Due to the slowness and time-delayed nature of many forms of virtual communication, research demonstrates that team members tend to reduce the overall amount of information conveyed, limiting their messages to problem-relevant (unique) information and curbing the amount of relationship-building communications (Mesmer-Magnus et al., 2011). While focusing communication on the task at hand might be beneficial at certain stages in the team's relationship, it is detrimental at early stages when trust and psychological safety need to be formed. This is particularly acute in newly formed global virtual teams where uncertainty is high due to the lack of familiarity among group members (Matook et al., 2015).

Finally, even when people are located in the same time zone, virtual work can impede informal (open information) conversations, sometimes forcing interactions onto a formal schedule rather than allowing them to happen casually and organically, and thus, frustrating relationship building (Waight et al., 2022). Waight et al. (2022) discuss the situation imposed by fully virtual interactions during the pandemic in Brazil in the following way:

> First, employees lost the informality of work-life; instead of informal, fluid communication and collaboration, participants had to book appointments and schedule time to discuss simple issues. Second, good-humored behaviors diminished, implicating connectedness. Third, nonverbal communication ceased, and employees lost facial expressions, eye contact, and other prevalent signs necessary for context. Fourth, the loss of unstructured exchange of experiences and ideas lessened tacit knowledge sharing. (p. 236)

So, when is the best time and what is the best timing for virtual communications? First, Glikson and Erez (2020) demonstrate that the exchange of relationally oriented information early in the formation of a global virtual team is an antecedent of a psychologically safe communication climate (PSCC) and that PSCC then has a positive influence on team performance. Such relationship-oriented information reduces team member uncertainty likely by reducing stereotypical thinking among the culturally diverse team, fostering familiarity, and promoting a sense of inclusion and common understanding (Lisak et al., 2016; Stahl & Tung, 2015). That first message among team members, full of both verbal and nonverbal content, is of key significance because relationship-oriented communication signals to the group the importance and appropriateness of such messages in the regular dynamics of team communication; in a sense, corresponding to a motivating leader's talk in the first co-located face-to-face team meeting (Glikson & Erez, 2020). Following up on this, predictable communication in line with the group's needs and schedule further cements trust among virtual teams throughout their lifecycle (Jarvenpaa & Leidner, 1999).

To foster more informal relationship building among team members, one suggestion is to use technology to support the "replication of work patterns and communication practices of more traditional office settings, such as using frequent meetings, ad hoc conversations, and shared documents" (Rhymer, 2023, p. 15). Promoting open access to information that anyone can obtain regardless of time zone, can lead to more transparency and reflects the idea of a "conversational firm," ultimately helping to eliminate hierarchy in employee voice (Rhymer, 2023; Turco, 2016). Another option is to set aside a time(s) during the day for synchronous virtual meetings (where everyone's camera is on) so team members can meet, talk, and share ideas. While there is no substitute for information-rich in-person chats at the water cooler, at least in synchronous face-to-face virtual meetings, there is a strong likelihood that verbal and nonverbal cues can be successfully sent and understood with engaged listening. Ad hoc conversations can then happen more organically via e-mail or group chat as per the various team members' schedules or inclinations; since team members are more familiar with colleagues' tone and manner, misunderstandings in more information-lean virtual media will be lessened.

Virtual Nonverbal Communication Cues in the Space Context

Early research on distributed work focused on the geographic distance between people. More recent research incorporates a multi-dimensional conceptualization of spatial distance, including factors such as time zones and cultural and linguistic differences (Rhymer, 2023; Wilson et al., 2013). Greater spatial distance between team members hampers verbal and nonverbal communication among the team – both open and relationally oriented information –hinders the sharing and coordination of knowledge and impedes outcomes such as innovation (Gibson & Gibbs, 2006; Waight et al., 2022). When teams are dispersed geographically, members are "embedded in different external contexts and thus have less shared contextual knowledge, with a far greater understanding of their own (geographical) context than others' context in the team" (Gluesing et al., 2003, p. 354). Members may take their tacit and common knowledge of the local context for granted and find it difficult to articulate how and why such context is relevant to the team (Gibson & Gibbs, 2006). This "situated knowledge" can lead to misunderstandings due to a lack of shared awareness among team members and hamper possible innovation (Gibson & Gibbs, 2006).

An additional challenge presented by the space context in virtual communications is the robust research finding that as the physical, social, or temporal distance from an object increases, individuals tend to rely on higher-level construals about that object (Trope et al., 2007; Wilson, Crisp & Mortenson, 2013). This suggests that the farther an individual is from someone, the more likely they are to construe or represent that person in terms of a few generalized, abstract features or traits; the closer an individual is to their interlocutor, the more likely they are to represent the person with more contextualized or concrete traits (Wilson, Crisp & Mortenson, 2013). Thus, the more distant virtual communicators feel from one another, the more likely they are to default to stereotyped cognitions of them. Furthermore, higher-level construals (from a further distance) lead to inferences about behavior that are dispositional rather than situational (Nussbaum et al., 2003). As suggested by Gibson and Gibbs (2006), these attributions about the motives of the other party can lead to a hesitancy to share information, once again hindering outcomes from the collaboration.

The withdrawal from the office environment during the pandemic meant that spontaneous meetings became formalized and planned (Waight et al., 2022), and the amount of open or relational information given and feedback received was reduced (Carillo et al., 2021). Many workers experienced feelings of isolation (Van Zoonen & Sivunen, 2022). Construal-level theory suggests that geographic distance does not equal psychological distance; although it may result in psychological distance, the relationship is likely bidirectional (Trope et al., 2007; Wilson, Crisp & Mortenson, 2013). A suggestion to address the challenge presented by virtual communication then would be to find ways to reduce the psychological distance between communicators. For virtual teams that are geographically distributed, plan co-located team retreats. In-person retreats provide crucial face-to-face interaction with team members, allowing for more interactions among them (Sytch & Greer, 2020). Such events provide members with an information-rich communication environment in which they can share information about their local communication context and more easily send and detect one another's nonverbal cues, information that will help interpretation and lessen miscommunication when they are once again separated and meet virtually.

To back up the need for some of the communication to occur synchronously and in-person, Mesmer-Magnus et al.'s (2011) research demonstrates that for teams that have a hybrid strategy – using both virtual tools and in-person meetings – the relationship between overall information sharing and team performance is stronger than for teams that met only in-person or only virtually. For cross-cultural interactants, communicators have the chance to interact in person and gain from that information-rich interaction in terms of the ability to recognize and understand nonverbal cues. Such understanding can be carried over to the less rich virtual environment, fostering greater overall understanding and more effective communication.

Future Directions

In this chapter, we have discussed the challenges posed by virtual interactions for the encoding and decoding of contextual cues in communication and possible ways to overcome them. We end with propositions yet to be examined regarding the implications of virtual communication media for the transmission and understanding of nonverbal messages.

One question to be explored is whether the positive relationship between emotional intelligence and the ability to decode and encode cues is sustained regardless of the information richness of the communication environment. If the proposition by Pitts et al. (2012) holds, the development of high EI in communicators has promise for reducing misunderstanding and miscommunication in both information-rich and lean virtual interactions.

> Proposition 1a: Relative to communicators low in emotional intelligence (EI), communicators high in EI have a greater ability to detect, understand and manage the cues being sent to them (or the cues they send) in information-lean communication environments such as those that occur with virtual communication.

The next question then is, how can such ability be developed. One solution, as suggested by Earley and Peterson (2004), is more extensive cross-cultural training, education that is inclusive not only of appropriate behaviors in a given situation but of the underlying social norms so that the reasons why people communicate the way they do can be understood. One such training is interCultural Edge (icEdge) (Adair et al., 2016). Through training with icEdge, communicators learn the socio-cultural roots of interaction styles, gain a detailed understanding of how context influences their own communication, and are able to compare their interaction style across the domains of message, relationship, time, and space to others in their group. In becoming more aware of their own style and those of their teammates, communicators gain agility in adapting their style to be more effective in interaction, ultimately, increasing understanding of both verbal and nonverbal communication with their interlocutors, and developing their EI and CQ.

> Proposition 1b: By promoting the development of emotional intelligence (EI) and cultural intelligence (CQ), cross-cultural training that helps communicators understand their own and others' visible behaviors, as well as underlying norms and values – that is, both verbal and nonverbal communication – will promote the development of greater ability to detect, understand and manage the cues being sent to them (or the cues they send) in virtual communication.

Similarly, the research by Presbitero (2021) and Richter et al. (2021) suggests virtual teams with members high in CQ display greater synergy (conflict-resolution and coordination), direction (moving forward toward goals) and social integration than teams with lower average CQ. Adair et al. (2016) demonstrated that more highly context-dependent communicators have higher CQ. This leads to the expectation that higher context communicators will similarly display higher levels of synergy, direction and social integration in virtual settings.

Proposition 1c: Communicators higher in context dependence, and hence higher in CQ, will display greater synergy, direction, and social integration in virtual interaction settings than communicators low in context dependence.

A second area of exploration concerns the optimal frequency, or timing, of virtual communications. Research has demonstrated that when interactions are conducted solely by virtual means, overall communication frequency likely increases, but (team) efficiency decreases (Marlow et al., 2017). This presents a quandary. While a first response may be to decrease "irrelevant" information, how does one determine what information is irrelevant? And for whom? For someone who is a low-context communicator, someone for whom the meaning of a communication is imparted through the words used, virtual messages containing open, relationship-oriented information may seem to be a waste of time; instead, closed, task-oriented messages are preferred. For the high-context communicator, someone for whom the meaning of interaction is contextualized within the time, space, and relationship of the interlocutors and the message itself, team processes and outcomes are much more dependent on the relationship among team members, and key information as to the functioning of each member can be found in the nonverbal messages contained in open, relationship-oriented communications. The optimal frequency of communication in virtual interactions will need to provide enough relationship-oriented communication for the high-context individual to be able to glean nonverbal communication about team members and processes while still limiting the amount of relationship-oriented communication so that the low-context communicator does not dismiss the communications entirely and miss task-oriented messages.

Proposition 2: To provide for optimal understanding and engagement by both higher and lower context communicators in virtual communication interactions, there needs to be a fine balance in the frequency, or timing, of virtual message communication between too much relationship-oriented communication (for the lower context communicator) and too little (for the high context communicator).

Finally, the research of Mesmer-Magnus et al. (2011) and others presented here occurred before the technology for online virtual meetings was as developed as it is now. Do their findings still hold? That is, is a hybrid communication strategy – combining virtual and in-person interactions – still better in terms of the relationship between information shared and team performance compared to either virtual or in-person interactions alone? At the heart of this question is how information-lean our current video interaction technology is compared to in-person interactions. How much more information-rich do the technologies need to become such that communicators can fully encode and decode nonverbal messages in virtual interactions?

And most importantly, who will most benefit from a hybrid communication strategy: communicators who are higher in context or those lower in context? Due to the enhanced ability to glean a deeper understanding of non-verbal cues during in-person interactions that can be extended to virtual interactions, we suggest communicators higher in context dependence reap more benefit from a hybrid communication strategy than communicators lower in context dependence.

Proposition 3a: A hybrid communication strategy – combining virtual and in-person interactions with current technology – will yield a stronger positive relationship between information shared and team performance than virtual or in-person interactions alone.

Proposition 3b: A hybrid communication strategy – combining virtual and in-person interactions with current technology – will yield a stronger positive relationship between information shared and team performance for communicators higher in context dependence than communicators lower in context dependence.

References

Adair, W. L., Buchan, N. R., Chen, X. P., & Liu, D. (2016). A model of communication context and measure of context dependence. *Academy of Management Discoveries, 2*(2), 198–217.

Anawati, D., & Craig, A. (2006). Behavioral adaptation within cross-cultural virtual teams. *IEEE Transactions on Professional Communication, 49*(1), 44–56.

Brew, F. P., & Cairns, D. R. (2004). Do culture or situational constraints determine choice of direct or indirect styles in intercultural workplace conflicts? *International Journal of Intercultural Relations, 28*(5), 331–352.

Brewer, M. B., & Kramer, R. M. (1985). The psychology of intergroup attitudes and behavior. *Annual review of psychology, 36*(1), 219–243.

Burke, K., & Chidambaram, L. (1999). How much bandwidth is enough? A longitudinal examination of media characteristics and group outcomes. *MIS Quarterly, 23*, 557–579.

Carillo, K., Cachat-Rosset, G., Marsan, J., Saba, T., & Klarsfeld, A. (2021). Adjusting to epidemic-induced telework: Empirical insights from teleworkers in France. *European Journal of Information Systems, 30*(1), 69–88.

Clark, H. H., & Brennan, S. E. (1991). Grounding in communication. In L. B. Resnick, J. M. Levine, & S. D. Teasley (Eds.), *Perspectives on socially shared cognition* (pp. 127–149). American Psychological Association.

Daft, R. L., & Lengel, R. H. (1986). Organizational information requirements, media richness and structural design. *Management Science, 32*(5), 554–571.

Daim, T. U., Ha, A., Reutiman, S., Hughes, B., Pathak, U., Bynum, W., & Bhatla, A. (2012). Exploring the communication breakdown in global virtual teams. *International Journal of Project Management, 30*(2), 199–212.

Detert, J. R., & Burris, E. R. (2007). Leadership behavior and employee voice: Is the door really open? *Academy of Management Journal, 50*(4), 869–884.

Earley, P. C., & Ang, S. (2003). *Cultural intelligence: Individual interactions across cultures*. Stanford University Press.

Earley, P. C., & Mosakowski, E. (2004). Cultural intelligence. *Harvard Business Review, 82*(10), 139–146.

Earley, P. C., & Peterson, R. S. (2004). The elusive cultural chameleon: Cultural intelligence as a new approach to intercultural training for the global manager. *Academy of Management Learning and Education, 3*, 100–115.

Gesteland, R. R. (2012). *Cross-cultural business behavior: A guide for global management* (5th ed.). Wiley.
Gibson, C. B., & Gibbs, J. L. (2006). Unpacking the concept of virtuality: The effects of geographic dispersion, electronic dependence, dynamic structure, and national diversity on team innovation. *Administrative Science Quarterly, 51*(3), 451–495.
Gibson, C. B., & Zellmer-Bruhn, M. E. (2001). Metaphors and meaning: An intercultural analysis of the concept of teamwork. *Administrative Science Quarterly, 46*(2), 274–303.
Gibson, C. B., Huang, L., Kirkman, B. L., & Shapiro, D. L. (2014). Where global and virtual meet: The value of examining the intersection of these elements in twenty-first-century teams. *Annual Review of Organizational Psychology and Organizational Behavior, 1*(1), 217–244.
Giles, H., & Ogay, T. (2007). Communication accommodation theory. In B. B. Whaley & W. Samter (Eds.), *Explaining communication: Contemporary theories and exemplars* (pp. 293–310). Lawrence Erlbaum Associates.
Glikson, E., & Erez, M. (2020). The emergence of a communication climate in global virtual teams. *Journal of World Business, 55*(6), 101001.
Gluesing, J. C., Alcordo, T., Baba, M. L., Britt, D., Wagner, K. H., McKether, W., Monplaisir, L., Ratner, H. H., & Riopelle, K. (2003). Virtual teams that work: Creating conditions for virtual team effectiveness. In C. B. Gibson & S. G. Cohen (Eds.), *The development of global virtual teams* (pp. 353–380). Wiley.
Graham, J. L., & Requejo, W. H. (2009). Managing face-to-face international negotiations. *Organizational Dynamics, 38*(2), 167–177.
Hinds, P. J., & Mortensen, M. (2005). Understanding conflict in geographically distributed teams: The moderating effects of shared identity, shared context, and spontaneous communication. *Organization Science, 16*(3), 290–307.
Hinds, P. J., Neeley, T. B., & Cramton, C. D. (2014). Language as a lightning rod: Power contests, emotion regulation, and subgroup dynamics in global teams. *Journal of International Business Studies, 45*, 536–561.
Jarvenpaa, S. L., & Leidner, D. E. (1999). Communication and trust in global virtual teams. *Organization Science, 10*(6), 791–815.
Johri, A. (2012). From a distance: Impression formation and impression accuracy among geographically distributed coworkers. *Computers in Human Behavior, 28*(6), 1997–2006.
Katriel, T. (1986). *Talking straight: Dugri speech in Israeli Sabra culture*. Cambridge University Press.
Kirkman, B. L., & Mathieu, J. E. (2005). The dimensions and antecedents of team virtuality. *Journal of Management, 31*(5), 700–718.
Kirkman, B. L., & Shapiro, D. L. (1997). The impact of cultural values on employee resistance to teams: Toward a model of globalized self-managing work team effectiveness. *Academy of Management Review, 22*(3), 730–757.
Klitmøller, A., & Lauring, J. (2013). When global virtual teams share knowledge: Media richness, cultural difference and language commonality. *Journal of World Business, 48*(3), 398–406.
Klitmøller, A., Schneider, S. C., & Jonsen, K. (2015). Speaking of global virtual teams: Language differences, social categorization and media choice. *Personnel Review, 44*(2), 270–285.
Kreijns, K., Kirschner, P. A., & Jochems, W. (2003). Identifying the pitfalls for social interaction in computer-supported collaborative learning environments: A review of the research. *Computers in Human Behavior, 19*(3), 335–353.
Lewis, R. (2010). *When cultures collide* (pp. 171–211). Nicholas Brealey Publishing.
Lisak, A., Erez, M., Sui, Y., & Lee, C. (2016). The positive role of global leaders in enhancing multicultural team innovation. *Journal of International Business Studies, 47*, 655–673.
Marlow, S. L., Lacerenza, C. N., & Salas, E. (2017). Communication in virtual teams: A conceptual framework and research agenda. *Human Resource Management Review, 27*(4), 575–589.
Martins, L. L., Gilson, L. L., & Maynard, M. T. (2004). Virtual teams: What do we know and where do we go from here? *Journal of Management, 30*(6), 805–835.

Matook, S., Cummings, J., & Bala, H. (2015). Are you feeling lonely? The impact of relationship characteristics and online social network features on loneliness. *Journal of Management Information Systems, 31*(4), 278–310.

Mayer, J. D., Roberts, R. D., & Barsade, S. G. (2008). Human abilities: Emotional intelligence. *Annual Review of Psychology, 59*, 507–536.

McKinsey & Company. (2023). *Reimagining the postpandemic workforce: How companies can make remote working a success*. https://www.mckinsey.com/capabilities/people-and-organizational-performance/our-insights/reimagining-the-postpandemic-workforce

Mesmer-Magnus, J. R., & DeChurch, L. A. (2009). Information sharing and team performance: a meta-analysis. *Journal of Applied Psychology, 94*(2), 535.

Mesmer-Magnus, J. R., DeChurch, L. A., Jimenez-Rodriguez, M., Wildman, J., & Shuffler, M. (2011). A meta-analytic investigation of virtuality and information sharing in teams. *Organizational Behavior and Human Decision Processes, 115*(2), 214–225.

Miao, C., Humphrey, R. H., & Qian, S. (2012). Emotional intelligence and authentic leadership: A meta-analysis. *Leadership & Organization Development Journal, 39*(5), 679–690.

Neeley, T. B., Hinds, P. J., & Cramton, C. D. (2012). The (un)hidden turmoil of language in global collaboration. *Organizational Dynamics, 41*(3), 236–244.

Newman, A., Donohue, R., & Eva, N. (2017). Psychological safety: A systematic review of the literature. *Human Resource Management Review, 27*(3), 521–535.

Nonaka, I., & Takeuchi, H. (1995). *The knowledge creating company*. Oxford University Press.

Nussbaum, S., Trope, Y., & Liberman, N. (2003). Creeping dispositionism: the temporal dynamics of behavior prediction. *Journal of Personality and Social Psychology, 84*(3), 485.

Oetzel, J. G., & Ting-Toomey, S. (2003). Face concerns in interpersonal conflict: A cross-cultural empirical test of the face negotiation theory. *Communication Research, 30*(6), 599–624.

Pitts, V. E., Wright, N. A., & Harkabus, L. C. (2012). Communication in virtual teams: The role of emotional intelligence. *Journal of Organizational Psychology, 12*(3/4), 21–34.

Presbitero, A. (2021). Communication accommodation within global virtual team: The influence of cultural intelligence and the impact on interpersonal process effectiveness. *Journal of International Management, 27*(1), 100809.

Purvanova, R. K. (2014). Face-to-face versus virtual teams: What have we really learned? *The Psychologist-Manager Journal, 17*(1), 2.

Raghuram, S., Hill, N. S., Gibbs, J. L., & Maruping, L. M. (2019). Virtual work: Bridging research clusters. *Academy of Management Annals, 13*(1), 308–341.

Rhymer, J. (2023). Location-independent organizations: Designing collaboration across space and time. *Administrative Science Quarterly, 68*(1), 1–43.

Richter, N. F., Martin, J., Hansen, S. V., Taras, V., & Alon, I. (2021). Motivational configurations of cultural intelligence, social integration, and performance in global virtual teams. *Journal of Business Research, 129*, 351–367.

Shapiro, D. L., Furst, S. A., Spreitzer, G. M., & Von Glinow, M. A. (2002). Transnational teams in the electronic age: Are team identity and high performance at risk? *Journal of Organizational Behavior, 23*(4), 455–467.

Stahl, G. K., & Tung, R. L. (2015). Towards a more balanced treatment of culture in international business studies: The need for positive cross-cultural scholarship. *Journal of International Business Studies, 46*, 391–414.

Sytch, M., & Greer, L. L. (2020, August 18). Is your organization ready for permanent WFH. *Harvard Business Review*.

Tenzer, H., & Pudelko, M. (2017). The influence of language differences on power dynamics in multinational teams. *Journal of World Business, 52*(1), 45–61.

Tenzer, H., Pudelko, M., & Harzing, A. W. (2014). The impact of language barriers on trust formation in multinational teams. *Journal of International Business Studies, 45*, 508–535.

Triandis, H. C., Marín, G., Lisansky, J., & Betancourt, H. (1984). Simpatía as a cultural script of Hispanics. *Journal of Personality and Social Psychology, 47*(6), 1363–1375.

Trope, Y., Liberman, N., & Wakslak, C. (2007). Construal levels and psychological distance: Effects on representation, prediction, evaluation, and behavior. *Journal of Consumer Psychology, 17*(2), 83–95.

Turco, C. J. (2016). The future of the conversational firm. In *The conversational firm* (pp. 173–182). Columbia University Press.

Van Dyne, L., Ang, S., Ng, K. Y., Rockstuhl, T., Tan, M. L., & Koh, C. (2012). Sub-dimensions of the four factor model of cultural intelligence: Expanding the conceptualization and measurement of cultural intelligence. *Social and Personality Psychology Compass, 6*(4), 295–313.

Van Zoonen, W., & Sivunen, A. E. (2022). The impact of remote work and mediated communication frequency on isolation and psychological distress. *European Journal of Work and Organizational Psychology, 31*(4), 610–621.

Von Glinow, M. A., Shapiro, D. L., & Brett, J. M. (2004). Can we talk, and should we? Managing emotional conflict in multicultural teams. *Academy of Management Review, 29*(4), 578–592.

Waight, C. L., Kjerfve, T. N., Kite, A., & Smith, B. (2022). Connecting and relating in Brazil: Implications of remote work. *Human Resource Development International, 25*(2), 231–253.

Walther, J. B. (2009). Computer-mediated communication and virtual groups: Applications to interethnic conflict. *Journal of Applied Communication Research, 37*(3), 225–238.

Wang, L., Chen, X.-P., & Yin, J. (2022). Leading via virtual communication: A longitudinal field experiment on work team creativity in an extreme context. *Asia Pacific Journal of Management*, 1–37. https://doi.org/10.1007/s10490-022-09846-5

Watson, W., Stewart, W. H., Jr., & BarNir, A. (2003). The effects of human capital, organizational demography, and interpersonal processes on venture partner perceptions of firm profit and growth. *Journal of Business Venturing, 18*(2), 145–164.

Whitener, E. M., Brodt, S. E., Korsgaard, M. A., & Werner, J. M. (1998). Managers as initiators of trust: An exchange relationship framework for understanding managerial trustworthy behavior. *Academy of Management Review, 23*(3), 513–530.

Wilson, J., Crisp, C. B., & Mortensen, M. (2013). Extending construal-level theory to distributed groups: Understanding the effects of virtuality. *Organization Science, 24*(2), 629–644.

Chapter 10
Contextualized Communication as a Path to Multicultural Understanding and Collaboration

In today's interconnected and globalized world, it is now commonplace for people of dissimilar world views, faiths and races to live side by side. It is a matter of great urgency, therefore, that we find ways to cooperate with one another in a spirit of mutual acceptance and respect. – Dalai Lama

This book expands existing literature on culture and communication in the workplace by introducing the four domains of communication context: message, relationship, time, and space, with a focus on how they influence nonverbal interactions. Field research finds that managers and employees who work in culturally diverse environments report misunderstanding, frustration, and conflict when direct, lower-context communicators work alongside higher-context counterparts who send nuanced, implicit messages through indirect, nonverbal channels (e.g., Behfar et al., 2006; Cohen, 1997; Trompenaars & Hampden-Turner, 2011). We reviewed the large body of empirical research examining cross-cultural communication in the workplace that offers behavioral (e.g., communication accommodation), cognitive (e.g., language fluency), and affective (e.g., uncertainty management) mechanisms explaining patterns of adaptation and adjustment for understanding communication in the global workplace. It offers recommendations for creating culturally inclusive communication climates. Our discussion of this literature across six organizational domains reveals a low-context bias, such that recommendations tend to emphasize employees adopting a direct, explicit, and open communication style to foster effective communication and collaboration. Our propositions throughout the book offer avenues for research to incorporate high-context communication approaches to improve cross-cultural understanding. In this concluding chapter, we build on previous chapters by offering new directions for framing cross-cultural communication as a holistic tool for intercultural collaboration.

Effective communication through verbal and nonverbal channels is essential and challenging for cross-cultural human connection and collaboration. Ting-Toomey (1999) explains:

> More often than not, nonverbal messages can create intercultural friction and confusion because (1) the same nonverbal signal can mean different things to different people in different cultures (e.g., the nonverbal OK sign means "victory," "insult," and "money," in

W. L. Adair et al., *What Isn't Being Said*, Springer Series in Emerging Cultural Perspectives in Work, Organizational, and Personnel Studies,
https://doi.org/10.1007/978-3-031-53645-8_10

> the United States, Brazil, and Japan, respectively); (2) multiple nonverbal cues are sent in each interaction, thereby creating interpretive ambiguities; and (3) factors of personality, gender, relational distance, socioeconomic status, and situation create tremendous variations of nonverbal display patterns in different cultures. (pp. 114–115)

Cross-cultural communication research, however, has largely focused on differences in styles and cognitions across cultural groups (Merkin et al., 2014; Sharma & Liu, 2023; Szkudlarek et al., 2020). An overwhelming theme in our literature review shows that cultural differences moderate the relationship between communication practices and outcomes and that a key to managing across cultures is to balance cultural universality to reduce uncertainty and decrease social distance with cultural specificity that may or may not align with communication norms in the comfort zone of the communicator.

We have reviewed ways in which employees from different and multiple cultural backgrounds communicate through the context surrounding a verbal message, imbued in parties' relationships, permeating through their uses of clock vs event time, and infused throughout their sensory space (Adair et al., 2016). We offer propositions for bringing communication context into cross-cultural organizational research in each of the six organizational domains. Here we categorize those propositions as to how they are related to more proximal effects, namely mutual understanding, and more distal effects, namely collaboration. Returning to our Interactive Model of Contextualized Communication, our propositions focus on the center of the model, maximizing the zone of overlap wherein communicators' culturally normative communication styles are acknowledged, respected, and adapted for the sake of communication effectiveness and shared understanding. Further, our propositions focus on increasing the ease and effectiveness of the communication loop between sender, receiver, and response so that the prospect for collaboration between the interactants is maximized (Fig. 10.1).

Increasing Cross-Cultural Understanding Through Contextualized Communication

Figure 10.2 overlays the propositions from chapters of this book onto the Interactive Model of Contextualized Communication in an outside-in manner, going from a general focus on understanding the sender's and receiver's environmental contexts to focus on specific strategies at the center of the model to increase the overlap between the interactants and make collaboration more likely and productive.

The propositions on the outside of the figure emphasize using the Recommended Proactive Strategies to better understand one's own and one's partner's fields of experience. Proactively explaining the culture-based meanings associated with spatial cues is suggested to increase participation and engagement between the parties and decrease misunderstanding and misattribution (4.4). Similarly, conducting one's due diligence regarding nonverbal spatial cues and planning interaction settings can signal prudent deliberation and respect for the other negotiator (5.4).

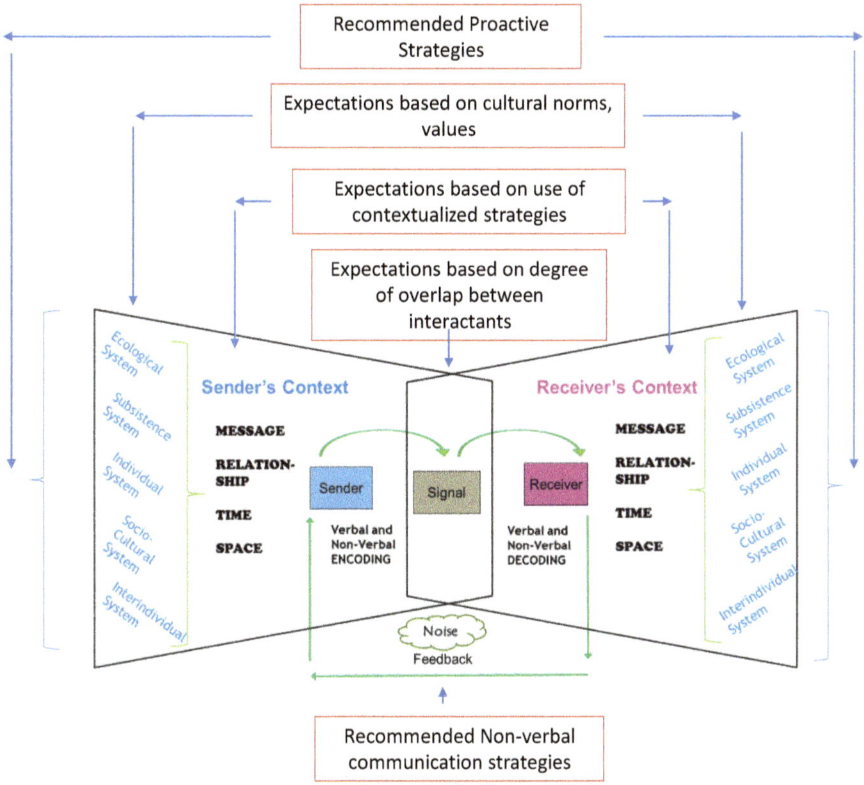

Fig. 10.1 Interactive model of contextualized communication

Cross-cultural communication training that helps communicators understand their own and others' visible behaviors and underlying norms is proposed to promote the development of emotional intelligence in communicators – ultimately increasing the understanding of nonverbal cues in interaction (9.1).

Moving inward, the next set of propositions focuses on understanding the influence of cultural norms held by the sender and receiver during communication. Employees higher in context dependence are proposed to be more likely to modify their voice, silence, gossip and feedback behaviors based on their relationship with the counterpart than lower context employees (6.2). Furthermore, higher-context employees are expected to use more indirect messaging than lower-context employees (6.1). In low-context environments, employees are expected to provide voice and feedback during regularly scheduled times. In contrast, in high-context environments, employee feedback is likely to occur spontaneously and outside of scheduled meetings (6.3). Higher-context communicators who use flexible time are more likely to be temporal brokers and fill coordination roles in lower-context organizations, thus again contributing to the increased understanding for both senders and receivers within communication (4.3). Finally, due to their higher levels of cultural intelligence (CQ), communicators with higher context dependence will display greater synergy, direction, and social integration in virtual interaction settings than communicators with lower context dependence (9.1).

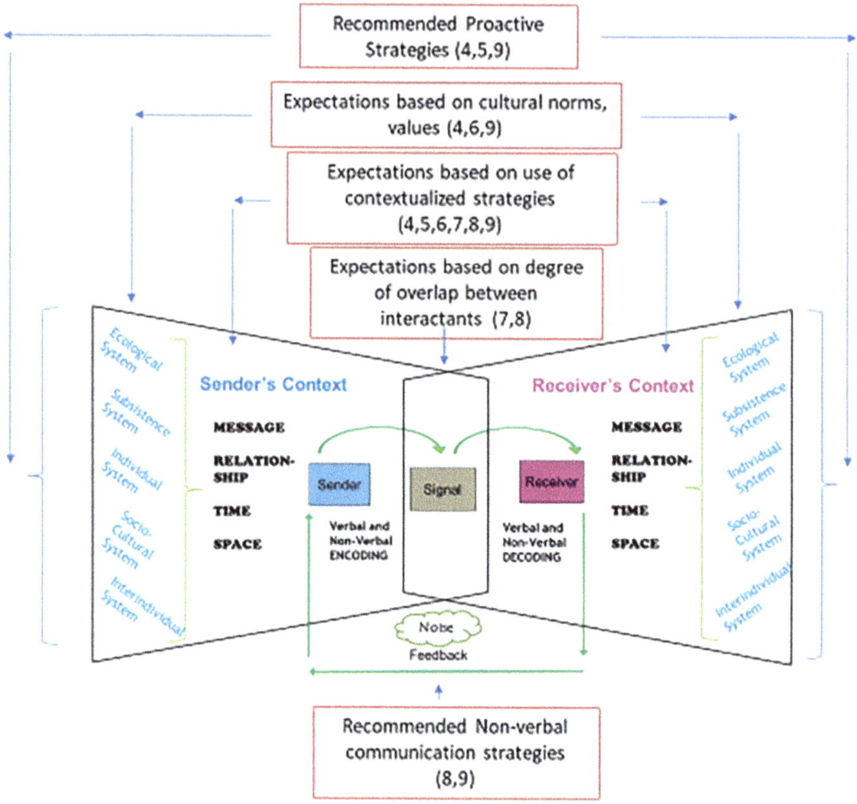

Fig. 10.2 A taxonomy of propositions (book chapters in parentheses) to increase understanding and collaboration

Closer to the middle of the model is a set of propositions emphasizing the use of and focus on contextualized, responsive communication strategies to increase the ease of transmitting and receiving messages. Increased attention to implicit messages and engaged listening in the message context is offered as a path to decrease misunderstanding in cross-cultural negotiation and multicultural teams (4.1, 5.1). Clear, explicit messaging is proposed for more productive leadership scenarios and to reduce workplace incivility (8.1, 7.1). We propose more research focusing on implicit, relational cues and relationship management in negotiation, conflict, team, and leadership settings as a way to decrease misunderstanding and increase effective communication between parties (4.2, 5.2, 7.2). Proactively discussing and managing different time orientations is proposed for research into negotiation and virtual interactions (4.4, 9.4). Finally, we suggest the optimal frequency of communication in virtual interactions will need to be such that enough relationship-oriented communication is imparted for more high-context individuals to be able to glean nonverbal cues about team members and processes, but still limiting the amount of relationship-oriented communication so that the lower context communicators do not dismiss the communications entirely and miss task-oriented messages (9.2). Together these propositions focus on managing the communication space between interlocutors to increase understanding and overlap in the feedback loop of communication interaction, easing interaction between them and making collaboration more likely and effective.

A final set of propositions focuses on the extent of overlap in contexts of the sender and receiver where true collaboration can occur. We propose that greater overlap between the intended meaning of the sender and the meaning interpreted by the receiver (7.1), the perspectives the two interlocutors have on time (7.3) and their understanding of silent language (7.4), will facilitate more understanding between the two parties as well as leadership effectiveness. Addressing the negative externalities in collaboration, it is proposed that cultural norm congruent ostracism will be less threatening than culturally incongruent ostracism (8.1).

At the bottom of the model is a proposition purely focused on fine-tuning the communication loop – particularly to increase understanding of nonverbal cues and meanings. A hybrid-communication strategy, combining virtual and in-person interactions, is proposed to yield more positive results between information shared and collaborative team performance compared to either virtual or in-person interactions alone (9.3).

Cross-Cultural Understanding

Reflecting on the process of communication, theorists Burgoon and Bacue (2003) surmised:

> It is the nature of the human condition that, try as we may, we cannot enter into the reality of another individual's experiences, thoughts, or feelings. Imprisoned as we are within our own bodies, the fallible process of communication is the primary agent currently available for crossing the psychological expanse between two or more individuals. (p. 179)

The fallible process of communication is even more perilous when considering nonverbal communication, particularly in light of the fact that any single nonverbal cue might be attended by a multiplicity of meanings and that multiple cues might substitute for the same meaning, and that often, such meanings are hidden (Hall, 1959). In such cases, "nonverbal skill must be examined at the level of constellations of cues and with cognizance of the social context and actors' goals, which may constrain and guide the selection of meaning" (Burgoon & Bacue, 2003, p. 187).

Let's focus on this idea of "cognizance of the social context." Consider, for example, a Japanese businessman with his eyes downcast, his tone quiet, and his use of silence vast. With these nonverbal behaviors, is he conveying respect for a more senior colleague in the room? Is he trying to impart disinterest in the business deal being proposed by another party? Is he angry? Does he not understand what has been said? To decode this constellation of nonverbal signals, the receiver (or listener) needs to understand the speaker's social context – and we assert in this volume that this context is broad and encompasses the speaker's entire field of experience, that is, his culture. In this example, the Japanese speaker's cultural context likely emphasizes respect for hierarchy and the show of respect through non-direct eye contact, conflict avoidance, and little display of emotion (Lewis, 2010). But we suggest his context also involves his relationship with the listener (relationship context), his position in space relative to any others in the room – is he at the head of the table or the end of it – (space context), and any spoken words that may have accompanied this constellation of nonverbal signals (message context). Thus, without an understanding of the Japanese businessman's context, or as illustrated in the Interactive Model of Contextualized Communication, without some overlap in the contexts of the sender and receiver, it will be impossible to bridge the "psychological expanse" and the receiver will be unable to interpret the message as the sender intended it.

However, as with Schramm's original communication model depicting the fields of experience of the sender and receiver, we suggest that to the extent that overlap in the culture and communication contexts of the sender and receiver occurs, effective communication can ensue. The sender's intention and the receiver's interpretation are more likely to be in sync, the more deeply they each understand the cultural context of the other and the message, relationship, time, and space contexts in which the signal was encoded or decoded.

Such effective communication can then be the seedbed for collaboration. Discussing successful business collaborations, Austin (2000) writes,

> To realize the full benefits of an alliance, the partners need to have means of communicating effectively, efficiently, and frequently. Multiple communication channels, formal and informal, are used. Partners stressed the importance of forthrightness and constructive criticism. Openness seems particularly powerful in social purpose collaborations, especially in the integrative-stage relationships. Good communication appears to foster trust and vice versa. (p. 86)

To this we add the need to create room in multicultural collaborations for a nuanced, culturally informed understanding of "openness" and "forthrightness." Openness for a more reserved, high-context communicator may give physical space for colleagues' ideas to be expressed and remain silent while openly considering them before responding with their own ideas (space context). Openness for a more expressive, high-context communicator may look like interruptions with different ideas that improve upon those currently under consideration (space context). Both reserved and expressive high-context communicators may lose face when a more low-context colleague expresses openness by offering forthright, constructive criticism, particularly if the colleague is perceived to have a higher status (relationship context). Employees in international and multicultural workplaces can foster safe and productive collaboration by understanding counterparts' fields of experience and communication styles and crafting complementary, contextualized messages and responses that increase overlap in the interpersonal communication space.

In our opening example (see Chap. 1, this volume), as Jasmin, a domestic student from North Carolina, introduces herself, the French exchange student Mathieu interrupts her with a request to "keep it short and get down to business." Here, Mathieu intends to propose a process management strategy. Team members who proactively learn about Mathieu's field of experience and a more low-context communication style (message and time context) may receive the message literally and interpret it as intended. Likewise, if Mathieu understands Jasmin's field of experience and more high-context communication style (relationship and time context), he will recognize that the message was interpreted as pushy and demanding when Jasmin's facial expression displays shock and she moves her chair back (space context). In this case, Mathieu, Jasmin, or any other teammate can use contextualized, responsive strategies to manage the communication space and avert potential miscommunication and conflict. This can take the form of active listening to reach a shared understanding of Mathieu's message, reinterpreting Mathieu's message through recognition of its context, or teammates' adapting to Mathieu's more low-context communication style, Jasmin's more high-context style, or a mutually developed emergent, hybrid style.

In a multicultural setting, articulating a message becomes an opportunity to establish common ground between and among parties for further interactions. Common ground and mutual understanding then support communicators in navigating individual, organizational, and cultural differences, weathering unexpected changes, and managing trust and relationship building. Thus, effective cross-cultural communication at a micro-level supports collaboration and the success of multinational ventures at a macro level. For example, through effective cross-cultural communication, US and Chinese filmmakers produced Kung Fu Panda (Dreamworks, 2008, 2011, 2016), ensuring that the film accurately represented Chinese culture that would be expressed in English and interpreted by viewers across the globe. US filmmakers worked closely with their Chinese counterparts to ensure that the film's story and characters were culturally appropriate and respectful of Chinese culture. They had to adapt their storytelling and animation techniques to align with Chinese aesthetics and cultural values. Yet, they had to tell the stories in a way that would be understood and accurately interpreted by viewers in a foreign language, in a non-Chinese cultural context. By embracing cultural differences and working together to achieve a common goal, the filmmakers were able to create a film that celebrated Chinese culture while also appealing to a global audience.

The Small World Machine campaign by Coca-Cola (2013) promoted communication and cultural understanding between the people of India and Pakistan, two countries with a history of political tensions and conflict. Interactive vending machines were placed in shopping malls in New Delhi, India, and Lahore, Pakistan. These machines were equipped with live-streaming video cameras, allowing people from both countries to see and interact with each other in real-time, in nonverbal ways. Participants were encouraged to complete simple tasks together, such as tracing peace symbols, dancing, or touching hands on the screen, which would result in a free Coke being dispensed to both users. The campaign aimed to emphasize the commonalities and shared humanity between the people of India and Pakistan via non-verbal communication despite their differences and political conflicts.

True understanding occurs when what is interpreted by a receiver is what was intended by the sender. As stated in Chap. 1 and echoed throughout this book, effective cross-cultural communication in the workplace requires understanding the socio-cultural roots of verbal and nonverbal communication styles in the self and others. Communicators must understand and recognize psychological and situational factors that can lead to misunderstanding. And they need motivation and flexibility to adapt and to use engaged listening for often unnoticed or misinterpreted nonverbal cues in all four domains of communication context.

Because so much information is contained in nonverbal cues in the message, relationship, time, and space contexts, employees in diverse and multicultural workplaces need to be aware of how different cultural groups communicate from, within, and through context. This cultural knowledge and attention to individual communication patterns are the foundational tools for employees embarking on the path to effective cross-cultural communication. Then, employees need self-awareness to recognize when nonverbal meaning is lost in translation and flexibility to modify the nonverbal channels through which they speak and listen. A holistic consideration of communication, including nonverbal cues in the message, relationship, time, and space contexts, can improve understanding and facilitate the social construction of human connections, which leads to downstream collaboration and cooperation within and across organizations.

References

Adair, W. L., Buchan, N. R., Chen, X. P., & Liu, D. (2016). A model of communication context and measure of context dependence. *Academy of Management Discoveries, 2*(2), 198–217.

Austin, J. E. (2000). Strategic collaboration between nonprofits and businesses. *Nonprofit and Voluntary Sector Quarterly, 29*(1), 69–97.

Behfar, K., Kern, M., & Brett, J. (2006). Managing challenges in multicultural teams. In Y. R. Chen (Ed.), *National culture and groups* (pp. 233–262). Emerald Group Publishing Limited.

Burgoon, J. K., & Bacue, A. E. (2003). Nonverbal communication skills. In J. O. Green & B. R. Burlson (Eds.), *Handbook of communication and social interaction skills* (pp. 179–219). Lawrence Erlbaum Associates.

Coca-Cola. (2013, May 19). *Coca-Cola small world machines – Bringing India & Pakistan together* [video]. https://www.youtube.com/watch?v=ts_4vOUDImE

Cohen, R. A. (1997). *Negotiating across cultures: International communication in an interdependent world.* US Institute of Peace Press.

Dreamworks. (2008, 2011, 2016). *Kung Fu Panda Directors' interviews, behind the scenes, and fansite.* https://www.youtube.com/results?search_query=kung+fu+panda+directors%27+interviews; https://dreamworks.fandom.com/wiki/Kung_Fu_Panda

Hall, E. T. (1959). *The silent language.* Random House.

Lewis, R. (2010). *When cultures collide.* London: Nicholas Brealey Publishing.

Merkin, R., Taras, V., & Steel, P. (2014). State of the art themes in cross-cultural communication research: A systematic and meta-analytic review. *International Journal of Intercultural Relations, 38*, 1–23. https://doi.org/10.1016/j.ijintrel.2013.10.004

Sharma, S., & Liu, L. A. (2023). Culture and communication. In M. J. Gelfand & M. Erez (Eds.), *Oxford handbook of cross-cultural organizational behavior.* Oxford University Press.

Szkudlarek, B., Osland, J. S., Nardon, L., & Zander, L. (2020). Communication and culture in international business – Moving the field forward. *Journal of World Business, 55*(6), 101126.

Ting-Toomey, S. (1999). *Communicating across cultures.* Guilford Publications.

Trompenaars, F., & Hampden-Turner, C. (2011). *Riding the waves of culture: Understanding diversity in global business.* Nicholas Brealey International.

Index

W. L. Adair et al., *What Isn't Being Said*, Springer Series in Emerging Cultural Perspectives in Work, Organizational, and Personnel Studies,
https://doi.org/10.1007/978-3-031-53645-8

GPSR Compliance
The European Union's (EU) General Product Safety Regulation (GPSR) is a set of rules that requires consumer products to be safe and our obligations to ensure this.

If you have any concerns about our products, you can contact us on

ProductSafety@springernature.com

In case Publisher is established outside the EU, the EU authorized representative is:

Springer Nature Customer Service Center GmbH
Europaplatz 3
69115 Heidelberg, Germany

www.ingramcontent.com/pod-product-compliance
Ingram Content Group UK Ltd.
Pitfield, Milton Keynes, MK11 3LW, UK
UKHW022210051026
15624UKWH00001B/95
* 9 7 8 3 0 3 1 5 3 6 4 4 1 *